Proceedings of the Sixth International Symposium on
Human Aspects of Information Security & Assurance (HAISA 2012)

Crete, Greece
6-8 June 2012

Editors

Nathan Clarke
Steven Furnell

Centre for Security, Communications & Network Research
Plymouth University

ISBN: 978-1-84102-317-5

Preface

It is now widely recognised that technology alone cannot provide the answer to security problems. A significant aspect of protection comes down to the attitudes, awareness, behaviour and capabilities of the people involved, and they often need support in order to get it right. Factors such as lack of awareness and understanding, combined with unreasonable demands from security technologies, can dramatically impede their ability to act securely and comply with policies. Ensuring appropriate attention to the needs of users is therefore a vital element of a successful security strategy, and they need to understand how the issues may apply to them and how to use the available technology to protect their systems.

With the above in mind, the Human Aspects of Information Security and Assurance (HAISA) symposium series specifically addresses information security issues that relate to people. It concerns the methods that inform and guide users' understanding of security, and the technologies that can benefit and support them in achieving protection.

This book presents the proceedings from the 2012 event, held in Crete, Greece, during June 2012. A total of 19 reviewed papers are included, spanning a range of topics including user attitudes and awareness, management and modelling of security, and the suitability of technologies that people are expected to use. All of the papers were subject to double-blind peer review, with each being reviewed by at least two members of the international programme committee.

We would like to thank the authors for submitting their work and sharing their findings, and the international programme committee for their efforts in reviewing the submissions and ensuring the quality of the resulting event and proceedings. We would also like to thank the local organising committee for making all the necessary arrangements to enable this symposium to take place. Special thanks go to Dimitris Gritzalis as the local host, for organising the venue and other facilities. Thanks are also due to the British Computer Society, Emerald (publishers of the sponsoring journal, *Information Management & Computer Security*), and the Colloquium for Information Systems Security Education (CISSE) as the co-sponsors of the event.

Nathan Clarke & Steven Furnell
Symposium Co-Chairs, HAISA 2012

Crete, June 2012

International Programme Committee

Helen Armstrong	Curtin University	Australia
William Buchanan	Napier University	United Kingdom
Jeff Crume	IBM	United States
Dorothy Denning	Naval Postgraduate School	United States
Ronald Dodge	United States Military Academy	United States
Paul Dowland	Plymouth University	United Kingdom
Jan Eloff	SAP	South Africa
Simone Fischer-Huebner	Karlstad University	Sweden
Sarah Gordon	Independent Professional	United States
Stefanos Gritzalis	University of the Aegean	Greece
John Howie	Microsoft	United States
William Hutchinson	Edith Cowan University	Australia
Murray Jennex	San Diego State University	United States
Andy Jones	Khalifa University	UAE
Vasilios Katos	Democritus University of Thrace	Greece
Sokratis Katsikas	University of Piraeus	Greece
Costas Lambrinoudakis	University of Piraeus	Greece
Michael Lavine	John Hopkins University	United States
Javier Lopez	University of Malaga	Spain
George Magklaras	University of Oslo	Norway
Maria Papadaki	Plymouth University	United Kingdom
Malcolm Pattinson	University of South Australia	Australia
Charles Pfleeger	Pfleeger Consulting Group	United States
Corey Schou	Idaho State University	United States
Rossouw von Solms	Nelson Mandela Metropolitan University	South Africa
Jeffrey Stanton	Syracuse University	United States
Kerry-Lynn Thomson	Nelson Mandela Metropolitan University	South Africa
Theodore Tryfonas	University of Bristol	United Kingdom
Kim Vu	California State University	United States
Jeremy Ward	ExecIA LLP	United Kingdom
Merrill Warkentin	Mississippi State University	United States
Wei Yan	Trend Micro	United States
Louise Yngstrom	Stockholm University	Sweden
Mary Ellen Zurko	IBM	United States

Contents

Cybersecurity Workforce Development Directions

R.C. Dodge[1], C. Toregas[2] and L. Hoffman[2]

[1] United States Military Academy, West Point NY, 10996
[2] The George Washington University, Washington, DC 20052
e-mail: ronald.dodge@usma.edu; {toregas1, lance.hoffman}@gwu.edu

Abstract

The cybersecurity workforce is one of the most critical employment sectors in the world. The systems supporting the information technology requirements of the world's government, power, and financial systems are interconnected more than any other system in the world. Despite the criticality and interconnectivity of these systems, the workforce has developed without a concentrated and standard view of its requirements. In this paper the authors report on efforts in the last two years to define the requirements for developing the cybersecurity workforce.

Keywords

Cybersecurity workforce, security education, training, awareness

1   Introduction

The cybersecurity workforce is failing to meet the demands of a society with deep reliance on information technology. This failure is abundantly evident in many security assessment reports. Identifying the requirements of this career field and creating a holistic approach to defining accreditation guidance to certify an individual's competence to be a part of this workforce has been the topic of several workshops in the USA in the past two years. While there was no overlap in planning or participation in the workshops, they arrived at the same conclusion – change is needed now in the way we develop and manage the cybersecurity workforce.

In 2011, the United States Department of Homeland Security sponsored a workshop executed by the Institute for Information Infrastructure Protection (I3P). In this workshop, approximately 40 representatives from the US government, international corporations, and academic institutions met to discuss and outline the demands within each sector for cybersecurity workforce professionals. The final report highlighted the sense that the cybersecurity workforce resembled an ecosystem comprised of expertise in complementary knowledge, skills, and abilities (Goodman et al., 2011). The domains of expertise, however, are nearly impossible to all master within a specific job function in the career field. Unfortunately, if one is lacking, the system is vulnerable to attack or failure.

A second effort sponsored by the National Science Foundation and executed by the Cyber Security Policy and Research Institute (CSPRI) of The George Washington University (GW) started to explore the integration of workforce development strategies into a plan that involves educators, career professionals, employers, and policymakers.

The healthcare and legal professions may serve as potential models for the development of a cybersecurity workforce management plan. In both of the fields, an educational foundation is important yet due to the very specialized nature of the many sub-disciplines within the career fields, a specialization path and possibly a certification structure could be helpful.

A first step in constructing a development model for a career field is to detail the components of the career field and the specific functional requirements within each component. In a multiagency effort, the United States launched the National Initiative for Cybersecurity Education (NICE), led by the National Institute of Standards and Technology (NIST) in partnership with the Department of Homeland Security. The goal of this effort is to create a Cybersecurity Workforce Framework that defines the architecture and specific functional requirements for all job functions within the cybersecurity workforce.

The referenced workshops and the proposed NIST workforce model serve as informed starting points in the discussion on how to rationally develop the cybersecurity workforce. The cybersecurity workforce career fields must transform to assist organizations managing and securing our IT infrastructures and services, to ensure the employees are competent, and to support the development of education and training programs. In this paper, we discuss the findings of the I3P and CSPRI workshops and how the NIST NICE workforce model can be used as a starting point in a full career development and management structure.

2   Three significant efforts

In order to develop new directions in cybersecurity workforce development, it is important to look at a variety of discussions and make sure that no one sector or special interest dominates the conclusions. Too much is at stake to develop the "favorite flavor of the month" approach to new directions in cyber security. The authors have identified three recent events in which significant number of important stakeholders assembled to discuss cyber security workforce issues, and present the problem they were organized to address, the discussion which took place and the recommendations which emerged. In this way, while not claiming exhaustive coverage, the paper is able to provide diverse ideas from an illustrative subset of discussions (which however surprisingly tend to similar conclusions and observations!)

2.1   I3P workshop on Cybersecurity Workforce Demand

Problem. Much attention has been paid to devising better ways to educate and train cybersecurity professionals; however this effort was supported only by calls for a more talented workforce, not by a specific problem statement. To begin to address the lack of originating guidance from the employment sectors, the Institute for Information Infrastructure Protection (I3P) ran a workshop in 2011 to gain a better understanding of the demand for cybersecurity workers in government and private industry.   At this workshop, participants listened to keynote talks from leading figures from government, industry, and academia and participated in collaborative working sessions to transpose the discussion points into statements about the need for cybersecurity workers.

The workshop participants shared their specific workforce needs in order to collectively develop a more complete and nuanced understanding of the demand. Among the workshop's goals were to:

1. Develop a more complete understanding of employer demand for cybersecurity skills so that employers and educators can work together to meet the demand.
2. Facilitate communication and cooperation between cybersecurity workforce customers and providers so that supply will more closely track demand.
3. Recognize emerging trends in cybersecurity workforce demand so that training programs can be developed or enhanced to provide new capabilities when they are needed.
4. Provide a framework for needed research and action in the future.

Discussion. The problem space presented while assessing the workplace requirements for cybersecurity professionals is daunting.   One aspect of the challenge was well articulated when one workshop participant summed up the pace of change by observing that none of the cybersecurity jobs he has held in the last 20 years existed when he started his career.   This is very characteristic of the career field.   Employers and employees have struggled to keep pace with change, making the development of a formalized career model very challenging.   Because specific job roles will shift with the advent of new threats and new technologies, participants agreed that competency in core skills is essential. These capabilities include both quantitative skills such as engineering, mathematics and computer science, as well as behavioral skills such as management, communication and the ability to think creatively.   Thus, the demand for cybersecurity expertise cannot easily be described with a uniform skill profile. Rather, needed expertise encompasses an ecosystem of complementary knowledge, skills and abilities

The workshop consisted of three primary keynote presentations, each followed by a breakout session to discuss the presentation and assess the viewpoints in context of the workshop goals.

First, Roberta G. Stempfley, Deputy Assistant Secretary for Cybersecurity and Communications and Principal Deputy Manager, National Communications System,

Department of Homeland Security, described the landscape she surveys from the perspective of leading the US federal government's efforts in this space: the challenges are constantly changing, the demand is outpacing the number of employees, and the workforce must understand the broad aspects of the mission. Using the automobile industry is indicative of the pressures being placed on the IT industry, she noted that Ford produces 2 million cars annually; Apple sells 12 million iPods in the same period. Ford executives therefore say they have no choice but to put iPod connectivity in every car. Consumers demand it, so Ford provides it. The Apple technology is integrated into Ford automobiles, presenting potential new threats to functions and features. Distributed computing and Smartphone are two more worrisome examples. During roughly this same year-long period, the cybersecurity workforce with the Department of Homeland Security grew from 38 to over 200 employees. The rapid pace of change and growing landscape of integration and services requires its employees to be well-rounded professionals who can make security decisions in the context of their organization's mission and resources.

The second keynote talk, by William G. Horne, Research Manager, Systems Security *Lab*, Hewlett-Packard, described the challenges posed to one of the largest technology providers in the world, consisting of 325,000 employees operating in 170 countries. He described the security workforce development challenges: a competitive recruiting and retention environment, the lack of a cybersecurity skills taxonomy, and an uncertain business environment.

He stated that no universal system exists to classify cybersecurity skill sets. HP employs 325,000 people, including a large and diverse cybersecurity workforce. Still, he noted, "there's no database I can query to find out how many of those people know government and risk management and how many people know incident response." This is further challenged by the large collection of corporations seeking to offer high performing employees lucrative offers to change companies. Lastly, Mr. Horne noted the complex environment that his cybersecurity professionals are responsible for. He noted that cybersecurity encompasses a broad and rapidly expanding group of capabilities, and it involves supporting activities in nearly every facet of the economy.

In this respect, security is much like health care. There's more to medicine than hiring the best doctors and nurses; an effective health care system requires a broad diversity of roles: EMTs, medical equipment providers, hospital administrators, pharmaceutical research and manufacturing, and insurance services. Similarly, cybersecurity requires an ecosystem of skills, both general and specialized, among them computer scientists, programmers, forensic analysts, cryptographers, white-hat hackers, and risk-management specialists. A Venn diagram of all these necessary skills would have very little overlap.

Finally, Stephen J. Lukasik, of the Center for International Strategy, Technology and Policy at The Sam Nunn School of International Affairs, Georgia Institute of Technology, discussed how to develop an integrated cybersecurity workforce. He advocated a multi-disciplinary approach to cybersecurity, rejecting "Edisonian" thinking in favor of a methodology based on established sciences that study active agents. He quoted James Lewis, Director of the Technology and Public Policy Program at the Center for Strategic and International Studies, saying that "there is no correlation between the training cyber professionals receive and the job they have to do." One of the greatest misperceptions is defining cybersecurity as a technical problem. Doing this only addresses about 50 percent of the problem, Lukasik said. Effective cybersecurity demands a mix of skills, including law, diplomacy, and management in addition to information technology. Additionally, the workforce at large needs to understand their responsibility to exercise due care and "IT hygiene".

Recommendation. The keynote presenters, while coming from varied positions within the "cyber economy", all posited viewpoints that were very consistent. Throughout the discussions the concept of a diverse workforce that requires both a broad understanding of the landscape and also a deep understanding of very specific areas kept reappearing. The lack of a taxonomy that defines the cybersecurity worker's initial and continuing education and training requirements is a significant deterrent to meeting the needs of the workforce.

To address the underlying concerns raised, the working groups adopted and expanded upon some recommendations from the keynotes and provided insight into additional areas. The first and foremost need was for a skills taxonomy that defines roles for the cybersecurity employee. This would serve as the foundation for a workforce management strategy. A strong recommendation from the working groups was to not exclude the non-cybersecurity workforce in the roles discussion. Every employee with computer access has a cybersecurity role as much as an employee is responsible to safeguard his or her door keys or access codes. This was commonly referred to as "cyber hygiene".

Once a taxonomy of roles is established, the initial and continuing education and training requirements must be established. We have seen an initial attempt at this in the United States Department of Defense with the 8500 series directive (DoD 8500.01E). In this model, a very rough roles taxonomy was created (and refined/expanded in subsequent updates) along with a representative commercial certification that must be obtained in order to serve in a specific role. (In Section 2.3 of this paper we review the new NIST proposed cybersecurity workforce framework.) The definition of frameworks however is not sufficient to ensure workforce competency due to the rapidly changing setting. The working groups proposed a system of practical internships and residency (to borrow a term from the medical field) where practitioners apply their education and training in order to gain an appreciation of the complex environment.

While creating a taxonomy and an educational/training support structure is an important foundation, without requirements for organizations to comply with the framework, the solution will not meet the demand of a highly interconnected IT infrastructure. The requirement for regulations that cross international borders was deemed an important facet of this proposed solution. However, it was admitted that this was the least likely to be adopted.

2.2   CSPRI Workshop on Cybersecurity Education and Workforce Development

Problem. Even while the education and development of cybersecurity professionals is increasingly seen as a priority, the cybersecurity workforce suffers from a fragmented cadre of training and development programs (Assante and Tobey, 2011). The breadth of cybersecurity activities requires a highly diverse workforce. Potential entrants into academic or training institutions come from very different, non-homogeneous backgrounds:

1. High school students with a general interest in computer science
2. Students in two-year community colleges who are eager to join the work force
3. The incumbent work force with needs for updating their skills
4. Workers who have been laid off in allied fields with a desire to re-enter the workforce
5. University students in a broad variety of fields that are tangent to cybersecurity

An October 2010 workshop organized by the George Washington University Cybersecurity Policy and Research Institute (CSPRI) and sponsored by the National Science Foundation explored issues related to post-secondary cybersecurity education and workforce development (CSEWD). Participants agreed that while the university model does not completely satisfy all cybersecurity education and training needs, employers are reluctant to provide that experience through internships or part-time work because (1) the return on investment is uncertain, (2) screening and training interns for meaningful work is expensive and time-consuming, and (3) organizations cannot afford to make their systems vulnerable to possible threats. Participants also agreed that cybersecurity requires a multi-disciplinary, holistic, approach. On the other hand, they could not reach consensus on how to integrate cybersecurity education into current academic settings, nor could they agree on whether barriers to cybersecurity education and training could or should be addressed through standardization. Details of the workshop findings and expanded work that uses it are available elsewhere (Hoffman, 2010; Hoffman et al., 2012).

Discussion. A holistic approach to developing the cybersecurity workforce is one that considers the many disciplines that produce cybersecurity professionals – technical and nontechnical alike, in a coherent fashion. It respects the relative contributions of these different subfields, and recognizes that cybersecurity professionals must develop expertise within their individual subfield while simultaneously understanding how their work fits into the rest of the field. Such an approach incorporates (1) activities that define the workforce structure; (2) continuous professional development opportunities to maintain the human resource; and (3) educational initiatives designed to build capacity in the pipeline.

The development of other professions provides a historical model for the structuring of this emerging field. For instance, cybersecurity today can be compared to 19th century medicine. Medical practitioners of the day, who were often self-taught and uneven in capabilities, functioned within an emerging field that addressed a complex, dynamic and somewhat unpredictable environment with no (or few) professional standards for performance. Needed was a landscape that was "coherent and consistent", much as cybersecurity doctrines are needed to foster those today (Schneider and Mulligan, 2011).

In 1908 the American Medical Association Council on Medical Education approached the Carnegie Foundation and asked their help in surveying and restructuring American medical education. A remarkable non-physician professional educator, Abraham Flexner, who also co-founded Princeton's Institute for Advanced Study, led the effort (Starr, 1982). Over time, efforts by diverse groups helped the medical field evolve into a profession, and today its structure includes a host of fields and sub-fields with distinct career ladders, differentiated training and development programs, and strong standards of professional practice. This model could inform the current cybersecurity workforce discussions and provide replicable models for consideration.

Recommendation. Workshop participants identified a number of cross-cutting principles—concepts that should be applied to any efforts to improve CSEWD. Some of these were:

1. **Curative—not palliative**—approaches to address causes rather than symptoms of the continuing security breaches in computer systems.
2. The **development of metrics and processes for evaluation** to identify successes and areas for improvement.
3. **Long-term integration** of CSEWD efforts including a **lifelong learning continuum**

Workshop participants also saw a need for the development and launch of coordination and disagreement resolution mechanisms for multiple organizations, since no single organization holds the key to preparing the cybersecurity work force of the future.

Finally, they agreed that non-traditional approaches to education and training should be incorporated side-by-side with university-delivered courses. These approaches include:

1. Well designed two-year community college curricula that either produce strong, desired skills for market-ready workers or articulate seamlessly to baccalaureate programs
2. Degrees which span, in a holistic manner, the entire offerings of a university and its diverse schools and departments and which prepare the cybersecurity worker with a full set of skills that truly address the problem
3. Academic and private efforts that enable job-specific challenges to be addressed in long term, educational environments
4. Different delivery mechanisms for education modules that take full advantage of today's technology capacity (for example, wikis, podcasts, social media, virtual laboratories, and cloud computing).

2.3   NICE Cybersecurity Workforce Framework

Problem. The Cybersecurity Workforce effort by the National Institute of Standards and Technology (NIST) was embarked on because there is very little consistency throughout the United States about how cybersecurity is defined and how the workforce is trained.   To have a comprehensive understanding of the cybersecurity workforce, additional human capital data beyond the competencies and data on knowledge, skills, and abilities (KSAs) is needed.   The framework developed by NIST presents a very detailed analysis of roles and responsibilities within the cybersecurity career field and is not limited to government roles.   It is possible to consider applying it across sectors and international lines.

Discussion. The Framework organizes the cybersecurity workforce into seven high-level categories, each comprised of several specialty areas (Homeyer and Maxson, 2012). In developing the framework, NIST coordinated with all sectors of the US federal and state government(s) as well as a large number of not-for-profit organizations including educational, security practitioners, and professional societies. The high-level categories are:

1. Securely Provision: Specialty areas concerned with conceptualizing, designing, and building secure IT systems.
2. Operate and Maintain: Specialty areas responsible for providing the support, administration, and maintenance necessary to ensure effective and efficient IT system performance and security.
3. Protect and Defend: Specialty area responsible for the identification, analysis and mitigation of threats to IT systems and networks.
4. Investigate: Specialty areas responsible for the investigation of cyber events or crimes which occur within IT Systems and networks.
5. Operate and Collect: Specialty areas responsible for the highly specialized and largely classified collection of cybersecurity information that may be used to develop intelligence.
6. Analyze: Specialty area responsible for highly specialized and largely classified review and evaluation of incoming cybersecurity information.
7. Support: Specialty areas that provide critical support so that others may effectively conduct their cybersecurity work.

Each of the categories is further defined to address the specific specialty areas. For example the "Operate and Maintain" category is further defined to include the following specialty areas: Data Administration, Information System Security Management, Knowledge Management, Customer Service and Technical Support, Network Services, System Administration, and Systems Security Analysis. These seven areas make up the functional requirements within this category.

While the breakdown of the categories into specific specialty areas is important, more details are needed to ensure the functions are uniformly understood and supported. To meet this requirement, each specialty area is further defined using the taxonomy shown in Table 1. Each of the rows in Table 1 are explained in detail for each specialty area so that the job functions within the specialty area are clearly articulated and measurable.

Cybersecurity Category	A generalized grouping of specialty areas	Can have one or more unique specialty areas associated with a category
Specialty Area (SA)	Defines specific areas of specialty within the cybersecurity domain	•Belongs to one and only one cybersecurity category •Can have any number of unique tasks and KSAs associated with it
Task	Defines high-level activities that codify a specialty area	•Belongs to one and only one cybersecurity specialty area •Tasks are not linked individually to competencies/KSAs
Competency	A measurable pattern of knowledge, skills, abilities, or other characteristics that individuals need to succeed and that can be shown to differentiate performance.	•One or more KSAs are assigned to each competency •The same competency is likely to be needed across multiple specialty areas
KSA	Defines a specific knowledge, skill, ability.	•Assigned to one or more specialty areas •Each KSA has exactly one competency associated with it

Table1: Function Framework Taxonomy

Recommendation. The details of the NIST cyber security workforce framework lay out a single component of a wide ranging program designed to meet the demand for our cyber workforce. The Department of Homeland Security in the United States is testing the framework to provide structure to its cyber security workforce, trying to develop consistency in terminology across all agencies and components. Lessons learned from the pilot should be gathered and integrated into larger adoptions of a workforce model.

3   Three efforts – fitting the puzzle pieces together

The workshops both identified the need for a new, more holistic way to look at cybersecurity education requirements from the government and commercial market places and major structural descriptors that a good solution must have in order to be viable. Inputs were sought from a wide group of stakeholders, and there was surprising agreement on this need to rethink cybersecurity education. At about the same time, the US Government began its NIST/NICE effort, identifying actual skill sets needed in a structured methodology. The workshop outcomes and NIST/NICE results are consistent with one another and represent a framework that begins to inform decision makers as to needed strategies to improve the workforce, both in quantity number as well as its ability to respond to market needs.

Of course there are many ways to address cybersecurity needs in the government and industry market place. A dominant one is the entire industry of training and accreditation which takes a skills-dominant approach and delivers in a manner authorized by a recognized national or international body a set of skills to workers and students alike. Many times, efforts to define needed reforms and changes in cybersecurity strategies come up short because the academic and training disciplines do not effectively integrate into a coherent set of action strategies for industry, government and academia to consider simultaneously. Figure 1 provides a pictorial flow diagram to help visualize and see the interconnections within the process for cybersecurity workforce development.

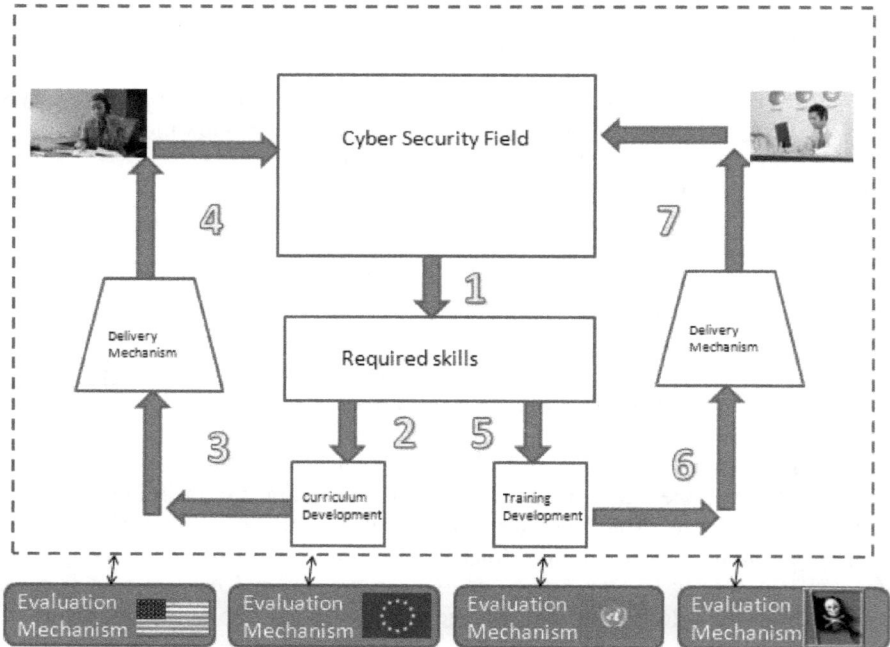

Figure 1: Process for Cybersecurity Workforce Development

Intervention strategies in various stages of the process flow can help fine tune the work force quality and quantity, and also establish the relativities with other parts of the interconnected system. As an example, creating a way to link a set of skills to curriculum development (#2 in the diagram) would modify the outcomes emanating from the related delivery mechanisms (#4).

The details of the NIST cybersecurity workforce framework layout a single component of a wide ranging program designed to meet the demand for our cyber workforce. The Department of Homeland Security in the United States is piloting the framework to provide structure to its cybersecurity workforce, gaining consistency in terminology across all agencies and components. Lessons learned from the pilot should be gathered and integrated into larger adoptions of a workforce model.

4   Conclusions and Recommendations

Cybersecurity workforce development is an international issue. Although the work described here was set in the United States, the cybersecurity workforce challenges are global.   Since 2009 an international group of educators has focused on the education aspects of workforce development in Information Assurance (IA).   (We consider IA to be a component of cybersecurity.)   Through the Innovation and Technology in Computer Science Education (ITiCSE,) working group meetings, faculty, researchers, and government officials from Australia, Sweden, the UK and the US collaboratively examined the "history of IA education efforts, current academic, government and industry guidelines, standards, and recommendations with respect to IA and computing education, and how the quality of IA programs might be assessed." In addition, ITiCSE participants are working "to develop a model of curricular guidelines for IA education," and to examine "the educational missions and curricula of two and four-year institutions with respect to IA education." (Perez et al., 2011). The focus of this work has been on creating a rigorous set of academic modules that work together and define a robust set of outcomes responsive to perceived cybersecurity education needs. The efforts of this group are consistent with the findings presented here.

The international cybersecurity education community can be strengthened through a coherent discussion of the entire Needs-->Responses-->Delivery mechanism action flows.   This paper attempts to establish an initial framework for this needed discussion.

5   Acknowledgements

This material is based upon work supported in part by the National Science Foundation under grants DUE-0621334 and CISE-103956 and in part upon work supported by the U.S. Department of Homeland Security under Grant Award Number 2006-CS-001-000001, under the auspices of the Institute for Information Infrastructure Protection (I3P)

Any opinions, findings, and conclusions or recommendations expressed in this material are those of the author(s) and do not necessarily reflect the views of the National Science Foundation.

6   References

Assante, M., Tobey, D. 2011. "Enhancing the Cybersecurity Workforce," *IT Professional*, vol. 13,   no.   1,   pp.   12-15,   Jan.-Feb.   2011, http://ieeexplore.ieee.org/xpl/freeabs_all.jsp?arnumber=5708280.

Department   of   Defense   Directive   8500.01E, www.dtic.mil/whs/directives/corres/pdf/850001p.pdf

Goodman, S., Lawrence Pfleeger, S., Dodge, R., Longstaff, T., I3P Workshop Report Workforce Development: Understanding the Demand, 27-28 April 2011. Available at: www.the**i3p**.org/docs/publications/432.pdf

Hoffman, L.J. 2010. Building the Cybersecurity Workforce of the 21st Century: Report of a Workshop on Cybersecurity Education and Workforce Development, *Report* GW-CSPRI-2010-3, December 15, 2010.   http://www.cspri.seas.gwu.edu/Seminar%20 Abstracts%20and%20Papers/2010-3a%20Building%20the%20Cyber%20Security %20Workforce%20of%20the%2021st%20Century.pdf

Hoffman, L.J., Burley, D., Toregas, C. 2012 Thinking across Stovepipes: Using a Holistic Development Strategy to Build the Cybersecurity Workforce, to appear, IEEE Security & Privacy Magazine, March 2012.

Homeyer, J., Maxson, M. 2012. Introduction to NICE Cybersecurity Workforce Framework, available at: http://csrc.nist.gov/nice/framework/documents/NICE-Cybersecurity-Workforce-Framework-printable.pdf, last accessed 17 Jan 2012

Perez, L., et al. "Information Assurance Education in Two and Four Year Institutions," http://www.iticse2011.tu-darmstadt.de/sites/default/files/wg3_0.pdf.

Schneider, F., Mulligan, "A Doctrinal Thesis," *IEEE Security & Privacy Magazine*, vol.   9,   pp.   3-4,   July-Aug.   2011,   http://ieeexplore.ieee.org/xpls/abs_all.jsp? arnumber=5968081&tag=1.

Starr, P. 1982. *The Social Transformation of American Medicine*. Basic Books, 1982.

Creating a Security Culture Development Plan and a Case Study

O. Olivos

Inca Garcilaso University, Lima, Peru
e-mail: olivosomar@gmail.com

Abstract

When developing training and awareness programs, information security specialists usually fail to consider the human element as an important component of the program (Kruger et al, 2006). They tend to focus on security policies and technical aspects leaving aside the human aspect of information security. We argue that it is necessary that the characteristics of the employees (roles and learning styles), the compliance with the current policies, the state of the security culture and the mission, vision and strategic planning of the organization be considered when setting up a security culture development plan. This paper describes the steps that should be followed to develop a Security Culture and reports a case study in an organisation where the development plan was applied.

Keywords

Social Engineering, Training, Awareness, Security Culture

1 Introduction

Organizations that are in the process of developing training and awareness programs need to take into account the audience. They need to provide information and case studies that the audience can relate to, not a one size fits all training program (Deloitte, 2007). The human resources need to be evaluated so that we get a better understanding of the different learning styles and needs of each individual. The security policies in place and the perception of security within the organization need to be evaluated too. The strategic business plan must also be considered for the goals of the program are to be aligned with the business goals. With all this information the organization is ready to design and implement its Security Culture Development Plan (see Figure 1) to fight Social Engineering attacks. The processes have been devised with social engineering in mind; however, they could be used in a wider scope.

Security is not a technology problem-it's a people and management problem. As developers continuously invent better security technologies, making it increasingly difficult to exploit technical vulnerabilities, attackers will turn more and more to exploiting the human element (Nolan and Levesque, 2005). Social engineering is defined as the social/psychological process, by which an individual, the social engineer, can gain information from an individual about a targeted organization (Thornburgh, 2004). Therefore physical and technical controls are not enough to protect the confidentiality, integrity and availability of the information. The human dimension is usually considered the weakest link in the overall ICT security chain (Tarimo et al, 2006). This paper describes the steps (see Figure 1) that should be followed to develop a security culture which will help the organization mitigate the risks of social engineering attacks.

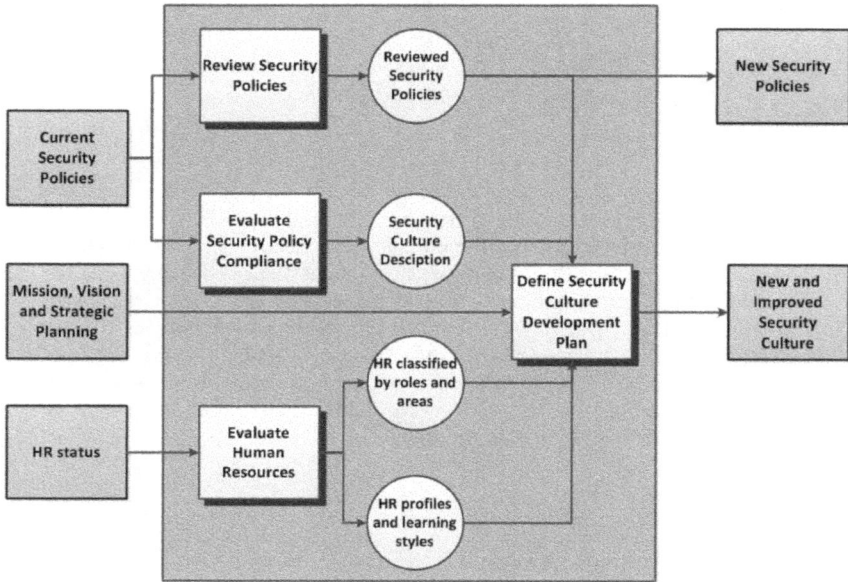

Figure 1: Security Culture Development Plan

The security culture development plan introduced in this paper is based on the conceptual model of information security culture described by Van Niekerk and Von Solms (2006, 2010). Their work is an extension of the model for corporate culture presented by Schein (1999). This model has become widely accepted amongst information security researchers (Schlienger & Teufel, 2003).

The adaptation of Schein's model is composed of 4 layers: Artifacts, Espoused Values, Shared Tacit Assumptions and Knowledge (Van Niekerk and Von Solms, 2006, 2010).

According to Schein and Van Niekerk and Von Solms, artifacts are what actually happen in the organization. Espoused values can be seen as the visible contributions of the organization's management towards the organization's culture. The mission, vision and policies form part of the espoused values. The shared and tacit assumptions layer consists of the beliefs and values of employees. Having adequate knowledge regarding information security is a prerequisite to perform any normal activity in a secure manner. Without adequate knowledge, information security cannot be ensured (Van Niekerk and Von Solms, 2006, 2010).

The artifacts layer will be evaluated by the Evaluate Security Policy Compliance process. The espoused values are assessed and standardized in the Review Security Policies process. They are also included in the Define Security Culture Development Plan process in the form of the mission, vision and strategic planning. The knowledge is instilled as part of the training and culturization process (Lower order thinking skills). The shared tacit assumptions will be dealt with in the training and culturization process when the instructor helps the employees develop their higher order thinking skills.

The remainder of the paper is organized as follows. Section 2 explains how to evaluate the organization's security policies. Section 3 gives details on the steps followed to determine what is the organization's perception and attitude towards security. Section 4 deals with the aspects that should be taken into account when evaluating the human resources of the organization. Section 5 explains in detail how the security culture development plan works and Section 6 how to measure its results. A case study is reported in Section 7. Finally, Section 8 concludes the paper with some general comments.

2 Review Security Policies

The security policy is basically a plan, outlining what the company's critical assets are, and how they must be protected. Its main purpose is to provide employees with a brief overview of the acceptable use of any of the Information Assets, as well as to explain what is deemed as allowable and what is not, thus engaging them in securing the company's critical systems (Danchev 2003).

Danchev (2003) also mentions that the main reasons behind the creation of a security policy is to set a company's information security foundations, to explain to employees how they are responsible for the protection of the information assets, and emphasize the importance of having secured communications while doing business online. Policies also have to address issues such as threats and possible countermeasures as well as defining roles and responsibilities (Mlangeni and Biremann, 2005).

Management should set a clear policy direction in line with business objectives and demonstrate support for, and commitment to, information security through the issue and maintenance of an information security policy across the organization (ISO 17799, 2005). Policies should reflect the overall attitude of top management about security controls and its importance to the organization (Dhillon, 2001).

Since information security culture emerges where specific behaviour is encouraged such as complying with a well-established standard (Martins and Eloff, 2002), we suggest that the current organization's security policies be compared with an international standard such as ISO/IEC 27002.

In this section of the paper we consider three aspects of security: Physical, Technical and Administrative. Since we focus on the human aspect of security and ISO 27002 does not specifically address social engineering we have taken into account only those elements or controls that are related to the human component of security. A checklist for each of the three aspects of security is provided so that the current security policies can be assessed. As a result of this process, an improved ISO 27002-compliant set of policies are suggested to the organization to provide better protection against social engineering attacks.

3   Evaluate Security Policy Compliance

In this process we evaluate the compliance with the security policies. This will help us understand the employee's perception and attitude towards security. This is important because inconsistent application of policies may lead to frustration by employees and thus undermine the effectiveness of policies (Stephanou and Dagada, 2008). Our goal is to develop an information security culture and to achieve this we need to provide knowledge, promote a positive attitude towards security and modify the behaviour because it's not what people know, or feel, or are aware of that is the final determinant of the quality of security — it's what they do (Roper et al, 2006 p7).

Good security practice goes beyond technical IT solutions. It is driven by a business strategy with associated security policies and procedures implemented in a culture of Security. These practices are supported by IT and Financial Resources dedicated to Security (Ang et al, 2006). As suggested by some authors, one way of measuring the level of an organization's information security culture is to use an information security culture assessment instrument (e.g. questionnaires or surveys) (Da Veiga et al, 2007) so a survey is applied to members of the organization and they are asked to rate a series of statements about their perception of security, specifically: The current state of that security issue within their organization and the importance of that security issue for their organization.

4   Evaluate Human Resources

In order to develop a successful security culture development plan the human component needs to be taken into account. In this step we suggest that the human resources be evaluated in two aspects:

4.1   Roles

An inventory of the roles that the employees have within the organization is required. These roles grant them access to different information systems and provide them with the appropriate level of information. Employees with different roles perform different tasks and also have different needs which make them vulnerable to different kinds of social engineering attacks. Due to the nature of their job, phone operators will benefit more from training on pretexting, mobile users will require more training on shoulder surfing and receptionists and guards on impersonation to name a few. Other topics like phishing among others will apply to all employees.

4.2   Learning Styles

Students learn in many different ways –by seeing and hearing; reflecting and acting; reasoning logically and intuitively; memorizing and visualizing and drawing analogies and building mathematical models; steadily and in fits and starts. How much a given student learns in a class is governed in part by the student's native ability and prior preparation but also by the compatibility of his or her learning style and the instructor's teaching style (Felder and Silverman, 1988). A learning style model classifies students according to where they fit on a number of scales pertaining to the ways they receive and process information (Felder and Silverman, 1988).

Adults have previous knowledge, experiences, relationships, believes that influence the way they behave and how they learn (Lowy and Hood, 2004 p 267). We should make use of this background when creating the groups and also when preparing the training and culturization sessions. Kolb's learning theory sets out four distinct learning styles (Figure 2), which are based on a four-stage learning cycle. Knowing a person's learning style enables learning to be orientated according to the preferred method (Kolb and Kolb, 2005).

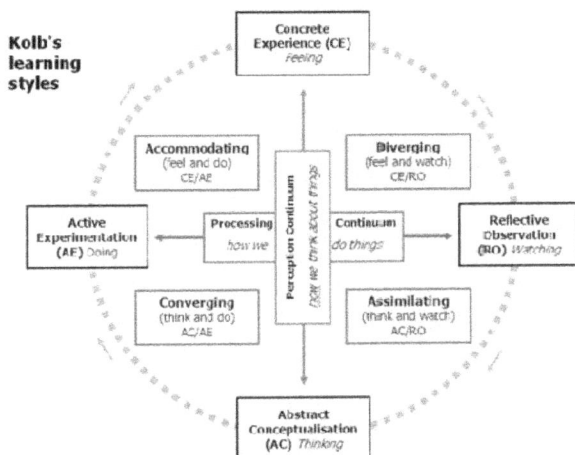

Figure 2: Kolb's Learning Styles (Chapman, 2005)

A learning style is a preference, not an absolute. All learners, regardless of preference, can function in all four styles when needed (Sharp, 1998). Assessing an individual's learning style is vital to the teaching and learning process (Hein and Budny, 2000).   There is vast collection of learning models amongst which Kolb Learning Style Inventory (KLSI) remained one of the most influential and widely distributed instruments used to measure individual learning preferences (Kayes, 2005). The original KLSI encountered serious attacks because of his low test-retest reliability and limited construct validity. In 1985, the inventory was reorganized and redeveloped in light of the psychometric criticism it received. The KLSI was redesigned with the aim of experimentally evaluating skills of individuals in learning process. The inventory was further redeveloped in 1996 (Lu et al, 2007; Yildirim, 2010). Researchers have examined and found support for the revised KLSI and found increased stability (Lu et at, 2007).

As shown in Figure 2, Kolb's model works on two levels - a four-stage cycle:
* Concrete Experience - (CE)
* Reflective Observation - (RO)
* Abstract Conceptualization - (AC)
* Active Experimentation - (AE)

And a four-type definition of learning styles, each representing the combination of two preferred styles:
* Diverging (CE/RO)
* Assimilating (AC/RO)
* Converging (AC/AE)
* Accommodating (CE/AE)

Each individual learning style should be taken into account by the Security Culture Development Plan team when setting out the groups and also by the instructor when preparing the lessons and activities that will be used in the culturization sessions.

5   Security Culture Development Plan (SCDP)

This is the most important process because here we will provide the necessary knowledge and will establish the foundations for the shared tacit assumptions. Without adequate knowledge, information security cannot be ensured (Van Niekerk and Von Solms, 2010).   The shared tacit assumptions consist of the beliefs and values of employees. If such belief should conflict with one of the espoused values, knowing why a specific control is needed might play a vital role in ensuring compliance (Schlienger & Teufel, 2003).

The main goal of the SCDP is to set the foundations to develop a new security culture that takes into account the needs and learning styles of each individual, their security perception, the security policies of the organization and its business goals.

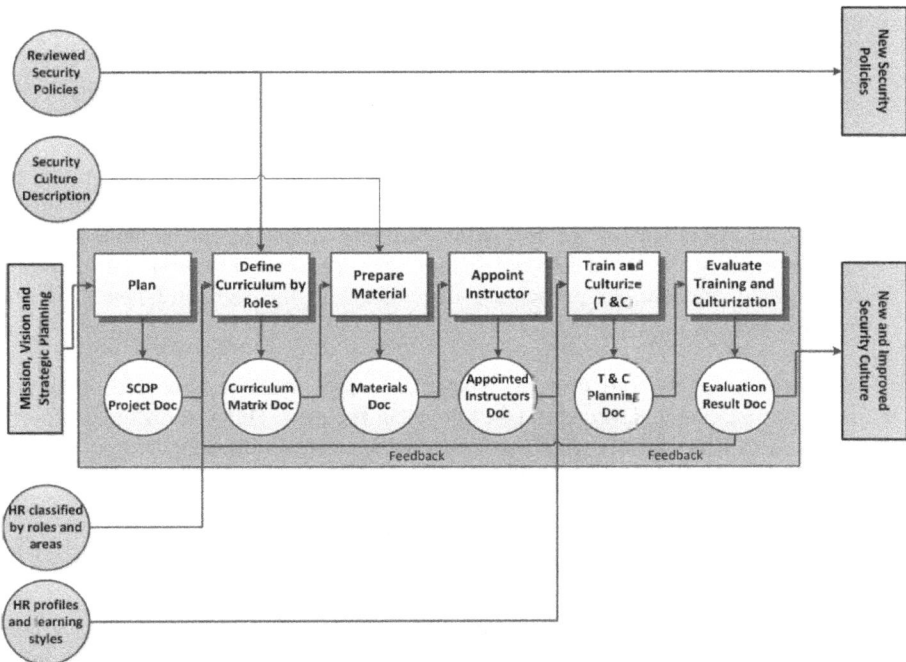

Figure 3: Define a Security Culture Development Plan

This process is composed of 6 sub processes and each of these processes produces a document that is used as the input for the following step. In Figure 3, we can observe the main and first feedback loop. The result of the evaluation of the training and culturization process provides the SCDP Team with the necessary feedback to reorganize and redefine the curriculum, prepare and acquire better material or appoint another instructor that fulfils the requirements.

5.1 Plan

It is a very important part of the process but is often overlooked. Just like in any other project the goals of the SCDP must be clearly stated and must be aligned with the organization's goals. The SCDP Team needs to make sure that the security program adapts to the changing business environment, requirements and technology (Tyukala et al, 2006). The necessary resources (people, money, time, etc.) must be allocated to the project and the support from the higher levels of the organization must be obtained. It is composed of four steps:

a) **Define Goals.** Goals must be in line with the organization's goals and must support the business needs of the organization and be relevant to the organization's culture and IT architecture (NIST 800-50, 2003, p.22).

b) **Appoint a champion.** It is the person that will lead the project and be the link with the stakeholders. This individual will provide leadership and should have overall responsibility for the preparation and implementation of the program (Baybutt, 2003). Since support and commitment from the top management is vital, it is suggested that the champion be a member of the senior management (Höne, 2004).

c) **Form the SCDP Team**. Since it is not just a training program but a project to develop a security culture, personnel from different areas will be required to participate. Members of the following business areas should be included: IT, HR, Marketing, Legal Department and Security. Representatives from other areas could and should participate depending on the size and needs of the organization.

d) **Allocate resources and budget**. A special budget must be allocated, it cannot be the same budget assigned to IT or physical security. This is a different project and as such it needs its own resources. The Security Culture Development Plan should not be seen as a spending cost but as an investment (Soon Lim et al, 2009).

5.2 Define curriculum by roles.

The first job of the SCDP Team is to prepare a list of relevant security topics that need to be addressed during the training and culturization process. Since not all areas have the same needs, these topics must be carefully mapped to the different business areas in the organization. The receptionist and assistants may need more training on pretexting and attacks over the phone while laptop users may need training on how to prevent shoulder surfing for instance. It is important to distinguish between job-specific and overall security training and practices (Kraemer and Carayon, 2005). The topics chosen must reflect the weaknesses identified during the revision of the security policies. Members of the IT department and the CIO/CISO play an important role in adding items to this list as they are aware of new threats and techniques used by social engineers.

5.3 Prepare material

This process receives the Security Culture Description document as an input from the Evaluate Security Policy Compliance process. This document will help the SCDP Team prioritize the topics that need urgent attention and that should be dealt with first.

The next step is to acquire or produce the marketing material necessary to spread the new ideas and information about training possibilities, security tips, etc. The marketing area of the organization will play an important role in this process. It is suggested that the direct marketing approach be used to spread the new ideas. Unlike mass marketing, direct marketing takes into account the characteristics of each individual such as the age, sex, role in the organization, experience and others (Stewart, 2009). Once the marketing material is acquired, it is recorded in the inventory and then using the Marketing Material Matrix the SCDP Team matches the marketing material with the topics listed in the Define Curriculum by Roles process.

Then SCDP Team needs to obtain training material (videos, books, presentations, CBT, WBT, etc.) that will be used during the training and culturization process. Ideas on how to develop and deliver awareness and training material can be found on NIST 800-50 (2003).

5.4 Appoint instructor.

Usually it is a member of the IT department who delivers the classes. We consider that it is extremely important that the instructor have teaching experience and knowledge of teaching techniques. We believe that one of the main reasons why training programs fail to achieve a change in attitude is because they only work on the lower order thinking skills (LOTS). Lower order thinking skills are related to remembering and understanding knowledge while higher order thinking skills (HOTS) are related to evaluating, judging, creating and formulating ideas. (Van Niekerk & Von Solms, 2008)

5.5 Train and culturise.

This is the most important process and it is the main contribution of this paper. Most training programs work only on LOTS and therefore accomplish neither a change in attitude nor a change in behaviour.

Users may know and understand their roles in the organization correctly but still don't adhere to a security policy because it conflicts with their beliefs and values (Schlienger & Teufel, 2003). It is therefore important to also ensure that the users have the correct attitude, and thus the desired behaviour, towards information security (Van Niekerk & Von Solms, 2006; Kruger et al, 2006). In order to ensure the desired user behaviour, it is necessary to cultivate an organizational culture of information security (Von Solms, 2000; Schlienger & Teufel, 2003; Tarimo et al, 2006).The Training and Culturization process is composed of five steps (see Figure 4)

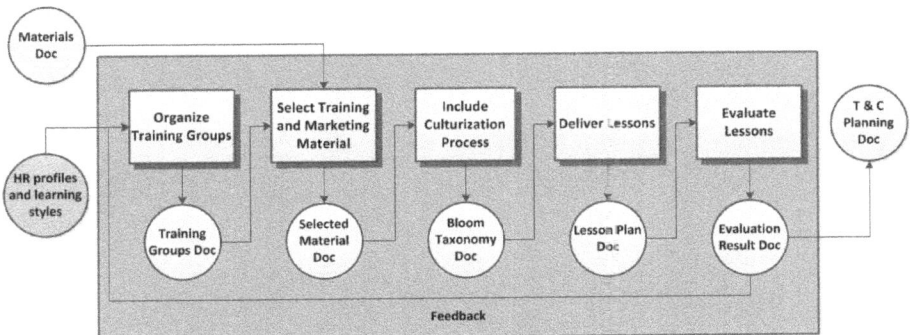

Figure 4: Training and Culturization process

a) **Organize Training Groups.** Employees are divided into groups based on the roles they play in the organizations, the tasks they perform, their learning styles and their availability. It is important to record the criterion that was used to form the groups so that the instructor is aware of it.

b) **Select Training and Marketing Material.** The material relevant to the topics listed in the Define Curriculum process and the groups formed is chosen from the available material acquired in the Prepare Material process.

c) **Include Culturization Process.** During the preparation of the training and culturization sessions the appointed instructor must take into account the different learning styles identified in the Evaluating Human Resources process. The activities that will be used in the training and culturization sessions should correspond to each of the Bloom's levels in order to make the participants reach the highest level of the taxonomy hence promoting a change in the attitude and behaviour. An information security specialist might think that teaching the users what a password is (or lecturing users on the organization's security policies), is enough, but research has shown that understanding why is essential to obtaining buy-in from employees (Van Niekerk & Von Solms, 2008). Table 1 shows examples of activities that can be used in each level during the training and culturization sessions on Password Management. Based on these examples, the instructor should create activities that will help users (considering their different learning styles) move from a passive role (remembering and understanding) to a more active role (evaluating and creating).

d) **Deliver Lessons.** The instructor will work on the activities designed in the previous step, see Table 1 for suggested activities. The lessons must be delivered using a variety of techniques that accommodate participants with different learning styles. We believe that the instructor must have some teaching experience as the goal is not just to make sure that the employees acquire knowledge but that they change their attitude towards security and behave in a secure manner.

Level	Activities
Create	Formulate a theory to explain why employees still write down their passwords and what the risks of doing so are. Propose solutions to this problem (Van Niekerk & Von Solms, 2006).
Evaluate	Judge and evaluate organization's security policies about passwords and suggest changes and improvements
Analyse	Compare the level of protection provided by passwords and other mechanisms (biometrics, smartcards, etc).
Apply	Use mnemonic techniques to create and recall a secure password.
Understand	Explain why the organization requires that the password includes non-alphanumeric characters and a minimum of 8 characters.
Remember	Describe the characteristics of a strong password as stated in the organization's security policies.

Table 1: Suggested Activities based on Bloom's taxonomy

5.6   Evaluate Lesson

It is extremely important to evaluate each and every training and culturization session or lesson delivered. It will provide feedback to make the necessary amendments to the lessons. Since our goal is to develop a security culture within each of the participants we believe that each session should be assessed. First, it should assessed by each employee who participated in the session using a form provided. Second, by the instructor to check if the goals set were achieved. And in some cases by the SCDP team. In a large organization it would impossible for the SCDP team to evaluate every session but it should definitely assess some. This process provides the inner feedback loop. This feedback allows the instructor to make the necessary amendments.

6   Evaluate Training and Culturization

Without effective measurement and evaluation, there is no real evidence from which to conclude that training and culturization have been effective - not just that awareness of information security issues has been raised, but also and more importantly that positive behavioural change towards information security has actually been effected (Davis, 2008).

Without this measurement, it is impossible to establish whether or not an appropriate return on the investment has been realized. Measurement also plays an important part in allowing organizations to adopt a risk-based approach to information security, as it allows a business to identify where there is a need for greater investment in training as well as where it may be possible to spend less without impacting the security risk profile adversely (Davis, 2008).

Once the Training and Culturization process has been completed it is necessary to evaluate its success. In the previous step, Evaluate Lesson, we assessed the success/failure of an individual lesson, in this process we look at the whole process that means the effect that it has had on the knowledge, attitude and behaviour of the individuals (Kruger and Kearney, 2005). It provides the outer and main feedback loop which allows the SCDP Team to make the necessary amendments and also to justify future investments in the program (Schlienger & Teufel, 2003).

To evaluate knowledge we suggest that multiple choice, True/False, fill in the blanks and matching definitions tests be used. They are all easy to administer and can be done through a virtual learning environment. Surveys, interviews and focus groups are the most effective methods to evaluate the change in attitude. Surveys, interviews and focus groups can also be used to evaluate the change in behaviour. Although they are time-consuming activities they are very effective.

Other methods such as the following can also be used:

* Internal and External Audits.
* Participation in coaching programs.
* Participation as security champions for their section or department.
* Posting in blogs and/or wikis about security.

One of the main focuses of this work is to make sure that the learning styles of each member of the organization be taken into account. Therefore it is important to keep a record of each individual. Social engineers will always look for the weakest link in the security chain so it is necessary that the organization keeps track of the development of each employee in terms of knowledge, attitude and behaviour towards security.

7   Case Study

The proposed Security Culture Development Plan was applied in an organization with over 20 years of experience in manufacturing and trading high-quality canned, fresh and frozen products. The organization has 40 employees in its main office and 8 admin employees in its two branches plus a large number of workers on the fields.

The first step was to review the security policies. We requested all the documents that the organization had related to information security (policies, procedures, guidelines and others). We also interviewed two of the managers, the head of the IT section and 5 employees from different sections. We found that the security policies were spread over several documents many of which are not known by the employees. No specific roles or responsibilities are defined in the documents. Some of the rules are not applicable in the organisation anymore. For example, one of the documents states that employees are responsible for backing up all their critical information stored in their computers and that they are to contact the IT department if they require any assistance with the process. In our interview with the Head of IT he mentioned that all backup was centralised and that the IT department was responsible for the backup and restore processes. In other cases, the employees are asked to perform certain tasks but are not explained how and are not provided with more information. For example, employees must change their password every three months but are not told what the password requirements are (length, use of symbols, etc). However, this information appears in a PowerPoint presentation available in a folder in the public network drive. None of the 5 employees interviewed had ever received copies of all these documents.

After this assessment, an improved ISO 27002-compliant set of policies were suggested to the organization. Management and the IT department made some changes and finally the new policies were approved.

The second step was to evaluate the Security Policy compliance so we applied a questionnaire to 3 of the managers, the 3 members of the IT department and 21 employees from different sections.

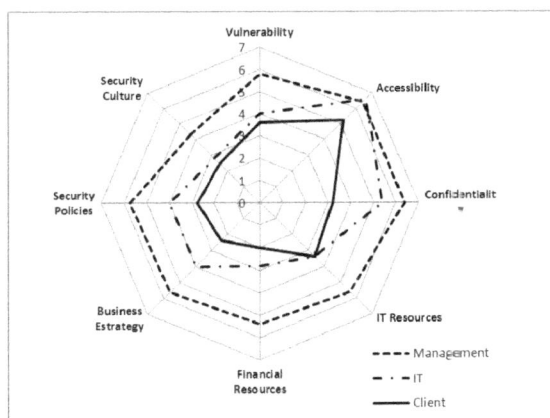

Figure 5: Security Assessment Results

The results (see Figure 5) show that the managers feel that the main weakness in information security in the organisation lies on people. They also feel that they are providing enough financial and IT resources for security purposes and that business strategies and security policies are well aligned. The three members of the IT department agree on the fact that security culture is an issue but think that they are not provided with enough resources to fulfil their roles in terms of information security. Finally the 21 employees who participated had a more pessimistic perception of security in the organization and assessed it very low in almost all the aspects of the questionnaire. As had been discovered earlier most employees are not aware of the existing security policies and do not feel that the organization management supports information security adequately.

Role/ Area	Employees		Learning Style	Employees
Manager / supervisor	6		Diverging	10
Administration	15		Assimilating	7
Commercial	9		Converging	7
Reception/Secretary	3		Accommodating	6
IT	3		Total	30

Table 2: HR classification by roles and learning styles

Members of the organisation were also classified according to the roles they have, the areas they belong and their learning styles (Table 2). Only 36 out of the 40 employees were considered as one employee was away on parental leave and 1 had a contract that was due in the next couple of weeks and would not be renewed. One was on holidays and another had been sent to one of the branches to replace the branch supervisor who was away on vacations. Out of the 36 only 30 completed properly and on time the learning style questionnaire.

The Chief of Admin and Finance was designated SCDP Champion and the SCDP Team was formed by 2 members of the IT department, 1 member from the commercial section and the human resources supervisor. One of their first tasks was to put together a list of security topics that need to be addressed during the training and culturization process. These topics included: Social Engineering, shoulder surfing, password management, dumpster diving, phishing, information classification, laptop/mobile security, internal threats, influence techniques and impersonation.

The next step was to map these topics to the clients based on their roles in the organisations (see Table 3). Some topics are specific to some clients, for example since laptops are only issued to managers and supervisors, the receptionist would not need special training on this area.

The SCDP Team then prioritized the suggested topics based on the needs of the organization. Password management, laptop security, phishing and information classification were considered the topics with the highest priority. Flyers related to the topics were downloaded from the European Network and Information Security Agency (ENISA) website and posted on the walls in different parts of the building. Some comic strips (taken from Dilbert's website) about password management and other security related topics were found by the SCDP Team. An employee volunteered to translate them into Spanish and emailed them to his colleagues. There was very positive feedback on this.

Due to budget constrains no books or videos were bought at this time. All material used during the Training and Culturization sessions was prepared in house. Since we have a teaching background, experience in information security and knowledge of the proposed methodology we became the instructor.

	Managers / Supervisor	Admin	Commercial	Secretary / Reception	IT
Social Engineering	√	√	√	√	√
Shoulder Surfing	√	√	√	√	
Password Management	√	√	√	√	
Dumpster diving		√	√	√	√
Phishing	√	√	√	√	√
Information classification	√	√	√	√	√
Laptop Security	√				
Internal threats		√	√	√	√
Impersonation			√	√	
Influence techniques			√	√	√

Table 3: Security topics by roles

The training groups were formed based on time availability, role in the organization and learning styles. Time availability became the main restriction. The first group was composed of 10 employees. Since all 4 learning styles were present in the group the activities were planned to accommodate all learning styles.

The activities presented in Table 1 were used during the training and culturization sessions. All sessions were planned using the provided lesson plan format. The lesson plan contained the topic, objectives, activities, material needed and assessment opportunities for each session (Figure 6).

Lesson Plan format		
Lesson Plan Title **Safe Passwords in the Organisation**		**Topic** **Password Management I**
Instructor **Omar Olivos**	**Time** **1h 15m**	**Sub Topics** • Mnemotechnic rules • Attack techniques
Main Objectives • Describe the Organisation security policies regarding the use of passwords • Apply Mnemotechnic rules to create and remember strong passwords		**Secondary Objectives** • Name common techniques used by social engineers to obtain passwords • Name god and bad habits on password management
Activities	**Materials**	**Assessment Strategies**

• Explain Objectives
• First Assessment (Pre Test)
 	
• Presentation
  o Organisation Security Policies
  o Social Engineer techniques.
  o Mnemotechnic rules (Group discussion)
  o Group presentation– Feedback
 	
• Final Assessment (Post Test)
	• Laptop
	• Projector
	• PowerPoint Presentation (ppt)
	• Memory Stick USB
	• Whiteboard / Markers / Large pieces of paper
	• Organisation Policies– hard copies
	• Paper / pens
	• Internet Access. The password meter
		Pre Test - Multiple Option
		
		Post Test - Multiple Option
		
		Group Work
		  • Discussion
		  • Presentation - Feedback

Notes Final Assessment (Post Test) can be handed in at the beginning of the following session if there is not enough time left at the end of Session I.		

Figure 6: Lesson Plan - Session I on Password Management

At the beginning of the session the First Assessment (Pre-Test) was distributed to all and out of the 10 participants:

Only 5	Knew what was the minimum password length as stated in the organization's policies
Only 2	Were able to identified a password that fulfilled all the requirements as stated in the policy documents
Only 2	Knew how often they needed to change their password
Only 3	Would not provide their password to another person under any circumstances

In this session we only worked on the lower order thinking skills (LOTS): remember, understand and apply.

At the end of the session the Post-Test was distributed to all and out of the 10 participants

All	Remembered what was the minimum password length as stated in the organization's policies
All	Identified the password that fulfilled all the requirements as stated in the policy documents
9	Knew how often they needed to change their password
All	Would not provide their password to another person

In a later session, we continued working on Password Management but with an emphasis on higher order thinking skills (HOTS): analyse, evaluate and create. Our goal is to promote a positive attitude towards information security and a change in the behaviour. During this session participants identified bad security practices in the organisation and provided solutions to these problems. A common problem was that managers shared their passwords with their assistants so that they could check and update their calendars. It was suggested that the calendars be shared and permissions be granted to the assistants so that they could access their bosses' calendars without knowing their passwords. Participants also came up with new techniques to create strong password that were easy to remember (like using two words in different languages and adding numbers and symbols to make it more complex).

Knowledge acquired was assessed with the Post-Tests in each session. Attitude was assessed during the group activities and also through their feedback and comments. Change in behaviour was assessed in later interviews with participants. Some participants mentioned that they had requested that their computers be changed positions as some other employees could shoulder surf them while entering their passwords. The SCDP champion supported this request and the workstations were repositioned. Another participant mentioned that now she shuts the blinds when the cleaners are cleaning her office windows to avoid them from looking at her computer screen. IT support granted assistants access to manager's calendar as requested by them and approved by their bosses. Another participant was very proud because she was able to teach her teenage son some techniques to create strong password. Even though the son spent a great deal of time in the computer he did not have good security habits. All the participants interviewed had changed at least one of their passwords in the last 10 days and their work password was different from the other passwords they had.

All the responses we got showed that all participants had acquired the required knowledge, that they had a different attitude towards security and that they had a more positive and proactive behaviour towards security in the organisation and in their private lives. A new security culture was emerging.

8   Conclusions

In this paper we presented a holistic approach on how to create a security culture development plan in an organization based on the conceptual model of information security culture described by Van Niekerk and Von Solms (2006). This approach considers the human component as one of the most important ones. Employees play different roles within the organization, they have different learning styles and have different backgrounds that need to be considered when creating groups, planning activities and delivering lessons. The training and culturization sessions cannot be just traditional lectures, it is important that different activities are used to reach all learning styles. The activities must also be carefully planned based on the different levels of Bloom's taxonomy. The instructor must have some teaching experience or pedagogical background as the main goal is not just to provide knowledge but to change the attitude and the behaviour which will later develop a security culture in the organization. Assessment of knowledge, attitude and behaviour is also necessary and the SCDP Team must keep track of the progress of members of the organization.

Policies are also very important and must reflect the organization's business strategy. Since support from the top management is necessary for the project to be successful, it is suggested that the SCDP champion be a member of the senior management.

Information security is not just the responsibility of the computer department but of every single member of the organization. Therefore we need to make sure that all business areas are part of the security culture development plan. Finally after applying the suggested methodology a change in behaviour was observed in all the employees that participated in the Training and Culturisation sessions.

9 References

Ang, W.H., Lee, Y., Madnick, S., Mistree, D., Siegel, M., Strong, D. and Wang, R. (2006), "Designing the house of security: Stakeholder perceptions of security assessment and importance", *MIT Sloan Working Paper* 4623-06, Proceedings of the Twelfth Americas Conference on Information Systems.

Baybutt, P. (2003), "Process security management systems: Protecting plans against threats". *Chemical Engineering*, Vol 110, No 1, pps 48-55.

Chapman, A. (2005), "The Kolb Learning Styles", www.businessballs.com/kolblearningstyles.htm (Accessed 10 June 2010) .

Da Veiga, A., Martins, N., Eloff, J. (2007), "Information security culture - validation of an assessment instrument". *Southern African Business Review*, vol. 11, no. 1, pp. 147-166.

Danchev, D. (2003), "Building and Implementing a Successful Information Security Policy", *Windows Security*.

Dhillon, G. (2001), "Violation of safeguards by trusted personnel and understanding related information security concerns". Computers & Security, Volume 20, pp 165-172.

Felder, R.M., Silverman, L.K. (1988), "Learning and teaching styles in engineering education", *Engineering Education*, 78(7), pp. 674–681.

Hein, T.L., Budny, D.D. (2000), " Styles and types in science and engineering education", *International Conference on Engineering and Computer Education (ICECE)*, Sao Paulo, Brazil. Article published in the ICECE proceedings.

Höne, K. (2004), "The information security policy - an important information security management control". *Faculty of economic and management science*, Rand Afrikaans University.

ISO. (2005), "Information technology. Security techniques. Code of practice for information security management", ISO/IEC 17799 (BS 7799–1: 2005).

Kayes, D.C. (2005), "Internal validity and realiability of Kolb's Learning Style Inventory version 3 (1999)". *Journal of Business and Psychology*, 20 (2), 249-257.

Kolb, A., Kolb, D. (2005), "The Kolb Learning Style Inventory, Version 3.1", Boston, Hay Group.

Kraemer, S., Carayon, P., (2005), "Computer and information security culture: Findings from two studies". *Proceedings of the Human Factors and Ergonomics Society 49th Annual Meeting.*

Kruger HA., Drevin, L., Steyn, T. (2006), "A framework for evaluating ICT security awareness". *Proceedings of the 2006 Information Security South Africa Conference*, Sandton, South Africa.

Kruger, HA., Kearney, WD. (2005), "Measuring information security awareness: A West Africa gold mining environment case study". *Proceedings of the 2005 Information Security South Africa Conference*, Sandton, South Africa.

Lowy, A., Hood, P. (2004), "The Power of the 2x2 matrix" Jossey-Bass, New York.

Lu, H., Jia, L., Gong, S.H. and Clark, B. (2007), "The relationship of Kolb learning styles, online learning behaviors and Learning outcomes". *Educational Technology & Society*, 10(4), 187-196.

Martins, A., Eloff, J. (2002), "Information Security Culture". Security in the information society, pp 203-214. *IFIP/SEC2002*. Boston, MA: Kluwer Academic Publishers.

Mlangeni, SA., Biermann, E. (2005), "An assessment of Information Security Policies within the Polokwane area: A case study". *Proceedings of the 2005 Information Security South Africa Conference*, Sandton, South Africa.

National Institute of Standards and Technology. (2003). "NIST 800-50: Building an Information Technology Security Awareness and Training Program". *NIST Special Publication 800-50*, National Institute of Standards and Technology.

Nolan, J. and Levesque, M. (2005). "Hacking human: data-archaeology and surveillance in social networks", ACM SIGGROUP Bulletin, vol. 25, no. 2, pp33-37.

Roper, C., Grau, J. and Fischer, L. (2005), "Security education, awareness and training: From theory to practice". Elsevier Butterworth Heinemann.

Schein, EH. (1999), "The corporate culture survival guide". Jossey-Bass Inc.

Schlienger, T., Teufel, S. (2003), Information Security Culture – from Analysis to Change, *Proceedings of the 3rd Annual Information Security South Africa Conference*, Sandton, South Africa.

Sharp, J., (1998) , "Learning Styles And Technical Communication: Improving Communication And Teamwork Skills". Proceedings, 1998 Frontiers in Education Conference.

Soon Lim, J., Chang, S., Maynard, S., Ahmad, A., (2009), "Exploring the relationship between organizational culture and information security culture". *7th Australian Information Security Management Conference* pp 88-95. AISM2009. Perth, Western Australia.

Stephanou, AT., Dagada R. (2008), "The impact of information security awareness training on information security behaviour: The case for further research", Information Security South Africa (ISSA), Johannesburg, South Africa.

Stewart, G,. (2009), "Maximising the effectiveness of information security awareness using marketing and psychological principles". *Technical Report,* RHUL –MA-2009-02. Royal Halloway, University of London.

Tarimo, C., Kuwe, J., Yngström, L., Kowalski, S. (2006), "A social-technical view of ICT security issues, trends, and challenges: Towards a culture of ICT security – The case of Tanzania". *Proceedings of the 2006 Information Security South Africa Conference,* Sandton, South Africa.

Thornburgh, T. (2004), "Social Engineering: The dark art". *InfoSecCD Conference'04,* Kennesaw State University.

Tyukala, M., Pottas, D., Van de Haar, H., Von Solms, R. (2006), "The organisational information security profile – a tool to assist the board". *Proceedings of the 2006 Information Security South Africa Conference,* Sandton, South Africa.

Van Niekerk, J., Von Solms, R. (2006), "Understanding information security culture: A conceptual framework". *Information Security South Africa (ISSA),* Johannesburg, South Africa.

Van Niekerk, J., Von Solms, R. (2008), "Bloom's taxonomy for information security education". *Information Security South Africa (ISSA),* Johannesburg, South Africa.

Van Niekerk, J., Von Solms, R. (2010), "Information security culture: A management perspective". *Computers & Security,* Volume 29, Issue 4, pp. 476-486, 2010.

Workman, M. (2007), "Gaining access with social engineering: An empirical study of the threat". *Information Security Journal*: A global perspective 16:6, 315-331, Florida USA.

Yildirim, N. (2010), "Increasing effectiveness of strategic planning seminars through learning style" . *Australian Journal of Teacher Education,* Vol 35, 4, July 2010.

Zakaria, O. (2004), "Understanding challenges of information security culture: a methodological issue". *2nd Australian Information Security Management Conference* pp 83-93. AISM2004. Perth, Western Australia.

Education in the 'Virtual' Community: Can beating Malware Man teach users about Social Networking Security?

A.A. Sercombe and M. Papadaki

Centre for Security, Communications and Network Research,
Plymouth University, United Kingdom
e-mail: info@cscan.org

Abstract

Social Networks have become part of daily life for millions of people and by their very nature they encourage information sharing. 2011 was a year that saw numerous targeted "Spear Phishing" attacks in which it was clear that attackers gained knowledge about victims prior to carrying out their attacks. There is evidence that social media has been utilised as the source for this information so therefore it is more important than ever that users are educated against the risks.

This paper starts by looking at the current threats and awareness strategies. It then describes the design and evaluation of an online game to help educate users. The game has a central 'Malware Man' character and a firewall which burns him if the player answers correctly. The success of the game was evaluated using an experiment with a group of participants who had played the game, and a control group who had not. 101 users participated in the study. The results suggest that the game was successful in educating users as the average percentage of correct answers was 77% for those who had played the game, compared to 55% for those who had not.

Keywords

Social Networking, Social Networks, Phishing, Spear Phishing, Education, Awareness, Game, Interactive

1   Introduction

Social Networks are defined as 'networks of social interactions and personal relationships' (Oxford Dictionary, 2011). They are used to build online communities of people who share associations with one another (Shin, 2010). Facebook alone, reports that it has over 800 million active users, of which more than 50% logon every day (Facebook, 2012). These statistics indicate that there is a large amount of data to mine and a plentiful supply of users that could be targeted. It is clear that social media is a very lucrative target and information source for attackers.

These threats do not only affect individuals, but also pose a risk to organisations, governments and infrastructure. 2011 has seen a decrease in the amount of spam detected, but at the same time, an increase in the number of targeted attacks. It has been proposed that this may be because attackers are moving away from spam and are choosing to use social networks to mine information so that they can perform more targeted attacks (Symantec, 2011).

A security intelligence company called Stratfor was the victim of a targeted attack in the last week of 2011. At around the same time they released an announcement on Facebook stating that they had evidence that users or employees who posted messages of support on social networking sites were being specifically targeted (BBC, 2011). This is further evidence that information on social media sites is being used by attackers as a standard information gathering tool and that it can also be used to target individuals.

2   Awareness Strategies

There are a number of different strategies used to raise awareness about security threats, and there has been considerable research in this area. The U.K. government, law enforcement and a number of large organisations sponsor a Get Safe Online initiative (www.getsafeonline.org) (Furnell, Bryant & Phippen, 2007). The web site offers videos, guides, reports and help for users and small businesses to raise their security awareness. Globally there are numerous initiatives, for example the European Network and Information Security Agency (ENISA), which provides an awareness raising program of workshops, conferences and literature.

In general, training materials are effective when users actually read them (Sheng et al., 2007). This is easier said than done in some contexts. For example, social networking users cannot be forced to read the material like in an organisational context.

An alternative is defined as 'embedded training' whereby users are taught during their normal use and techniques, like role playing can be employed. A game called 'Anti-phishing Phil' (Sheng et al., 2007) was developed to complement the research in this area and the evaluation of it has shown it to be effective in educating users about Phishing attacks. The limitation of this game is that it is only focusing on one area of awareness. The danger might be that users have a false sense of security because they have 'educated' themselves in this one area but may have missed other threats. To complement the existing research that has been carried out, this project will attempt to educate social networking users about security threats whilst in the context of a game. The aim is to make the game fun to ensure that users want to play it and also to ensure that it educates them. Games like Anti-Phishing Phil have tended to focus on a particular threat whereas this game will aim to cover a range of threats and will be a more general security awareness tool.

3   Malware Man Design

A number of requirements were collated as a result of learning and education research and a literature review. The key requirements for the education game are listed below:

3.1   Requirements

3.1.1   Non-functional

- The game must captivate player attention (Dondlinger, 2007).

- The game design should promote and foster learning (Dondlinger, 2007).

- A narrative context should be used to ensure that the game is engaging and fun (Sheng et al, 2007).

- The game must have a strong character and story to help motivate players (Sheng et al, 2007).

- There should be an emphasis on skill as there must be a challenge to keep player attention.

3.1.2   Functional Requirements

- The game should be dynamic and easily configurable for different types of Social Networks.

- The game should also be customisable so that it is relevant for different types of users.

- It is important that the game is available to as wide a group of users as possible so it should be as platform independent as possible.

3.2   Design

The game was developed using Adobe Flash Builder 4.5 using the Adobe Flex development language to build a .swf file that can be played using Adobe's Flash Player. This ensures that the game will run on any browser as long as it has Flash Player 10 or above installed.

There are three game states; 'Start', 'InGame' and 'End'. If the user answers correctly, a flickering animated firewall increases in size and a speech bubble appears giving the impression that Malware Man is being hurt.

Help information appears providing the user more information about the question and the correct answer after they have submitted their answer. If the user answers correctly then the text will be coloured green.

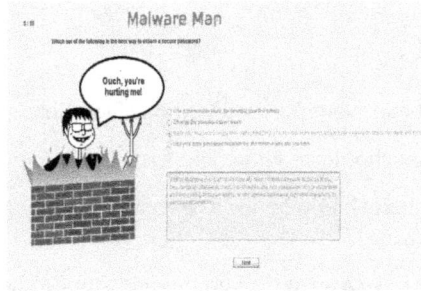

**Figure 1: Game Image (Malware Man image sourced from
LakeSuperiorityComplex (2011).**

If the user answers incorrectly then the firewall stays the same size, and the wrong answer and hint text are coloured red. The right answer is coloured green, so that the user can immediately see where they went wrong.

The design of the questions is centred around the main threats briefly outlined earlier in this paper. The questions were all multiple choice with four possible answers. Some questions included images from social networks, for example a wall posting from a Facebook feed to make the question more relevant to the user. Three sets of ten questions were created for three different versions of the game.

4   Evaluation Design

A user study was used to evaluate how successful the game was in educating users. The study consisted of a group of users who had played the game and a control group who had not. Both groups were given the same survey to complete. The survey included social networking security questions similar to that used in the game and the hypothesis was that the users that had played the game would answer more questions correctly. The questions were multiple choice and reflected the areas that were covered within the game. The research is mainly quantitative in nature but there was also an informal feedback field in the survey for participants to give some qualitative feedback on the game.

The two sample groups included Plymouth University Masters and Undergraduate students and UK Met Office employees. All participants were over 18 years old and the study did not include vulnerable adults. An invitation email and a consent page outlined the aims of the research, contact details, a clear description of the right to withdraw at anytime and a reinforcement that participation is voluntary.

5   Results

104 participants took part in the study, of which three results were discarded due to all blank answers to the questions. The overall percentages are 32% female, 65%

male and 3% undisclosed. 51% of participants were aged between 26-35 and 32% were between 36-45. The other 17% were either 18-25, 46-55 or 56-65.

Figure 2 below shows that that the % of Correct answers is significantly higher for those users that played the game compared to those who had not. The results indicate that the overall percentage of correct answers for those users who played the game was 77%, as opposed to 55% for those who had not played. The first 8 questions in the survey were the same for all users so these are split out in the results. The other questions were Facebook or Twitter specific and only appeared if users played those specific versions of the game but also provided very similar results.

	Correct Answers	Incorrect Answers	Un-answered	Total	% Correct out of Total	% Incorrect out of Total
No Game - 1st 8 Questions	215	177	0	392	54.847	45.153
Game - 1st 8 Questions	322	92	2	416	77.404	22.115
No Game - All Questions	276	239	73	588	46.939	40.646
Game - All Questions	439	116	69	624	70.353	18.590

Figure 2: Table of overall Results

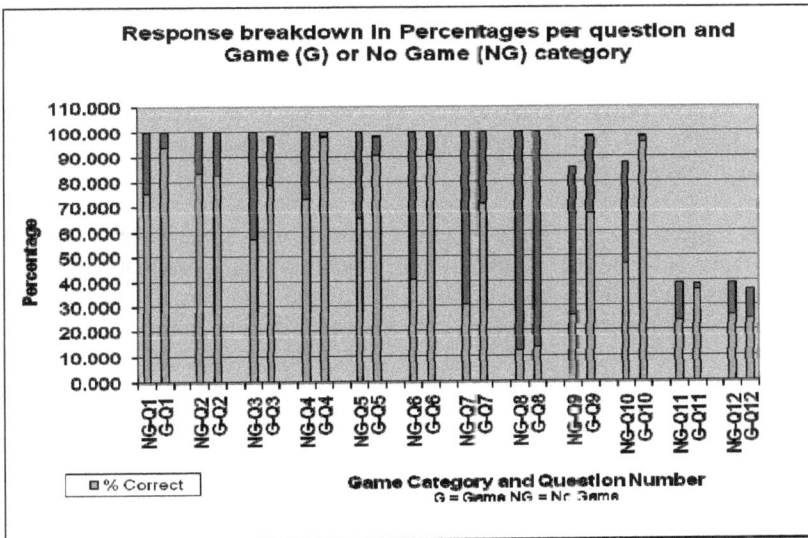

Figure 3: Graph showing a breakdown of the results

Figure 3 shows a breakdown of the results for each question for users who had played the game compared to those who had not. There was one question out of the eight that all answered that was statistics based (Q8 in the graph above). The question was ' During a 3 month period in 2010, what percentage of all malicious URLs observed on social networking sites made use of URL shortening? (According to Symantec threat report 2010).' Before analysing the results, it was thought that as the users had seen these statistics in a similar question when they played the game, they should do better than those who had not played. In actual fact only 13.5% answered correctly compared to 12.3% who had not played. This is interesting as it may suggest that more descriptive questions are more effective in embedding learning. The idea was that the users would be shocked by the percentage and then be more aware of the risk. They may have remembered the principle without the actual percentage and it is not possible to draw conclusions from one question but may warrant further investigation.

Another question where there is a similar percentage for those who played or did not play is question 2. This question was ' Shortened web addresses are more secure because they are harder for hackers to amend?'. A high percentage of both groups answered correctly so this question may have been more obvious for both groups. It was also a true or false question so there is a higher chance that they may have guessed the correct answer.

The informal feedback on the game showed that participants found the game to be generally fun and informative, but there were some concerns over the clarity of the colours for users with colour blindness. One participant suggested that a leader board may have added to the experience so they could see how they performed compared to other users.

6   Conclusions and Future Work

This paper has provided an overview of the current social networking threats and awareness campaigns and has then presented the design and evaluation of the Malware Man Game.

The results suggest that the game was successful in educating users as there was a large difference between the number of correct answers for those that had played the game, compared to those who had not. The sample size was not sufficient to be conclusive and the participants belonged to a specific demographic.

Future research could include looking at different cultures and demographics of users, as well as using a larger sample size. It could also include extensions to the game for different levels and could give forms of reward to see if this improves the user experience.

Trialing the game against other forms of online educational material and carrying out a study to determine how well the game performed comparatively would give a better understanding of how effective the game is in educating users in comparison to other techniques. It would also be worth investigating further whether different types of questions may be more effective than others as a result of this research.

7   References

BBC, 27/11/2011, *'Anonymous' hack victims face repeat attacks*, BBC. Available from: <http://www.bbc.co.uk/news/technology-16338680>.[27/12/2011].

Dondlinger, MJ 2007, 'Educational video game design: A review of the literature', *Journal of Applied Educational Technology*, vol. 4, no 1, pp. 21-31.

Facebook,   *Statistics-Facebook*,   Facebook.   Available   from: <https://www.facebook.com/press/info.php?statistics>. [05/01/2011].

Furnell, SM, Bryant, P & Phippen, AD 2007, 'Assessing the security perceptions of personal Internet users', *Computers & Security*, vol. 26, no. 5, pp. 410-417.

Hogben, G 2007, 'Security issues and recommendations for online social networks', *Position Paper ENISA European Network and Information Security Agency*, vol. 80211, no. 1.

Jagatic, TN, Johnson, NA, Jakobsson, M & Menczer, F 2007, 'Social phishing', *Communications of the ACM*, vol. 50, no. 10, pp. 94-100.

LakeSuperiorityComplex   2011,   *Evil   Nerd*   (Image).   Available   from: <http://lakesuperioritycomplex.wordpress.com/2010/06/29/therewoman/>.[01/04/11]
OxfordDictionary 2011, *Oxford Dictionaries - Definition of Social Network* in Oxford Dictionaries,   Oxford   University   Press,   [01/06/2011].
Sheng, S, Magnien, B, Kumaraguru, P, Acquisti, A, Cranor, LF, Hong, J & Nunge, E 2007, 'Anti-Phishing Phil: the design and evaluation of a game that teaches people not to fall for phish', in, ACM, pp. 88-99.

Shin, D-H 2010, 'The effects of trust, security and privacy in social networking: A security-based approach to understand the pattern of adoption', *Interacting with Computers*, vol. 22, no. 5, pp. 428-438.

Symantec, CW- 2010, 'The Risks of Social Networking', *Symantec - Security Response*[12/05/2011].

Symantec, PW- 2011, *Symantec Intelligence Report: November 2011*, Symantec, [20/12/2011].

Development of Cognitive Functioning Psychological Measures for the SEADM

F. Mouton[1], M.M. Malan[2] and H.S. Venter[2]

[1]CSIR (Defence, Peace, Safety & Security), Command, Control & Information Warfare, Pretoria, South Africa
[2]University of Pretoria, Information and Computer Security Architecture Research Group, Pretoria, South Africa
e-mail: moutonf@gmail.com

Abstract

Social engineering is a real threat to industries in this day and age, even though its severity is extremely downplayed. The difficulty with social engineering attacks is mostly the ability to identify them. Social engineers often target call centre employees, as they are normally underpaid, under-skilled and have limited knowledge about the information technology infrastructure. These employees are, thus, seen as easy targets by the social engineer. This paper improves on a previously-proposed model, Social Engineering Attack Detection Model (SEADM), by proposing and incorporating a cognitive functioning psychological measure in order to determine the emotional state and decision-making ability of the call centre employee. The cognitive analysis combined with the social engineering attack detection model provides one with a quick and effective way to determine whether the requester is trying to manipulate an individual into disclosing information for which the requester does not have authorization.

Keywords

Cognitive analysis, decision making, emotional state, SEADM, social engineering, Social Engineering Attack Detection Model, social psychology, information sensitivity.

1 Introduction

Social engineering, in the context of this paper, refers to various techniques that are utilised to obtain information through the exploitation of human vulnerability in order to bypass security systems (Mitnick & Simon, 2002). As clearly stated by various authors, the human element is the 'glitch' or vulnerable element within security systems (Scheeres, et al., 2008), (Mitnick & Simon, 2005), (Debrosse & Harley, 2009). It is the basic 'good' human-natured characteristics that make people vulnerable to the techniques used by social engineers, as it activates various psychological vulnerabilities that could be used to manipulate the individual into disclosing the requested information (Orgill, et al., 2004).

Individuals make themselves even more vulnerable to social engineering attacks by not expecting to ever be a victim of such an attack. Many may never even know that they were a victim of such an attack. The majority of the public, thus, may not fully comprehend the extent to which these techniques to obtain such information, can be used. They also do not know the potential it holds for dire personal, economic and social consequences and losses for the individual as well as the institution. An individual may believe that the information they possess are of no particular value to another person, nor that it can be used for a malicious act. They may thus be more willing to disclose information freely. However, the social engineer is dedicated to researching various aspects and gathering information from various sources. Combined, the acquired information can have dire consequences.

On the other end of the spectrum, the individual may believe that they will not fall prey to such an attack, as they will be able to recognise such an attack. However, the social engineer is a skilled human manipulator, preying on human vulnerabilities using various psychological triggers that could foil human judgment.

The problem is to successfully detect social engineering attacks whilst working in a stressful environment, where decisions must be made instantaneously and under pressure. It is for this reason that the previously-proposed social engineering attack detection model (SEADM) by Bezuidenhout, Mouton and Venter (2010), has been improved upon by proposing a procedure in order to perform a cognitive functioning psychological measure. This cognitive functioning psychological measure is used to determine whether there is a change in the emotional state of the individual. It is also recommended that the model should be used in combination with training on various social engineering techniques, the psychological vulnerabilities it may elicit, and on institutional policies and procedures.

This research improves the SEADM by combining the two main perspectives of social engineering: the psychological perspective, and the computer science perspective. The psychological perspective focuses on the emotional state and cognitive abilities of the individual, whereas the computer science perspective focuses on information sensitivity. In essence, this research extends the existing SEADM with the addition of a cognitive functioning psychological measure.

The remainder of the paper is structured as follows. Section 2 provides background about social engineering. Section 3 introduces the previously-proposed SEADM in order to provide the reader with background knowledge of the original model. Section 4 proposes a new psychological measure to incorporate into the model by discussing the aim, the content and the results of such a measure. Section 5 provides an explanation of how the psychological measure should be incorporated into the model and what additional advantages it has to the previously-proposed model. Finally, Section 6 concludes with a summary on how the social engineering attack detection model has been improved on and provides suggested future work.

2 Social engineering

According to Mitnick & Simon (2002), social engineering is defined as the techniques used to exploit human vulnerability to bypass security systems in order to gather information. As indicated by this definition, social engineering attacks imply interaction with other individuals, indicating the psychological aspect of social engineering.

Various psychological vulnerabilities and triggers, used by social engineers, have been identified, which aim to influence the individual's emotional state and cognitive abilities in order to obtain information. To successfully defend against these psychological triggers, the individual will need to have a clear understanding of these triggers in order to recognise each during a social engineering attack. There are several psychological vulnerabilities, the most common ones are defined as: strong affect, overloading, reciprocation, diffusion of responsibility and moral duty, integrity and consistency, authority and finally deceptive relationships (Mitnick & Simon, 2005), (Gragg, 2002), (Workman, 2008), (Chantler & Broadhurst, 2006).

These triggers could be used to perform a social engineering attack on an unsuspecting victim, which could lead the victim to experience a sense of discomfort, whether just an uneasiness or even anxiety, as all these attacks prey on the victim's psychological vulnerabilities. One would expect that a victim would be able to use these clues of discomfort to detect that he is being targeted by a social engineering attack. However, this is the ideal and not reality, as the human reasoning and decision-making process is extremely complex, and prone to error.

The following section provides the practical application model, SEADM, which is used to determine whether a social engineering attack is being performed.

3 Social Engineering Attack Detection Model (SEADM)

In previous research, the authors have already proposed a social engineering attack detection model (SEADM). This model makes use of a decision tree by breaking the process down into more manageable components and guidelines to aid decision making. Figure 1 provides a shortened version of the SEADM, which consists of the two decision states which are focused on in this paper.

This model is used as a baseline throughout this paper and will improve on the parts where the individual is required to describe his or her own emotional state or provide their experienced level of discomfort. Throughout the remainder of the paper, the term *individual* is defined as the person dealing with the incoming call, as this model is proposed to be deployed within a call centre environment.

The first necessary step in this model would be for the individual to be conscious of, and able to evaluate, their emotional state on an ongoing basis. This implies a consciousness of emotion and how it can affect the individual's decisions.

In the same manner, the individual should evaluate the emotions that the person responsible for initiating the incoming call elicit within themselves, as the psychological vulnerabilities that might be triggered by a social engineering attack is directly aimed at creating certain emotional states, in order to obtain information.

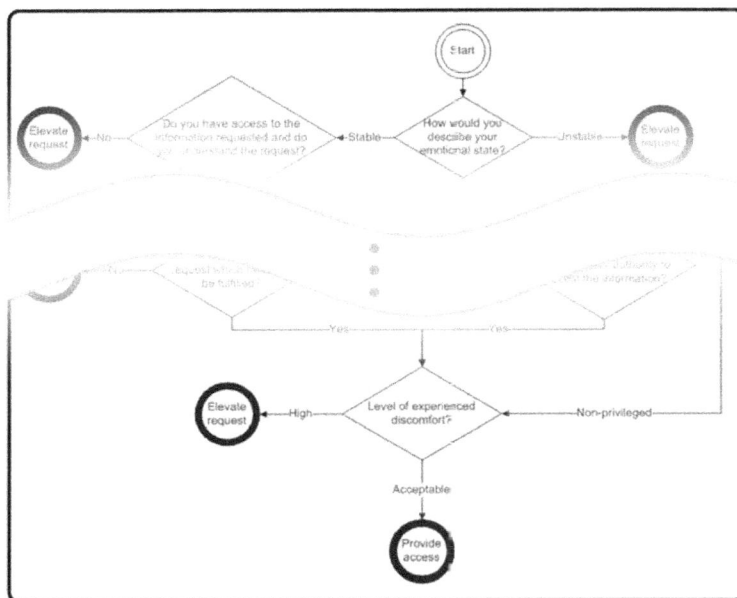

Figure 1: Social Engineering Attack Detection Model

One way or another we are all familiar with experiencing a bad day. Typically, such a bad day that starts off with some kind of bad experience and may seem to continue in such fashion throughout the day. For example, the car may break down on the way to work, followed by a negative emotional experience whether it results from family problems or an argument with a spouse or colleague. All factors and negative events influence our emotional state and hamper our ability to make rational, thought-through decisions (Siponen, 2008). Once a person finds themself in such a negative emotional state, that person is more likely to be a victim of social engineering: one's level of concentration may be low whilst irritability and frustration levels may typically be high, in which case an individual may be willing to provide a requester with certain information they rationally would have withheld, simply in a bid to get rid of the requester.

It is necessary to emphasise again the critical role an individual's emotional state can play in the safekeeping of privileged information. If an individual is in a negative emotional state, the individual will not always be able to make a rational decision on the sensitivity level of the information of a request, or to whom it may be disclosed. This can result in costly losses to the institution and the individual.

The following section focuses on the development of a psychological measure which can be used to determine an individual's emotional state.

4 Developing a psychological measure for the SEADM

Awareness and consciousness of one's emotional state is not an easy task, or even always a possible task, for individuals. It is important to note that judging one's own emotional state could be a difficult task and some individuals are unable to perform this task in a rational way when their emotions are irrationally challenged. It is for this reason that an automated psychological measure is required.

The initial steps for the development of a psychological measure are that one clearly has to specify the aim of the measure, identify the content of the measure and analysing the assessment of the measure. These steps are discussed in the following respective subsections.

4.1 Specifying the aim of the psychological measure

It can be determined from the SEADM, as seen in figure 1, that one would need to determine both the emotional state and the level of experienced discomfort of the individual. This is a tedious task for individuals to determine their own emotional state, as each individual have their own interpretation and perception of emotional states as well as their level of experienced discomfort.

Initially, it is required to determine how one would go about determining both the emotional state and the level of experienced discomfort of an individual. It is important to note that the level of experienced discomfort is only a single attribute, which exists within an individual's emotional state. For this reason, if one is able to correctly determine the emotional state of an individual, this emotional state will encompass the level of experienced discomfort of an individual.

There are psychological measures which have already been developed to accurately determine one's emotional state and the level of experienced discomfort (Lopes, et al., 2003). These psychological measures which are able to determine the emotional state of an individual mostly comprise personality-based tests. The results of such personality-based tests can clearly indicate the emotional state of well-being of an individual (Lopes, et al., 2003). However, the major drawback of these personality tests is that they are lengthy and too cumbersome to be incorporated within this model.

Another issue to consider whilst assessing one's emotional state is that the emotional state of an individual is something which can stay constant for long periods of time. The emotional state of an individual only illicit a change when the individual is exposed to issues such as experiencing severe stress, has a major life crisis or when the emotional well-being of the individual is affected by a health issue like illness.

It is for these reasons that it has been deemed impractical to assess the emotional state and level of experienced discomfort of the individual, by means of a psychological measure based on personality testing. In literature, it has been shown that there is a direct link between the performance of an individual on cognitive functioning based tests and the emotional state of an individual (Mathews, 1990), (MacLeod & Mathews, 1991).

According to Mathews (1990), "in any specific emotional state the cognitive system is organized in a manner appropriate for dealing with the new set of priorities arising from the particular event." As shown previously, if an individual is under attack by a social engineer, their stress levels would rise due to manipulation techniques exerted by the social engineer. Due to the increase in stress levels of the individual, the emotional state of the individual will change and, according to Mathews (1990), one can conclude that the change in emotional state will have an influence over the individual's cognitive functioning.

Social engineering attacks have also been shown to increase one's anxiety levels. This provides more evidence that any type of social engineering attack should have a direct influence over one's emotional state. This, in turn, will then have a direct influence over one's cognitive functioning.

Due to the intense effect that the emotional state has on the cognitive functioning of the individual, the aim of the psychological measure is to determine the level of cognitive functioning of an individual. The next section focuses on defining the content of the psychological measure.

4.2 Defining the content of the psychological measure

As it has been determined, by the authors, the aim of the psychological measure is to determine the level of cognitive functioning of an individual. This paper only examines pre-existing psychological measures which assess cognitive functioning. The field of cognitive functioning in psychology has been very well developed and several psychological measures have already been developed and are available for use (Eriksen, 1995), (Monchi, et al., 2001).

The advantage of using such psychological measures is that these psychological measures have already been approved and accepted by the American Psychological Association. The other advantage is that these psychological measures can also be analysed by a registered psychologist in order to determine the assessment results. It is very important to remember that, by law, one needs to be a registered psychologist in order to be allowed to draw conclusions and interpret the results of any psychological measure.

Whilst deciding which psychological measures to incorporate into the SEADM, it is important to remember that the entire model must be worked through during each call taken by the individual. Only three psychological measures are considered for this paper due to space constraints, however, several other psychological measures can also be incorporated.

The three psychological measures that are considered can all be found in the Psychology Experiment Building Language (PEBL), which is an open source project that allows easy creation of computer based psychological measures (Mueller, 2012).

The three psychological measures, Wisconsin Card Sorting Test, Eriksen's Flanker Test and the Dot Judgement Test, which are discussed in the following subsections, are depicted in figure 2 (Eriksen, 1995), (Monchi, et al., 2001), (Cicchetti & Rourke, 2004).

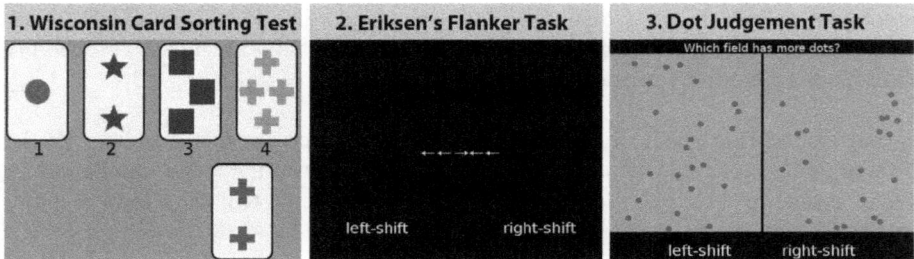

Figure 2: Psychological measures in PEBL

1. Wisconsin Card Sorting Test

The Wisconsin Card Sorting Test is normally used to test the ability to display flexibility in the face of changing schedules of reinforcement (Monchi, et al., 2001).

In the Wisconsin Card Sorting Test the individual is presented with a number of stimulus cards. The shapes on the cards are in different quantity, colour and design. The task of the individual is to match any additional cards by means of quantity, colour or design. The individual is then presented with a stack of cards in a specific order and is required to match each card to one of the stimulus cards. However, the individual is never told by which attribute the cards should be matched. The individual is only told if the match is correct or wrong. During the course of the test the rules of the game are changed. The time it then takes the individual to learn the new rules is measured as well as the amount of mistakes made in that time. The time taken and amount of mistakes which are made when the rules are altered, is used to determine the level of cognitive functioning of the individual.

2. Eriksen's Flanker Test

The Eriksen's Flanker Test assesses the ability to suppress responses that are incorrect in a specified context. Typically, in this test, a directional response is required from the individual when presented with stimuli which portrays conflicting or corresponding information about the directional response (Eriksen, 1995). In this psychological measure, the individual is presented with five arrows of which the direction of the middle arrow is requested from the individual. If the middle arrow is pointing to the right-hand side, the individual is required to press the right-shift button. Similarly, when the middle arrow is pointing to the left-hand side, the individual is required to press the left-shift button. The arrows on either side of the middle arrow can provide either corresponding information, by pointing in the same direction as the middle arrow, or conflicting information, by pointing in an opposite direction. This psychological measure determines the time it takes for the individual to respond to the stimuli and the amount of errors which are made during the test.

3. Dot Judgement Task

The Dot Judgement Task assesses the space perception of an individual by requesting the individual to briefly count the amount of dots on a screen and indicate which of two sides has more dots (Cicchetti & Rourke, 2004).

In this psychological measure the individual is provided with two blocks containing red dots. This screen is only displayed to the individual momentarily. After the screen has been cleared, the individual is required to indicate which of the two sides of the screen has more dots by pressing either the left-shift button or the right-shift button. The psychological measure determines the time it takes for the individual to respond to each of the stimuli and the amount of errors made during the test.

All the psychological measures discussed previously are computer based tests and can be performed very briefly by an individual, and be assessed afterwards. The analysis of the assessment of the psychological measures is discussed in the following section.

4.3   Analysis of the assessment of the psychological measure

All of the psychological measures return numerical values, which need to be analysed before a conclusion can be drawn on the level of cognitive functioning of an individual. As mentioned earlier, the results of the assessments may only be interpreted by a registered psychologist. This obstacle can however, be overcome as one knows that a specific state of cognitive functioning is indicated by the numerical values. Thus, an in-depth interpretation of the numerical values is not needed.

In order for the SEADM to function, it is required to determine whether there was a change in the emotional state of the individual. This can be determined by examining whether there was any change in the level of cognitive functioning of an individual, as the emotional state and cognitive performance influence each another. Determining if the emotional state of an individual has changed, requires only a comparison of the current level of cognitive functioning of the individual, versus the individual's normal level of cognitive functioning.

This comparison of cognitive functioning can be made using a feedforward neural network. Using a neural network allows one to determine if the emotional state of an individual has changed without performing a psychological analysis on the data. The neural network can determine if the results of the psychological measure is significantly different from what is expected to be the constant level of cognitive functioning of the individual and, thus, the emotional state. This task of comparison is legally allowed to be done without the participation of a registered psychologist, as only the neural network interprets the data and detect changes in the level of cognitive functioning of the individual.

The feedforward neural network is an artificial neural network which uses a set of inputs with an associated output in order to correctly predict the outcome of any other similar input (Bebis & Georgiopoulos, 1994). The neural network is trained over time during the normal office duties of the call centre agent. Each new call provides one with new training data for the neural network for the specific individual. During each call, the individual is required to perform a psychological measure at both the start and the end of the call. On the initial step of evaluating one's emotional state, the psychological measure is used to determine if the level of cognitive functioning correlates to the individual's normal level of cognitive functioning and then returns a value, which is fed into the SEADM. The final step of the model, determining the level of discomfort, is performed by assessing whether the individual's level of cognitive functioning has been influenced during the call. In the case where the individual's level of cognitive functioning changes at any time between the start and the end of the SEADM, the individual would be deemed unfit to continue with the call, as the individual's emotional state would have been compromised. If the individual's emotional state has been compromised, the call is escalated to a more capable person whom can handle the call appropriately.

The training data for the neural network is collected continuously, whilst the individual is performing their normal office duties. This data is then used as a baseline when determining the individual's emotional state. The continuous updating of the training data allows the neural network to adapt to certain life conditions or life events which may occur to the individual.

Each separate test can have its own independent neural network associated to it, which is able to provide an output result. All the tests can also have a combined neural network which provides another independent output result. Having two independent sources, which can indicate if the emotional state has been compromised, allows one to have more accuracy and less false positives from the neural network. This is because both of the neural networks provide an indication whether the emotional state of the individual has been compromised or not.

The following section is devoted to incorporating the suggested psychological measures into the SEADM, as well as how to keep the assessments as short as possible whilst providing feasible results.

5   Incorporating psychological measures into the SEADM

It has been shown that incorporating cognitive functioning, psychological measures are an effective way to determine the level of an individual's emotional state. Both the initial state, where one has to evaluate one's own emotional state, and the state where one has to evaluate one's level of experienced discomfort are replaced with incorporating the cognitive functioning psychological measure in the SEADM.

The individual is required to perform two, shortened versions from the group of the psychological measures, one at the initial state and one at the end state of the SEADM. The psychological measures provided to the individual only takes up to a maximum time span of thirty seconds, per measure, so that the efficiency in the call centre environment is not compromised. The shortening of the psychological measures has no adverse effects on the end result of the assessment, as the individual will complete several of these short versions during their normal office duties. This leads to an increase of one minute per call, thirty seconds at the start and thirty seconds at the end. It is a small price to pay to ensure that the individual in a call centre environment do not divulge any sensitive information, leading to a potential social engineering attack.

Randomising the order of the psychological measures reduce the repetitiveness of the tasks at hand. Using several different psychological measures has the advantage that the individuals will not get bored of having to complete the same psychological measure over and over again. This will also ensure that the user is presented with a new challenge each time. The order in which these psychological measures are completed is not important as each test has an independent neural network which is specifically trained on the individual associated with it.

It is, however, important to remember that the automated testing will only become effective when the individual has completed several attempts of each of the psychological measures. It is due to the design of the neural network that a large set of training data is required before it can be used to predict the output result, i.e. whether the individual's emotional state has been compromised. As the individual deals with more calls, the effectiveness of the automated testing improves as the neural network is provided with more training data. The initial training data can be acquired during an induction session directly after an individual is appointed. Collecting the training data during the induction session guarantees that there exists training data for each individual already. This ensures that when the individual starts his or her call centre agent duties, the neural network will already be trained to a sufficient level. During the initial training sessions, it is required that the individuals manually evaluate their own emotional states in order to provide training data to the neural network with the correct outputs. The accuracy of the neural network will be dependent on how accurately the neural network has been trained and on the amount of training data provided to the neural network.

The following section concludes the paper with a brief discussion of the improved SEADM and provides avenues for future research.

6   Conclusion

Social engineering is very difficult to detect, as the social engineer has various skills and effective techniques, preying on human vulnerabilities making these attacks often go without notice. What makes detection even more difficult is that many people are unaware of this technique. Even though some people are aware of this technique, they might still not be aware of the potential threat and dire consequences it holds for the individual and for institutions.

It has been previously-proposed that a visible, practically applied, user-friendly aid, such as the SEADM, will aid in the daily awareness of the threat of social engineering attacks and, thus, protection against social engineering attacks. The purpose of this paper was to enhance the existing SEADM by changing the way individuals have to evaluate their own emotional state. This paper proposes to evaluate the individual's emotional state by making use of a cognitive functioning psychological measure using a feedforward neural network.

It has been shown that the emotional state of an individual is directly linked to the level of cognitive functioning of an individual. Due to this link between the emotional state and level of cognitive functioning, cognitive functioning psychological measures have been proposed. This psychological measure is able to determine if there has been any change in an individual's level of cognitive functioning. This change, in turn, would then indicate that the individual's emotional state has been compromised and that there may be a chance that the individual is being targeted by a social engineering attack. This improved model makes a valuable contribution to the field of social engineering, as it aids in the detection of social engineering attacks.

In further research one can also further explore research by Scheeres, Mills and Grimaila (2008) to illustrate the probable increase in awareness of an individual's own vulnerability to a social engineering attack through practical application of social engineering in a training environment. It would also be useful to perform some action research in a call centre in order to verify the usability of the improved SEADM.

7   Bibliography

Bebis, G. & Georgiopoulos, M., 1994. Feed-forward neural networks. *IEEE Potentials,* 13(4), pp. 27-31.

Bezuidenhout, M., Mouton, F. & Venter, H. S., 2010. *SEADM: Social Engineering Attack Detection Model.* Johannesburg, Information Security for South Africa (ISSA).

Chantler, A. N. & Broadhurst, R., 2006. *Social Engineering and Crime Prevention in Cyberspace,* Brisbane: Queensland University of Technology.

Cicchetti, D. V. & Rourke, B. P., 2004. *Methodological and Biostatistical Foundations of Clinical Neuropsychology and Medical and Health Disciplines.* 2nd ed. London: Taylor & Francis.

Debrosse, J. & Harley, D., 2009. *Malice through the looking glass: behaviour analysis for the next decade.* Geneva, Virus Bulletin Conference.

Eriksen, C. W., 1995. The flankers task and response competition: A useful tool for investigating a variety of cognitive problems. *Visual Cognition,* 2(2-3), pp. 101-118.

Gragg, D., 2002. A Multi-Layer Defense Against Social Engineering. *Sans Institute Reading Room,* December.

Lopes, P. N., Salovey, P. & Straus, R., 2003. Emotional intelligence, personality, and the perceived quality of social relationships. *Personality and Individual Differences,* 35(3), pp. 641-658.

MacLeod, C. & Mathews, A., 1991. Biased cognitive operations in anxiety: Accessibility of information or assignment of processing priorities?. *Behaviour Research and Therapy,* 29(6), pp. 599-610.

Mathews, A., 1990. Why worry? The cognitive function of anxiety. *Behaviour Research and Therapy,* 28(6), pp. 455-468.

Mitnick, K. D. & Simon, W. L., 2002. *The art of deception: controlling the human element of security.* Indianapolis: Wiley Publishing.

Mitnick, K. D. & Simon, W. L., 2005. *The art of intrusion: the real stories behind the exploits of hackers, intruders and deceivers.* Indianapolis: Wiley Publishing.

Monchi, O. et al., 2001. Wisconsin Card Sorting Revisited: Distinct Neural Circuits Participating in Different Stages of the Task Identified by Event-Related Functional Magnetic Resonance Imaging. *The Journal of Neuroscience,* 21(19), pp. 7733-7741.

Mueller, S. T., 2012. *PEBL: The Psychology Experiment Building Language.* [Online] Available at: http://pebl.sourceforge.net/ [Accessed 13 January 2012].

Orgill, G. L., Romney, G. W., Bailey, M. G. & Orgill, P. M., 2004. *The urgency for effective user privacy-education to counter social engineering attacks on secure computer systems.* Salt Lake City, Information Technology Education.

Scheeres, J. W., Mills, R. F. & Grimaila, M. R., 2008. *Establishing the human firewall: reducing an individual's vulnerability to social engineering attacks.* s.l., 3rd International Conference on Information Warfare and Security.

Siponen, M. T., 2008. A conceptual foundation for organizational information security awareness. *Information Management & Computer Security,* 8(1), pp. 31-41.

Workman, M., 2008. A test of interventions for security threats from social engineering. *Information Management & Computer Security,* 16(5), pp. 463-483.

Proceedings of the Sixth International Symposium on
Human Aspects of Information Security & Assurance (HAISA 2012)

Psychosocial Risks: Can Their Effects On The Security of Information Systems Really Be Ignored?

E. D. Frangopoulos[1], M. M. Eloff[1] and L. M. Venter[2]

[1]School of Computing, University of South Africa (UNISA), Pretoria, South Africa
[2]Director: Research Support, North-West University, South Africa
e-mail: vfrangopoulos@hol.gr; e-mail: eloffmm@unisa.ac.za;
lucas.Venter@nwu.ac.za

Abstract

Psychosocial risks at the workplace is a well-researched subject from a managerial and organisational point of view. However, the relation of psychosocial risks to Information Security has not been formally studied to the extent required by the gravity of the topic. An attempt is made to highlight the nature of psychosocial risks and provide examples of their effects on Information Security. The foundation is thus set for methodologies of assessment and mitigation and suggestions are made on future research directions.

Keywords

Information Security, Psychosocial Risks

1. Introduction

It has been well established in the standard literature that major vulnerabilities of Information Systems can be attributed to their human element, i.e. the users. When these users are themselves targeted, the compromise of information security becomes imminent, irrespective of technical measures that strengthen information security as well as physical security. In previous work, it was shown that there are many human psyche aspects that attackers can use effectively against any user they set their sights on (Frangopoulos et al., 2010). Social aspects of Information Security were also examined (Frangopoulos et al., 2008) and their significance in successful attacks was discussed. In addition to breaches caused by such attacks, one must also not overlook those insider security incidents that are caused deliberately or accidentally, where due to user action, negligence, fault or oversight, information security is ultimately compromised. This again has to do with the fact that Information System users are humans with individual abilities and shortcomings that cannot be categorised and dealt with in bulk from an Information Security point of view. In this context, even though "to err is human", when these errors -deliberate or not- are aggravated by psychosocial factors, there may be dire consequences on Information Security. Hence, ways must be found to reduce such occurrences by ensuring that the causal factors of psychosocial risks that are inevitably present in any modern organisation are effectively controlled.

Social sciences have been dealing with the field of psychosocial risk mitigation for many years and no course in business management disciplines can be deemed complete without proper reference to this issue. The obvious conclusion is thus that if psychosocial factors affect all forms of business operations and a clear concern exists on how to control these factors and reduce their adverse effects, then it is only reasonable to assume that the security of Information Systems, viewed from this angle, is also exposed to risks of a psychosocial nature. This paper identifies psychosocial risks that affect Information Security, shows how this effect comes about and suggests ways and research directions for the assessment and mitigation of such risks.

2. Background

The term "Psychosocial" itself has two components: "Psyche" which pertains to one's own psychological predispositions and "Social" which has to do with external factors, stemming from the role of the individual in society and the interaction with others. By combining the two notions into one term and using it to describe risk, the emphasis is placed on those risks that result from the individual's own perceptions and psyche as he/she reacts to stimuli from his/her societal environment.

The currently prevailing notion of system security from a systems engineering perspective, as presented by Larson et al. (2009, p.114), is that system security (along with system safety) is yet another design constraint which *"relates to attributes that enable the system to comply with regulations and standards"*. Clearly, by adding the intricate parameter of Psychosocial Risk into the equation of Information Systems security, the above notion becomes insufficient. This, however, does not mean that, in designing a more secure system, one has to do away with standards and start from scratch. The standards are there and should be followed as they provide commonly acceptable and effective solutions to a number of different security problems. In a holistic approach to the Information Security issue however, standards should be complemented by those techniques and practices that mitigate risks of a psychosocial nature. In such a holistic approach, the people and their individual characteristics cannot be ignored. Designing secure Information Systems and applications becomes a much more intricate exercise when the individual problems of potential users that may affect Information Security need to be pro-actively addressed. In Bruce Schneier's own words: *"...the mathematics are impeccable, computers are vincible, the networks are lousy and the people are abysmal. I've learned a lot about the problems of securing computers and networks, but none that really helps solve the people problem"* (Schneier, 2004, p.255).

Barring a handful of researchers such as Greitzer et al. (2010; 2010a; 2011) and Vyhmeister et al. (2006) who deal with psychosocial risks in the particular context of Information Security, limited work has been done in this direction. Hence, it would be prudent to set the ground for the current work by examining the idea of psychosocial risks (or "psychosocial hazards" – the two terms seem to be used without distinction in the literature) from the usual managerial and organisational points of view, where extensive research has been and is being carried out.

The International Labour Organisation defines "psychological factors" in terms of the interactions between employee's skills and needs on one side, and job content, work organisation, work management and environmental and organisational conditions, on the other. In this context, "psychosocial hazards" refer to those of the above interactions that have a hazardous influence over employees' health, through the employees' perceptions and experience (ILO, 1986).

Cox (1993) considers that psychosocial hazards may have a direct or indirect adverse effect on both psychological and physical health, through the experience of stress. In a more recent work, he presents a definition for psychosocial hazards as "*those aspects of the design and management of work, and its social and organisational contexts, that have the potential for causing psychological or physical harm*" (Cox et al., 2003, p.195).

Haubold (2008, p.7) defines "psychosocial risks" as the human tensions potentially generated by the application of enterprise strategy. She continues by identifying some of these tensions as stress, the impression of being harassed, violence (in all forms), mental burden etc. In the same text, the author lists a few positions on psychosocial risks adopted by respected researchers in the field, which are included here in order to set the foundation for further discussion:

1. Employee satisfaction determines employee punctuality or absence (Spector, 1997, p.104).
2. Half of the days of absence from work are due to a problematic work environment or stress (Cooper, 1994).
3. Personnel involvement is associated with low running costs and high performance (Mathieu and Zajac, 1990).
4. Employee satisfaction is directly related to client satisfaction (Heskett et al., 1997, p.320)
5. Job satisfaction is founded on personnel involvement. (Vandenberg et al., 1999)
6. Employee satisfaction stemming from job security, compensation and satisfaction in general are directly related to the financial performance of the enterprise. (Schneider et al., 2003)

One has to bear in mind that the above statements view psychosocial risks from a business management angle but, nevertheless, conclusions can be drawn for the research at hand. It is immediately visible though, that if steps are taken to minimize psychosocial risks and keep employees happy, the enterprise benefits.

In order to further highlight the gravity of psychosocial risks, it suffices to mention that according to the European Agency for Health and Safety at Work, one third of the European worker population (i.e. more than 40 million people) report that they are affected by stress at work (EASHW, 2002). On this basis, psychosocial risks are currently recognised as a major challenge to occupational health and safety (EASHW, 2007). In 2007, 13.6% of all workers who responded to surveys carried out in the U.K. by the Health & Safety Executive, when asked to rate how stressful they felt their job was, reported that they found their job either very or extremely stressful (Webster, 2007). From these three statements, in conjunction to the list of accepted positions regarding psychological risks above, it becomes evident that, up to one third of an enterprise's workforce, could conceivably pose a significant threat to the enterprise's prosperity because of exposure to psychosocial risks.

It is interesting to note that from a managerial and organisational point of view, the issue of psychological risks at the workplace is well-established and well-researched. Furthermore, its importance to the well-being of the organisation is highlighted. However, from the extensive bibliographical research carried out in the course of the present work, only a handful of publications were found to relate psychosocial risks with Information Security in general, and the security of Information Systems in particular. It seems that even though some effort is invested on the general human aspect of Information Security, only a small group of scientists, primarily led by Greitzer, investigates psychosocial risks as a significant factor of Information Security in an effort to mitigate insider threat (Greitzer et al., 2010; 2010a; 2011).

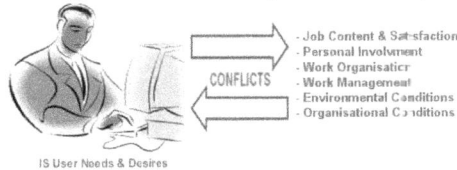

Figure 1: Psychosocial Risks affecting Information Systems users

The conclusion to be drawn is hence that Psychosocial Risks, being such an important factor in the general well-being of an enterprise, can and must not be ignored in the context of Information Security.

3. Common causes and general effects of psychosocial risks

Irrespective of the *nature* of the effects of Psychosocial Risks on the various aspects of an enterprise's prosperity, the *causes* of Psychosocial Risks have been thoroughly investigated in the past. Even though new causes may appear as society and technology progress, there already is a well-defined foundation that can work as the basis for the scope of this paper.

The International Labour Organisation in its invitation to "The New SOLVE" conference (ILO, 2011), lists the following among factors which place high emotional demands at work and contribute to work-related stress:

- Downsizing and outsourcing
- Greater need for flexibility both in functions and skills
- Increasing temporary contracts
- Greater job insecurity
- Higher workloads
- Long working hours
- Work intensification
- Poor work-life balance

Obvious and immediate results of the psychosocial risks caused by the above factors are absenteeism, diminution of employee efficiency and decrease in productivity. Second-order results vary from excessive drinking and smoking, drug abuse, eating and sleep disorders to workplace violence. Another interesting fact is that workers of all categories and occupations are affected, both in developing and developed countries (ILO, 2011).

According to Brun (2003), the psychosocial risks at work can be attributed to events taking place in the private life of the individual, in the organisation where he/she works or in the society in which he functions and progresses. Causal factors of psychosocial risks are also listed as:

- Quantitative work overload
- Qualitative work overload
- Lack of esteem by peers
- Job instability
- Lack of career advancement
- Insufficient compensation for given skills and professional experience
- Poor relations with superiors
- Poor relations with colleagues
- Poor relations with clients
- Lack of participation at the organisational level
- Lack of participation at the individual's level
- Lack of information flow at the organisational level
- Lack of participation at the individual's level
- Insufficient workload
- Unrealistic time constraints
- Conflict of work roles
- Work role ambiguity
- Lack of autonomy
- Lack of decision-making power
- Difficulties in the work environment and the working conditions
- Irregular working hours
- Extended working hours
- Centralised organisational structure

To these, Michie (2002) adds:

- Lack of breaks during work
- Lack of variety in work
- Poor physical work conditions (light, space, temperature etc)
- Working far away from home
- Taking work home
- Job relocation

Other lists of causes of psychosocial risks were also found during the relevant research, but, generally speaking, they revolve around the same themes as above. A detailed comparative description of such causes lies beyond the scope of this work and the interested reader is directed towards the bibliography presented in the references section of this paper.

It is noteworthy that as the design of Information Systems influences job design and workflow, management practices, organizational policy and other issues, it may itself constitute a causal factor of psychological distress (Vyhmeister, 2006) and, hence, psychosocial risk.

Irrespective of cause, psychosocial risks lead to a variety of problems, many of them quite serious and complex in nature. Haubold (2008, p.14) presents a table of such consequences, which is compiled to show the relations between different manifestations of various problems:

Physical consequences	Psychological Consequences	Behavioural Consequences
Headaches	Depressive mood	Absenteeism
Sleep disorders	Despair	Drug addiction
Muscular tension	Annoyance	Drug abuse
Weight issues	Anxiety	Sexual problems
Gastrointestinal disorders	Memory lapses	Impatience
Elevated blood pressure	Dissatisfaction	Aggressiveness
Allergy	Frustration	Alimentary problems
High cholesterol levels	Irritability	Drop in creativity and in taking initiatives
Skin conditions	Discouragement	Poor interpersonal relations
	Pessimism	Frequent mood swings
		Superficial relations
		Limited tolerance of frustration
		Disinterest
		Isolation

Table 1: Consequences of Psychosocial Risks

As expected, any of the above may lead to errors, reduction in productivity and sick-leave. Other outcomes are diminished job-satisfaction and commitment, generally unsafe behaviour at the workplace and an increased propensity for accidents (Cooper et al., 1997). To make matters worse, many of these issues are interrelated and often co-exist (Probst et al., 2008).

4. Effects on information security

Having established the gravity of the general effects of psychosocial risks, given that the people who are subject to these may be the users of information systems and thus the handlers of information, it becomes evident that Information Security is directly affected.

Whether intentional or by accident, breaches of Information Security in this context fall under the general category of "insider threat". The person directly or indirectly responsible for such a breach, is by definition an employee of the organisation who, out of malice or because of plain disregard for Information Security rules, allows information to be compromised.

According to recent data breach studies, insiders may directly or indirectly be behind a significant percentage of breaches, whether intentional or not (Verizon, 2009; 2010; 2011). The reported insider threat percentages varied from 17% to 48% of all data breach cases that were studied in the three-year period from 2009 to 2011. The significant fluctuation in the obtained percentages is due to the nature and total volume of the data breach cases examined each year (Verizon, 2011). However, even at the minimum level of 17%, insider threat is still quite substantial and must be examined, analysed and controlled.

In this context, an employee experiencing diminished job satisfaction becomes less committed to the organisation or enterprise he/she works for and may use the enterprise's confidential information as a bargaining chip for alternate employment by a competitor, or, simply, for monetary gain. For an employee who has become indifferent to his/her work, it will be very difficult to go through the sometimes tedious processes to ensure Information Security. Hence, when shortcuts are taken and security rules are not followed, information becomes liable to compromise. For those users afflicted by the physically debilitating consequences listed in table 1, it becomes evident that the employee's judgement may become erratic and accidents will inevitably follow. Insofar Information Security is concerned, accidents such as using an insecure channel to distribute sensitive information can be detrimental.

In order for Information Security policies to be effective, the co-operation of end-users is of paramount importance. When the end-users' abilities and will to co-operate towards better Information Security are curtailed as a direct effect of psychosocial risks, Information Security policies are bound to fail in some degree. It has already been shown that Social Engineering attacks play a major role in Information Security (Frangopoulos, 2007). In order to withstand such an attack, the end-user must be in a state of alertness. This state is impossible to attain under the light of most of the consequences of psychosocial risks listed in table 1.

In order to deal with attacks against Information Security in a centralised way, it is important to have an incident co-ordination and response centre. This centre relies on information from automated systems such as Intrusion Detection Systems and analyses of system log files. In addition to that, an important contribution comes in the form of feedback on attacks (even attempted ones) received from users. Hence, if the users' ability to contribute in this manner is impeded, the centre's function will be inherently limited.

Poor man-machine interface design on an otherwise secure information system or application may also lead to the compromise of Information Security. The users affected by psychosocial factors, who are already burdened by the interface's bad design and the required time-consuming sequences of actions, when they find themselves pressed for time due to a pending deadline, may opt for a less time and effort-consuming solution, albeit an insecure one.

These few and non-exhaustive examples show how psychosocial risks affect the users of Information Systems and consequently, Information Security. Irrespective of the level of security incorporated in systems and policies, the responsibility for Information Security largely lies with the end-user who has already been established as the weak link in the Information Security chain. When the user's abilities and will to protect the information he/she handles have been reduced by psychosocial factors, this information will inevitably be at peril. Hence, even though the user will always be expected to comply with policy requirements, every effort must be made to ensure that he/she is not hindered by psychosocial factors in doing so.

5. Proposed methods of assessment and mitigation – future work

By the discussion so far it should be clear that technological "add-ons" cannot solve all of the Information Security problems of an organisation upon deployment, as Information Security has to also address people issues and organisational aspects. To achieve this goal, all aspects of Information Systems and organisational issues must be designed or re-designed with Information Security as an element of the design process. Existing systems, applications and the complete information lifecycle must be re-examined, bearing in mind plausible Information Security principles.

There is little point in allowing psychosocial risks to go unchecked and then attempting to counteract their effects. This would be equivalent to treating the symptoms of a disease and not the disease itself. The best approach is to try and pro-actively diminish the psychosocial risks in the first place. To this end ILO provides detailed and up-to-date instructions (ILO, 1998; 2012). In order to be reduced, the psychosocial risks must first be identified and assessed. Following identification, the evaluation of psychosocial risks need not be obtained in absolute terms. It is more practical to obtain a base-line assessment of the situation at a given point in time and re-evaluate, after steps are taken towards psychosocial risk mitigation. Mitigation will take place by designing proper processes to this effect and incorporating appropriate controls. The virtuous cycle of perpetual re-assessment in order to evaluate the effectiveness of the controls has to be repeated periodically.

As this is both a tedious method to design and follow and expensive in terms of resources, senior management commitment is of paramount importance. To obtain such a commitment may be easier said than done, as described by Gagné et al. (2008, p.73): *"all other IT activities are perceived more as enabling the business to do their work, where security is the one group that is perceived as the opposite"*.

The assessment can take place using two methods: surveillance and questionnaires (Dollard, 2007). Surveillance relies on obtaining statistical data from sources like the Human Resources and Health departments of an organisation regarding personnel absences, complaints, decreased departmental efficiency, common ailments etc. Questionnaires can be based on 5-point balanced Likert scale structures (Likert, 1974) with gradations from "Not at all stressful" to "Extremely stressful" or "Very happy" to "Very unhappy" depending on the question subject. Also depending on the question subject, other forms of questionnaires may be used (Friedman and Amoo, 1999). The questionnaires having the capacity for much more accurate targeting of the effect of psychosocial risks on the security of Information Systems, they would be preferable to any other method of assessment that, nevertheless, can still be used to complement the questionnaire-based survey results and/or guide questionnaire design. This will be one of the topics of further research in this field.

A detailed examination of psychosocial risk mitigation being beyond the scope of this paper, future research in this area will be based on (among other sources) the work of Greitzer et al. (2010; 2010a; 2011) on combining psychosocial data with traditional cyber-security data and modelling towards insider-threat mitigation; on the work of Da Veiga and Eloff (2010) for Information Security culture assessment; on the writings of Vyhmeister et al. (2006) for risk assessment with respect to the implementation of information and communication systems; on Trompeter and Eloff (2001) for the implementation of socio-ethical controls in Information Security and on the works of Carlotto (2010) and Cifre et al. (2004) that deal with information technology-induced psychosocial risks and tools for their assessment.

6. Conclusions

In this paper, two existing research areas, that of psychosocial risk identification and management and that of Information Security, both well-researched in their own right, are brought together. Combining the two areas in research may bring us closer to an answer to the question of why Information Security fails when all prescribed measures and controls are in place and active. It may help us better understand the specificities of the effects of human nature on Information Security and in doing so, ameliorate the general environment in which humans are called upon to function in a secure manner. It may also help set a new paradigm on what constitutes a "reasonable request" from human operators of an information system when they are asked to uphold Information Security. Under this light and through a virtuous cycle of survey and re-assessment using specially constructed questionnaires, the real effect of psychosocial risks on Information Security will be established.

7. References

Brun, J.-P. 2003. *La Santé Psychologique au Travail... de la Définition du Problème aux Solutions*, Québec: Université Laval/IRSST, ISBN: 2-9807808-2-0

Carletto, M. S. 2010. Fatores de risco do tecnoestresse em trabalhadores que utilizam tecnologias de informação e comunicação. *Estud. psicol. (Natal).* **15**(3) 319-324. Available on-line from: http://www.scielo.br/scielo.php?script=sci_arttext&pid=S1413-294X2010000300012&lng=en&nrm=iso. Last access: 20.2.2012

Cifre, E., Salanova, M., Martínez-Pérez, M.D., Martínez, I., Llorens, S., and Grau, R. 2004. Developing a new tool to assess specific psychosocial risks among teleworkers: The RED-TT questionnaire. In: *Proceedings of the Third International Conference on Occupational Risk Prevention (ORP2004).*

Cooper C. L. 1994. The Costs of Healthy Work Organizations in: Cooper, C. L. and Williams, S. (Ed.) *Creating Healthy Working Organizations,* p. 1-5, Chichester: John Wiley & Sons. Cited in Haubold B. 2008. *Les risques psychosociaux. Identifier, analyser, prévenir les risques humains.* Paris: Éditions d' Organisation Groupe Eyrolles

Cooper, C.L. Liukkonen, P., and Cartwright, S. 1997. *Stress Prevention in the Workplace: Assessing the Costs and Benefits for Organisations.* Dublin, Ireland: European Foundation for the Improvement of Living and Working Conditions. ISBN: 978-9282765036

Cox, T. 1993. *Health & Safety Executive Contract Research Report No 61/1993. Stress research and stress management: Putting theory to work.* UK:HSE Books. ISBN: 0717606848

Cox, T., Griffiths, A. and Randall, R. 2003. A Risk Management Approach to the Prevention of Work Stress. In: Schabracq, M., Winnubst, J. and Cooper, C. (Ed.) *The Handbook of Work and Health Psychology,* Ch. 10, p.191-206, Chichester: John Wiley & Sons, Ltd., ISBN: 9780470013403

Cox, T. and Griffiths, A., 2003a. Commentary III: Monitoring the changing organization of work: A commentary. *Sozial- und Präventivmedizin / Social and Preventive Medicine.* **48** 354-355

Da Veiga, A. and Eloff, J. H .P., 2010. A Framework and assessment instrument for Information Security Culture. *Computers & Security.* **29**(2) 196-207

EASHW - European Agency for Health and Safety at Work, 2002. *European Week 2002: Preventing psychosocial risks at work.* Website. http://ew2002.osha.europa.eu/. Cited in Leka, S. and Cox, T. (Ed.) 2008. The European Framework for Psychosocial Risk Management: PRIMA-EF, Nottingham: I-WHO Publications, ISBN: 978-0-9554365-2-9

EASHW - European Agency for Health and Safety at Work, 2007. *Expert forecast on emerging psychosocial risks related to occupational safety and health,* Luxembourg: Office for Official Publications of the European Communities. Cited in Leka, S. and Cox, T. (Ed.) 2008. The European Framework for Psychosocial Risk Management: PRIMA-EF, Nottingham: I-WHO Publications, ISBN: 978-0-9554365-2-9

Frangopoulos, E. D., 2007. *Social Engineering and the ISO/IEC 17799:2005 Security Standard: A Study on Effectiveness,* MSc Dissertation, University of South Africa.

Frangopoulos, E. D., Eloff, M. M. and Venter, L. M., 2008. Social aspects of Information Security. In: *Peer-reviewed Proceedings of the ISSA 2008 Innovative Minds Conference.* ISBN 978-1-86854-693-0.

Frangopoulos, E. D., Eloff, M. M. and Venter, L. M., 2010. Psychological Considerations in Social Engineering – The Ψ-Wall as defense. *IADIS International Journal on Computer Science and Information Systems.* **5**(2) 1-20. ISSN: 1646-3692.

Friedman, H. H. and Amoo, T. 1999. Rating the Rating Scales. *Journal of Marketing Management.* **9**(3) 114-123

Gagné, A., Muldner, K. and Beznosovet K. 2008. Identifying Difference between Security and other IT Professionals: a Qualitative Analysis. In: *Proceedings of the Second International Symposium on Human Aspects of Information Security & Assurance (HAISA 2008).* 69-79

Greitzer, F. L., Noonan, C. F., Kangas, L. J. and Dalton, A. C. 2010. *Identifying at-Risk Employees: A Behavioral Model for Predicting Potential Insider Threats – PNNL 19665.* Available on-line from: http://www.pnl.gov/main/publications/external/technical_reports/PNNL-19665.pdf. Last access: 24.2.2012

Greitzer, F. L. and Frincke, D. A. 2010a. Combining Traditional Cyber Security Audit Data with Psychosocial Data: Towards Predictive Modeling for Insider Threat Mitigation. In: Probst, C. W., Hunker, J., Gollmann, D. and Bishop, M., (Ed.) 2010. *Insider Threats in Cyber Security.* New York: Springer. ISBN: 978-1-4419-7133-3

Greitzer, F. L. and Hohimer, R. E. 2011. Modeling Human Behavior to Anticipate Insider Attacks. *Journal of Strategic Security.* **IV**(2) 25-48

Haubold B. 2008. *Les risques psychosociaux. Identifier, analyser, prévenir les risques humains.* Paris: Éditions d' Organisation Groupe Eyrolles, ISBN: 978-2-212-54240-0.

Heskett, J. L., Sasser, W. E. and Schlesinger, L. A. 1997. *The Service Profit Chain: How Leading Companies Link Profit and Growth to Loyalty Satisfaction, and Value.* New York: Free Press. Cited in Haubold B. 2008. *Les risques psychosociaux. Identifier, analyser, prévenir les risques humains.* Paris: Éditions d' Organisation Groupe Eyrolles

ILO – International Labour Organisation, 1986. *Psychosocial factors at work: Recognition and control. Occupational Safety and Health Series no: 56,* Geneva: International Labour Office, ISBN: 92-2-105411-X

ILO – International Labour Organisation, 1998. *Technical and ethical guidelines for workers' health surveillance. Occupational Safety and Health Series no: 72,* Geneva: International Labour Office, ISBN: 92-2-110828-7

ILO – International Labour Organisation, 2012. *Stress prevention at work checkpoints: Practical improvements for stress prevention in the workplace,* Geneva: International Labour Office, ISBN: 978-92-2-125637-3

Larson, W. J., Kirkpatrick, D. H., Sellers, J., Thomas, L. D. and Verma, D. (Ed.) 2009. *Applied Space Systems Engineering,* McGraw Hill, ISBN: 978-0073408866

Likert, R. 1974. The Method of Constructing an Attitude Scale. In: Maranell, G. M., (Ed.) 1974. *Scaling: A Sourcebook of Behavioral Scientist,* Ch. 19, 233-243, Chicago, IL: Aldine Publishing Company, ISBN: 978-0-202-36175-8

Leka, S. and Cox, T. (Ed.) 2008. *The European Framework for Psychosocial Risk Management: PRIMA-EF,* Nottingham: I-WHO Publications, ISBN: 978-0-9554365-2-9

Mathieu, J. E and Zajac, D. M. 1990. A Review and Meta-Analysis of the Antecedents, Correlates and Consequences of Organizational Commitment. *Psychological Bulletin*. **108**(2) 171-194. Cited in Haubold B. 2008. *Les risques psychosociaux. Identifier, analyser, prévenir les risques humains*. Paris: Éditions d' Organisation Groupe Eyrolles

Michie, S. 2002. Causes and Management of Stress at Work. *Occupational Environmental Medicine*. **59** 67–72

Probst, T. M., Gold, D. and Caborn, J. 2008. A Preliminary Evaluation of SOLVE: Addressing Psychosocial Problems at Work. *Journal of Occupational Health Psychology*. **13**(1) 32–42

Schneider, B., Hanges, P. J., Smith, D. B. and Salvaggio, A. N 2003. Which Comes First: Employee Attitudes or Organizational, Financial and Market Performance? *Journal of Applied Psychology*. **88**(5) 836-851. Cited in Haubold B. 2008 *Les risques psychosociaux. Identifier, analyser, prévenir les risques humains*. Paris: Éditions d' Organisation Groupe Eyrolles

Schneier, B. 2004. *Secrets and Lies: Digital Security in a Networked World*, New York: John Wiley & Sons, Inc., ISBN: 978-0471453802

Spector, P. E. 1997. *Job Satisfaction: Application, Assessment, Causes, and Consequences*. Thousand Oaks: Sage Publications, Inc., p. 104. Cited in Haubold B. 2008. *Les risques psychosociaux. Identifier, analyser, prévenir les risques humains*. Paris: Éditions d' Organisation Groupe Eyrolles

Trompeter, C. M. and Eloff, J. H. P., 2001. A Framework for the Implementation of Socio-ethical Controls in Information Security. *Computers & Security*. **20**(5) 384-391

Vandenberg, R. J., Richardson, H. A. and Eastman L. J. 1999. The Impact of High Involvement Work Processes on Organizational Effectiveness: a Second Order Latent Variable Approach. *Group and Organization Management*. **24**(3) 300-339. Cited in Haubold B. 2008. *Les risques psychosociaux. Identifier, analyser, prévenir les risques humains*. Paris: Éditions d' Organisation Groupe Eyrolles

VERIZON Data Breach Investigation Report, 2009. Available on-line from: http://www.verizonbusiness.com/resources/executivebriefs/eb_2009_DBIR_snapshot_en_xg.pdf. Last access: 20.2.2012

VERIZON Data Breach Investigation Report, 2010. Available on-line from: http://www.verizonbusiness.com/resources/executivesummaries/es_2010-data-breach-report_en_xg.pdf. Last access: 20.2.2012

VERIZON Data Breach Investigation Report, 2011. Available on-line from: http://www.verizonbusiness.com/resouces/executivesummary/es_2011-data-breach-investigations-report_en_xg.pdf. Last access: 20.2.2012

Vyhmeister, R., Mondelo, P. R. and Novella, M. 2006. Towards a Model for Assessing Workers' Risks Resulting from the Implementation of Information and Communication Systems and Technologies. *Human Factors and Ergonomics in Manufacturing & Service Industries*. **16**(1) 39–59

Webster, S., Buckley, P. and Rose I, 2007. *Psychosocial Working Conditions in Britain in 2007*, Health & Safety Executive (HSE). Available on-line from: http://www.hse.gov.uk/statistics/pdf/pwc2007.pdf. Last access: 19.2.2012

Human Aspects of Information Security: An Empirical Study of Intentional versus Actual Behavior

A. Komatsu[1], D. Takagi[2] and T. Takemura[1,3]

[1] Security Economics Laboratory, Information-Technology Promotion Agency
Tokyo, Japan
[2] Graduate School of Humanities and Sociology, The University of Tokyo
Tokyo, Japan
[3] Research Institute for Socionetwork Strategies, Kansai University
Osaka, Japan
e-mail: a-koma@ipa.go.jp

Abstract

A significant amount of empirical research has been conducted on the socio-economic (sociological, psychological, economic) aspects of information security such asthe phenomena of individuals who are willing to take security measures, but often do not. There is a growing body of research relating to individual behaviour and decision-making. To promote effective information security measures, this paper refers to research on the psychology of persuasion from the field of social psychology. A survey was conducted into determinants for changing attitudes through persuasive messages, and the results were analysed. A questionnaire was used and the authors built a demonstrative experimental environment, which analysed in detail attitudinal changes in an individuals' behaviour.. As a result, the authors found differences in behaviour regarding the intent to implement measures discovered from the responses to the questionnaire as well as from actual conduct in the demonstrative experiment.

Keywords

Information Security, sProtection Motivation Theory, Elaborative Likelihood Model

1 Introduction

In Japan, according to the "Survey Report of Information Security Incidents" released every year by the Japan Network Security Association, 1032 security incidents happened in 2005, and theft and loss resulting from individual human error accounted for 42% of all incidents and was the largest category. In response to these types of situations, many products aimed at preventing information leaks have become available in the market and management practices, such as ISMS, have been implemented. However, in the 2009 survey, information leakage incidents had failed to decline, with the number reaching 1539 incidents. Although individual human error incidents had declined to 7.9%, incidents caused by administrative error had increased from 5.1% in 2005 to 50.9% (JNSA, 2010). Based on these statistics, new approaches for information security measures have arisen. One such approach is research focusing on the behaviour of individuals as standard practice and decision-making. In this paper, we analyze a survey on the behaviour of individuals who implement information security measures. In particular, we refer to existing research on attitudinal change using persuasive communication from the field of persuasion psychology.

The structure of this paper is as follows. In Section 2, the background to the motivation of our research is discussed. In Section 3, related works and the models our research is based on are discussed. In Section 4, the outline of the questionnaire and the experiment we designed is explained. In Section 5 the results are given as well as an explanation of the analysis and a discussion. In Section 6, this paper is summarized.

2 Background

A Bot is a malware program which allows a malicious attacker (referred to simply as an 'attacker' hereinafter) to gain control of a computer for fraudulent purposes. Once a computer is infected with a Bot, the attacker remotely controls the computer externally. Therefore, the user can cause damage to the entire network without recognizing that their PC is infected. The Cyber Clean Center (CCC) (2011) is an organization supported by the Ministry of Economics, Trade, and Industry (METI), and the Ministry of Internal Affairs and Communications (MIC) with the collaboration of ISPs. With the help of ISPs, the CCC sends an attention-grabbing warning email to the users of Bot-infected computers (Figure 1).

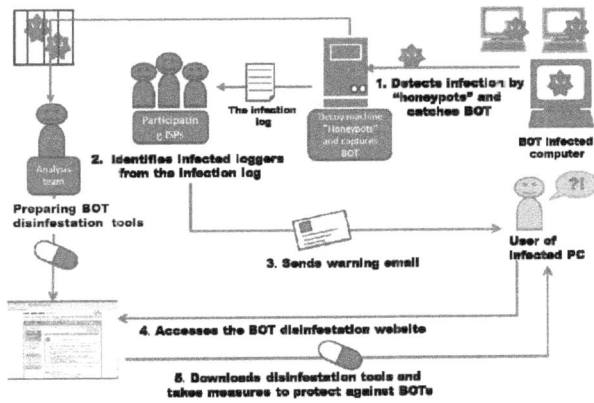

Figure 1: Activity by the Cyber Clean Center

CCC also provides a cleaning tool on its Website. People who are notified of an infection are expected to download the cleaning tool, install it on their PCs, and take necessary steps accordingly. This activity has proven to be effective, leading to the relatively low rate of Bot infections in Japan, compared to the rest of the world. However, among the users who received such an e-mail warning from the CCC, those who implemented the recommended measures (i.e., downloading the cleaning tool) account for only about 32.5 percent, thus underscoring the need to improve this rate. Despite being warned of the Bot-infection and urged to implement specific countermeasures, why do only 32.5 percent of users follow the recommendation? The answer might be that users think downloading and installing such a cleaning tool on their PCs might incur costs as well as cause further trouble. One survey in the field discusses the hypothesis that this phenomenon is a "Social Dilemma" and tries to verify the cognitive elements which are the feature of "Social Dilemma" (Komatsu et al., 2010). The results of the survey revealed that a users' attitude (based on stated preference) does not match that users' behaviour (based on revealed preference). For this reason, an analysis of the cause for this difference is necessary. Also, additional surveys and experiences need to be conducted. The authors found that the cognitive element that most affects a users' behaviour is a sense of crisis. Therefore, the authors refer to both Protection Motivation Theory (PMT), which can create the sense of a threat and the Elaboration Likelihood Model (ELM), which is a behavioural model using persuasibility in the decision-making process.

3   Related Research and Trends

Since 2001, a field of research called "Security Economics" has emerged with Ross Anderson at the forefront (2001). Far from being a Western-only interest, security economics has also garnered considerable interest in Asia (Sugiura et al., 2008). Also, Egelman et al., (2008) provide an insightful study that creates effective security indicators within the context of phishing. These indicators are clearly needed, as 97% of participants believed in phishing enough to visit the URLs. For the participants who saw the active warnings, 79% chose to heed them and close the phishing sites, whereas only 13% of those who saw the passive warnings obeyed them. Without the active warning indicators, it is likely that most participants would have entered personal information. However, the active indicators did not perform equally. In other words, this study has substantiated the effectiveness of the active warning alerts used in the experiments. A current and important result in terms of potential malware problems also exists. Christen et al., (2011) examined the cost for an attacker to pay users at home to execute arbitrary malware and then asked these users to download and run an executable program they wrote without being told what it did and without any way of knowing how it works .

3.1   Persuasion Psychology

Persuasive communication is a type of communication used for the adoption of certain beliefs in people.. Persuasion is defined as a socially effective process or a socially effective action that causes attitudinal or behavioural changes with a receivers' consent under a non-enforcing manner. This type of communication is mainly accomplished through language (Fukuda, 2002).

3.1.1   Protection Motivation Theory

Rogers (1983) discussed how communication that constructs threats is not a single communication, but several, which include three stimulus variables. The negative factors which define attitudinal change are "perceived severity", "probability of occurrence", and "cost". The positive factors include "response efficacy" and "self-efficacy". When reflecting on information security measures with these kinds of factors in mind, it is evident that behaviours related to information security measures are not just conducted by individuals, but by multiple people. In other words, it is necessary to investigate collective behaviour in order to persuade people to adopt coping behaviours for information security measures. This type of protection motivation theory is proposed by Fukuda and Tozuka (2005), to explain the effect of threat persuasion, which requires a collective coping behaviour. The factors for collective coping behaviour are defined as "perceived responsibility", "perceived ratio of others "and "perceived social norms". The "perceived ratio of others" means recognition of the ratio of others implementing security countermeasures. Research concerning information security using PMT on state of individual cognition under threats of home wireless security already exists by Tam et al., (2005).

The present authors consider the intention to implement security measures as dependent upon the situation and include such factors such as the capability of coping , past experience regarding incidents of information security, and the literacy of the Internet environment. Because of these reasons, the discussion is extended to the Elaboration Likelihood Model.

3.1.2   Elaboration Likelihood Model

The Elaboration Likelihood Model (ELM) designed by Petty and Cacioppo (1986) is considered to be high in explanatory power among models dealing with attitudinal change caused by personal circumstances upon receiving a persuasive message. The model defines two processing routes for a persuasive message as follows:

a) Central route: A persuasive message is scrutinized, understood, and then a logical coping behaviour is adopted..

b) Peripheral route: The receiver of the message does not have sufficient ability to understand its content, and so is affected by factors not directly related to the message content, such as the level of trust in the sender of the message

When a person changes their attitude through the peripheral route, their attitude is relatively temporary and is generally influenced by other information. On the other hand, when an attitude change occurs through the central route, the attitude is relatively sustained, regardless of whether the coping behaviour is employed or not. We introduced central route factors such as "persuasiveness of message" and "level of comprehension", and as peripheral routes "trust in sender" and "trust in message". We assume that these factors are influenced by individuals' IT-skills, knowledge, or intention in implementing security measures.

4   Survey and Demonstration Experiment

4.1   Preparations and questionnaire

To analyse the difference in actual behaviour and implementation intention, observation of the behaviour of people who are pressured to take actual measures when they received a persuasive message is needed. More specifically, factors for a persuasive message that needs to be satisfied become clear by clarifying the process that leads to an actual behaviour and the cognitive factors that trigger such attitudinal changes.. Therefore, we first conduct a preliminary survey on the implementation of intention, then link this survey with a demonstration experiment, and analyze each individual's behaviour and its linkage with the questionnaire. Below, we summarize the issues:

a) Regardless of whether or not there is an intention to implement measures, what are the circumstances of individuals who do not implement them?

b) What kind of persuasive message will give rise to attitudinal changes?

According to the ELM, to effect attitudinal changes from a warning alert email, the factors which will cause attitudinal change will depend on whether or not the individual has the ability to deeply comprehend the content of the warning alert mail. Therefore, it could be inferred that the attitudinal change will depend to some degree on the difference in IT skills and the degree of the user's involvement in security incidents. The procedure of the questionnaire was as follows: Subjects were presented with an explanatory text about Bots, followed by an warning alert mail, and then given a download method for a Bot-removal tool as a countermeasure. Subsequently, the demonstration experiment was conducted after selecting the participants from the respondents that answered the questionnaire. Furthermore, to elicit accurate intentions, the true purpose of the questionnaire was not disclosed. Also, the contents of the questionnaire varied widely so that the participants could not deduce the overall purpose of the questionnaire.

4.2   Experimental set-up

An experimental system was developed and constructed in the laboratory with a LAN connected to the Internet. One hundred participants were extracted from respondents of the questionnaire and were composed so that the number of participants who have experienced a computer virus infection was equal to the number of participants who did not. The experiment was conducted in three anechoic rooms with PCs set up so that there was no external influence (Figure 2). Also, monitoring PCs were prepared so that the authors could observe the PC screen used by each test participant (Figure3).

4.3   Ethical considerations

The experiment was conducted based on the Japanese Psychological Association "Code of Ethics" in regard to conducting a psychological experiment (JPA, 2011). The participants were told that the name of the experiment was, "A psychological experiment about a game environment that uses collective knowledge".

5   Findings and Discussion

The survey was conducted over the Internet using a Web survey environment from Cross Marketing Ltd. (2012). The reason we adopted an Internet survey was because the topic of this survey was Bot viruses, and people that used the Internet had to be selected effectively. The survey period was from 9 March 2010 to 10 March 2010, and the total number of respondents was 2254. Table 1 shows the number of respondents per gender and in each age group.

age	Male	Female
20-29	280	266
30-39	287	276
40-49	284	275
50-59	293	293
total	1144	1110

Table1: Gender and Age Composition of the Respondents of the Questionnaire

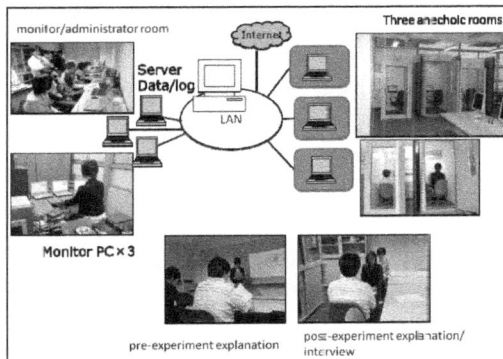

Figure 2: Overview of Experimental Environment

From 17 April 2010 to 29 May 2010, we conducted the experiment with three participants at one time, for a total of 35 times. We interviewed the participants about their behaviour in the game after the experiment. As a result, 93 samples were available because 7participants claimed that they did not take the indicated countermeasures because the PC was not their own. Table 2 shows the results of whether or not participants implemented the measures during the experiment with respect to having the intention for implementation in the questionnaire. Thirty-four participants in the questionnaire responded that they intended to implement the measures, whereas of these, thirteen actually implemented the measure and twenty-one failed to do so.

5.1   Findings from result of the questionnaire

Variables related to IT-skill level had 11 question items; "degree of involvement" had 3 items. For each respectively, we executed a principal component analysis with the median of the first principal component as the dividing line. PMT cognition factors with values of 1-4 indicate the level of cognition in descending order. According to multinomial logistic regression, "response efficacy" was the element within the collective PMT that was shown to significantly influence the implementation intention the most ($p<0.05$). As for factors in ELM, "trust in sender" influenced the intention of those in the low IT-skilled group the most. The statistics tool "stata11" was used because of its overall reliability in various areas of research.

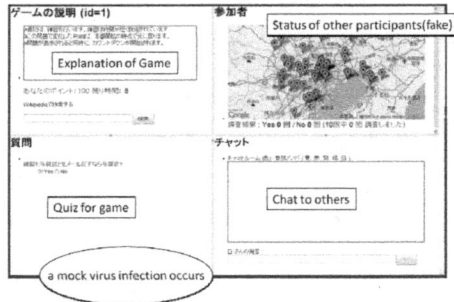

Figure 3: Snapshot of Participant's PC Screens

Questionnaire (number of respondents)		Measured in Experiment (number of participants)	
Intention	34	Implemented	13
		Not implemented	21
No intention	59	Implemented	24
		Not implemented	35
Total	93		93

Table2: Implementation Intention in the Questionnaire and Actual Implementation Results in the Experiment

5.2   Analysis of participants whose intentions and actual implementations were different

Since the total sample number is only 93, sample numbers for each four cases divided by intention/no-intention and behaviour (implement/not implement) were too small to run statistical analysis. Therefore, the authors introduced a multiplicative dummy with intention and cognitive elements defined by PMT and ELM Next, a stepwise multinomial logit regression was used to extract significant elements efficiently. The criteria for stepwise regression is $p<0.15$. The result of the stepwise analysis is shown in Table 3. Multiplicative dummies are indicated using the prefix "in_" with the original elements. The elements which affect actual behaviour without intention include "ITskill(+)" and "self-efficacy"(-). With intention, the elements include "perceived cost"(-), "perceived response efficacy"(-), "perceived social dilemma"(-), "persuasiveness of message"(-), "social norm"(+), "perceived severity"(+), " level of involvement"(-), and "responsibility"(+). Therefore, these positive elements affect the promotion of actual behaviour while cost, perceived response efficacy, perceived social dilemma, persuasiveness of message and level of involvement prevent actual behaviour.

Behaviour	Coef.	Std.Err	Z	P>|z|
IT-skill	1.546	0.924	1.67	0.094
in_ Perceived Cost	-2.708	1.237	-2.19	0.029
Level of comprehension	1.007	0.347	2.91	0.004
In_Perceived response efficacy	-4.688	2.177	-2.15	0.031
Trust in sender	-1.512	0.624	-2.42	0.015
In_Trust in sender	4.749	1.712	2.77	0.006
In_Perceived social dilemma	-6.264	2.641	-2.37	0.018
In_Perceived ratio of others	-4.778	1.715	-2.79	0.005
In_Persuasiveness of message	-2.083	1.407	-1.48	0.139
In_Perceived norm	1.764	1.000	1.76	0.078
Perceived self-efficacy	-1.080	0.513	-2.10	0.035
In_Perceived severity	5.844	2.499	2.34	0.019
Perceived ratio of others	1.030	0.516	2.00	0.046
In_ involvement	-2.062	1.057	-1.98	0.053
In_level of comprehension	-2.779	1.039	-2.67	0.007
In_responsibility	5.514	2.158	2.56	0.011
_cons	-4.569	3.237	-1.41	0.158

n=93,, Pseudo R2 = 0.354

Table 3: Result of stepwise logit analysis

A coefficient for the multiplicative dummy (e.g. in_the Perceived ratio of others) represents the impact of an element under intention and for a corresponding non-multiplicative dummy (e.g. Perceived ratio of others under no intention). Using the sign of the estimated coefficients for these items, the estimation results can be interpreted as follows:

- Level of comprehension is positive, but comprehension level with intention is negative: Comprehension promotes actual behaviour under non-intention, but prevents actual behaviour under intention.

- Trust in sender is negative, but in-trust is positive: Trust in sender prevents actual behaviour under non-intention, but promotes actual behaviour under intention.

- The perceived ratio of others is positive, but the in-perceived ratio of others is negative: Perceived ratio of others promotes actual behaviour under non-intention, but prevents actual behaviour under intention.

The above results seem to suggest that intention affects the actual behaviour of participants not directly but indirectly via cognitive elements. To be precise, we think that intention affects the elements and, then, subsequently, influences actual behaviour.

In the case where an Internet user trusts a sender, the former is unlikely to take measures if she/he has no intention, whereas the opposite is likely to hold true otherwise. In the case where the level of comprehension is high, an Internet user is unlikely to take measures if she/he has intention. Here, she/he observes a surrounding experimental environment carefully, understands the situation well, and, then concludes that she does not have to take measures. That is, she/he does not take measures unless she/he *really* thinks it is necessary. A similar argument applies to the case for the perceived ratio of others.

5.3   Requirements on a Persuasion Message

We summarize the requirements for a persuasive message. The results showed that in order to form the implementation of intention, it is necessary to communicate in a simpler manner "what kind of effect" an information security measure has on an individual, and to send a message which appeals to the low IT-skills group's trust in the sender. Also, the fact that these groups will process the message through a peripheral route is assumed, and therefore, presenting information that is intuitively satisfying is believed to be more effective than the accuracy of the message.

The results of the analysis between intention and actual behavior are more complicated than previously thought. The message should be sent by a trusted entity. While existing research shows that many people have an intention to heed the email warning, effective elements of an intention include social norms, the degree of severity of the message of persuasion, and a sense of responsibility, which are not always considered as well. If a user has the intention to heed an email warning and carry out the measures needed, then this intention will be effective for conducting actual behavior because the user will trust the sender. When a user has the intention of measuring implementation, the other users enforcement of the notification is not needed, and when a user's own degree of comprehension is high, it does not necessarily effect actual behavior.

5.4   Future Topics

Previously we believed that cognitive elements affected actual behavior through intention. However, the result shows the possibility that intention affects cognitive elements. We would like to consider the relationship among intention, actual behavior, and cognitive elements.

6   Conclusion

We conducted this psychology experiment to observe an actual, individual behavior after the questionnaire. The difference in intention and actual behavior was revealed.

Several cognitive elements related to PMT and ELM were effective in promoting the implementation of security measures. We will apply the results to activities that promote information security measures. However, the relationship between complex structures remains when considering intention, actual behaviour, and cognitive elements.

7   Acknowledgments

The authors wish to thank Professor Nicolas Christin of Carnegie Melon University for his valuable comments. We also wish to thank Professor A.Yoshikai of Nihon University, Associate Professor A.Inomata of the Nara Institute of Science and Technology, Assistant Professor M.Ueda of the National Institute of Informatics, and Dr. H.Numata of Excellead Technology Inc., for carrying out the survey and experiment.

References

Anderson, R. (2001). Why Information Security is Hard- An Economic Perspective, ACSAC '01: Proceedings of the 17th Annual Computer Security Applications Conference, 2001, IEEE Computer Society, Washington, DC.

CCC: Cyber Clean Center in Japan. (2011), "Achievements of the Cyber Clean Center", https://www.ccc.go.jp/en_report/201101/index.html

Christin, N., Egelman, S., Vidas,T, and Grossklags, J. (2011) "It's All About The Benjamins: An empirical study on incentivizing users to ignore security advice," Financial Cryptography & Data Security.

Cross Marketing Ltd., Web Site(2012), http://global.cross-m.co.jp/(Accessed 25 April 2012)

Egelman, S, Cranor, L, and Hong, J. (2008) "You've Been Warned: An Empirical Study on the Effectiveness of Web Browser Phishing Warnings." CHI '08: Proceedings of the SIGCHI conference on Human Factors in Computing Systems.

Fukada, H.(2002) "Handbook for Persuasion Psychology", Kita-ohji Publishing(in Japanese), 2002.

JNSA Japan Network Security Association. (2010). "Survey report for the information security incident in 2009" (in Japanese), http://www.jnsa.org/result/incident/2009.html.

JPA: The Japanese Psychological Association, "JPA code of ethics," http://www.psych.or.jp/members/rinri.html

Komatsu, A., Takagi, D., and Matsumoto, T., (2010) "Empirical study on cognitive structures and personal gain in information security countermeasure", Journal of IPSJ, (in Japanese), Vol.51, pp.1711-1725.

Tozuka, T., Fukada, H., (2005) "Study of the collective protection model for Threat appeal persuasion," The Japanese Journal of Experimental Social Psychology, Vol.44, No.1, pp.54-61.

Petty, E.,Rechard, Cacioppo, J.,.(1986), "The Elaboration Likelihood Model of persuasion," Advances in Experimental Social Psychology, Vol.19, 1986.

Rogers, R.W.,(1983), Cognitive and Physiological process in fear appeals and attitude change," A revised theory of protection motivation theory, Social Psychophysiology. Press,pp.153-176, New York.

Sugiura, T., Komatsu, A., Ueda, M., and Yamada,Y., (2008) "Challenge to Information Security Economics," Proc. of Computer Security Symposium 2008 (in Japanese), pp.725-730.

Woon, I., Tan, G.-W., and Low, R.(2005) "A Protection Motivation Theory Approach to Home Wireless Security," International Conference on Information Systems, Proc. of ICIS2005, Paper31.

Usable Secure Email Communications - Criteria and Evaluation of Existing Approaches

C.T. Moecke and M. Volkamer

TU Darmstadt / Center for Advanced Security Research Darmstadt, Germany
e-mail : cristian.moecke@cased.de; melanie.volkamer@cased.de

Abstract

Email communication has been used for many years and replaces more and more traditional letters. Compared to postal service the mail service is easier, faster and free of charge. However, the standard email is from a security point of view comparable to post cards and not to letters. While end-to-end secure email communication is possible with PGP and S/MIME, only few people use it due to a lack of awareness, low usability, and lacking an understanding of PKIs. Recently, some new approaches for secure email communication have been proposed. In order to enable a comparison of all these different email services we define security, usability, and interoperability criteria and apply them to existing approaches. Based on the result, we propose future directives for usable secure email communication.

Keywords

Secure email, Usable Security, Criteria

1 Introduction

Ray Tomlinson sent the first network email in 1971 using the ARPANET. With the conversion from ARPANET to the Internet in the early 1980s, email communication became broadly available. Since then, email has become more and more popular. Nowadays, email accounts are free of charge and much faster than traditional letters sent via postal services. Many people have several email accounts. Email replaces traditional letters more and more in many areas including in the private, business, and governmental sector. Critical, sensitive, personal and business information are sent via email although it is well known that emails are less secure than traditional letters. They can easily be forged; and provide neither strong sender authenticity nor message confidentially. Secure email communication is in general available i.e. based on PGP or S/MIME. These techniques are far from being broadly used. Studies like (Whitten, 1999) and (Sheng, 2006) show that these solutions are not usable. People in particular do not understand the concept of standard Public Key Infrastructures (PKI).

Solutions for more usable secure email communication have recently been proposed to improve the situation. Examples are the E-PostBrief (http://www.epost.de), De-Mail (https://www.bsi.bund.de) and Hushmail (http://www.hushmail.com/). These approaches do not provide end-to-end secure email communication but users need to trust the service providers. As in addition some of these solutions are closed systems and users need to pay for them; it is unclear whether they will be accepted like common emails. As an optimal solution for usable and end-to-end secure email communication is not yet available, users need to find an adequate trade-off for their needs. This paper defines the most relevant criteria that should be taken into account for such a decision. In addition we analyse existing security mechanisms in the context of email communication (namely DKIM, SPF, PGP, S/MIME and TLS) and popular mail service providers (namely Gmail, Hushmail, E-PostBrief and DE-Mail) according to these criteria.

The paper is structured as follows: In Section 2, we analyse related work. In Section 3 we define the security criteria, which are applied to available security techniques in Section 4 and existing email providers in Section 5. In Section 6 we present our conclusions and directions for future work.

2   Related Work

There is little published literature that proposes criteria for classifying and analysing the security of an email system. We analyse this work and how it compares to our work: NIST (National Institute of Standards and Technology) published Guidelines on Electronic Mail Security (NIST, 2007). The guide "is intended to assist organizations in installing, configuring, and maintaining secure mail servers and mail client" (NIST, 2007). The guide is based on available technology and on assisting administrator and users to apply this technology in the most secure way. Our work proposes criteria independent from available email systems and technologies. Alperovitch et al. (Alperovitch *et al.*, 2007) analyses some of the previous work on email reputation systems (systems that calculate a score for an email, usually for spam filtering) and provide a "taxonomy that examines the required properties of email reputation systems, identifies the range of approaches, and surveys previous work" (Alperovitch *et al.*, 2007). While their work classifies and organizes a broad range of reputation criteria, they do not analyse whether current systems ensure these criteria. Garfinkel (Garfinkel, 2005b) focuses on usability aspects of email security, and includes a survey on how users act regarding signed emails. There are also previous works on usable security analysis of secure email systems (Whitten, 1999) (Garfinkel, 2005a) (Sheng, 2006), which provide important usability criteria, which we also consider on our work.

3   Email usable security criteria

This section defines the evaluation criteria used to later analyse existing email security techniques and email providers. They include security, interoperability, and usability requirements. Due to space constraints, we leave aspects like malware spreading, spam, traceability, long-term authenticity and confidentiality, legal aspects and anonymous communication including aliases for future work.

Security: The security properties are divided into sender authenticity (A), integrity (I), confidentiality (C), and one requirement addressing trust in the service under evaluation (Tr). These criteria are deduced from our threat analysis of different email communication scenarios and possible attacks. We distinguish the following requirements: **(A.1)** It should be possible to verify that the sender is the owner of the email account that belongs to the stated sender email address. **(A.2)** It should be analysed which methods are used to verify the authenticity of the user i.e. password, two-factor authentication, or asymmetric cryptography (This authenticity information, especially how strong the authentication method was, are of interest to the receiver of a message. However, none of the later evaluated approaches provide this kind of information to the receiver.). This also includes whether passwords are securely transmitted or not. **(A.3)** It should be possible to deduce the real identity of the person sending the email. **(I)** It should be possible to detect modification of the content/the subject of the received email. **(C)** No one else except the receiver of the email should gain access to the content/subject of the email. **(Tr)** It should be analysed whether the user needs to trust the email provider or any other party like certification authorities regarding any of the security requirements defined previously.

Interoperability: Interoperability is important, as services are not ready for large-scale usage without it. Correspondingly, the sub criteria are related to security and trust aspects that are important for the acceptance of the corresponding service. This class of criteria is divided into the following sub criteria (Note, not all requirements are addressed here. Another one for instance is that the email service should provide all the functionality provided by standard email like searching in the inbox or accessing the account from different devices.): **(IN.1)** It should be possible to communicate with people who do not use the same email provider. **(IN.2)** It should be possible to securely communicate with people who do not use the same email provider. **(IN.3)** It should be possible to setup and run your own email service. **(IN.4)** There should be more than one provider offering the corresponding service. **(IN.5)** It should be possible to use the system with the security techniques discussed in Section 4.

Usability aspects: The usability criteria are deduced from papers on usable security analysis of email communication systems. The most important are: **(U.1)** It should be evaluated how much work is necessary to setup and start using the service. **(U.2)** Adequate metaphors should be used for functions like encryption, signing, and certificates. **(U.3)** It should only require less and easy to make trust decisions. **(U.4)** Sender and receiver should not need to understand the underlying PKI concepts to make any trust decisions. **(U.5)** It should not be necessary to obtain and/or compare some information via out of bounds mode like comparing hashes.

4   Security techniques available for email

In this section we describe the security techniques that are currently available and could be used to improve email security by integrating them in existing email services or by installing a corresponding plugin into the email client or web browser. The list contains techniques related to sender authentication, Public Key Infrastructure (PKI) support, and securing the network. We analyse which of the above security and usability criteria they fulfil while we only discuss those security requirements that are at least partially ensured and only those usability requirements that can be applied but are not fulfilled. We also do not address interoperability requirements as the analysed techniques do not stand on their own but can only be used as an add-on to the email services discussed in Section 5. For all techniques we make the trust assumption (Tr) that the software running the corresponding security operations and checks is trustworthy, and that cryptographic secret keys are securely stored.

An *SPF (Sender Policy Framework)* (RFC4408) record is a list of IP addresses that are authorized to send emails for a particular domain. The DNS server responsible for this domain publishes this list. This list can be used to partially verify the authenticity of a received email, confirming that it came from an authorized server. If we trust the DNS server regarding the integrity of this list and the email provider behind this domain (Tr), i.e. the provider only delivers emails from authenticated users with the correct address in the "from" field, and there is also no MITM attack (A Man-In-The-Middle attack could modify the list since it is not authenticated.) when fetching the list, A.1 is ensured. However since this assumption is not true for all DNS servers and all mail providers, hard trust decisions remain for the user (U.3). *Sender ID Framework - SIDF* (RFC4406) extends the SPF verification, but with no relevant improvements considering our criteria. *DKIM (Domain Keys Identified Mail)* (RFC4871) is a digital signature from the email service provider on sent emails. It allows verifying that this provider really sent the message. The corresponding public key is published on the DNS server associated to this domain. Thus, regarding A.1, one needs to trust that the DNS server provides the proper key and that the email service only delivers emails from authenticated users. Correspondingly, the trust assumptions (Tr) regarding A.1 and the limitations for U.3 identified for SPF also hold for DKIM, including the non-occurrence of a MITM attack (In this case the MITM attack could be used to inform the wrong key to the receiver). In addition, the integrity property (I) is partially ensured because the signature provides message integrity after being processed by the mail server of the sender under the same trust assumption required for A.1.

PGP (Pretty good Privacy) (RFC2015) provides end-to-end security to email messages. It is not necessary to trust a central trust anchor as it is based on the Web-of-Trust (WoT) model. It fulfils property C and I. Authenticity depends on the adequate use of the WoT. In a restricted environment where people verify carefully the keys they sign, A.1 and even A.2 can be considered as fulfilled, but with the cost of hard trust decisions (conflict with U.3) and the fact that out-of-bounds data (i.e. verifying key hashes before setting keys as trusted) is required (conflict with U.5). PGP requires some PKI understanding (conflict with U.4) and it takes a while to get started (conflict with U.1). Adequate metaphors (U.2) are very important for a user friendly implementation of PGP, while studies (Whitten, 1999) (Garfinkel, 2005a) showed that this is not the case for PGP (conflict with U.2). *S/MIME (Secure/Multipurpose Internet Mail Extensions)* (RFC2311) provides end-to-end security to email messages. It is based on X.509 PKIs. A certificate for a corresponding key pair should be obtained from a trusted Certification Authority (CA) which is usually not free of charge. However, the use of self-signed certificates is also possible. S/MIME with CAs fulfils A.1, C and I, and if the CA also verifies the personal identity (i.e. for Qualified Certificates on E.U. (RFC3739)) it fulfils A.2, as well. The receiver needs to trust the CA that issued the certificate of the sender (Tr). While major CAs are already set as trusted on most plugins, it leads to hard trust decisions if the sender's certificate is issued on an untrusted/unknown CA (conflict with U.3). Without CAs (self-signed certificates), S/MIME only fulfils C and I. In this case it is hard to decide if the authenticity of the message should or should not be trusted (conflict with U.3). The user needs out-of-bounds information to verify the authenticity (conflict with U.5). In both cases, it takes a while to get started (conflict with U.1). Similar to PGP, adequate metaphors are very important for a user-friendly implementation. In addition, in cases in which the verification fails (i.e. failure on obtaining revocation information, or an intermediate CA certificate), it is required to understand the underlying PKI (conflict with U.4).

Opportunistic Encryption (RFC4322) in general means that a system tries to use encryption to secure any communication, while using unencrypted communication if corresponding keys are not available. The keys are not necessarily authenticated. Thus, if there is any known key to communicate with the receiver (even in a self-signed certificate) encryption is used. Garfinkel (Garfinkel, 2003) proposed a system that implements opportunistic encryption for email communication. It acts like a proxy for sending and a proxy for receiving an email (While he does not provide clear information about the proxy, we assume that it runs as a plugin locally and is considered trusted (Tr).). The proxy manages the keys (including certificates), the encryption and the decryption process. Whenever the sending proxy is able to encrypt an email to the receiver, it will encrypt this message. It is also possible to specify that a message should only be delivered if it can be encrypted. There is no authentication of the keys in the system. The receiver proxy learns new keys from emails previously received and stores them in its own database. It gives a warning only if a new key is detected for an already-known email address. Furthermore, emails are not signed. It therefore provides confidentiality (C) under the trust assumption (Tr) that the proxy is trustworthy (i.e. a local proxy) and there was a previous legitimate communication between sender and receiver so the correct key is known. This idea avoids the need to understand PKI concepts (U.4 is ensured) and hard trust decisions (U.3 and U.5 is in general ensured - except when a conflict occurs). There is also a low setup effort (U.1).

TLS (Transport Layer Security) provides a secure communication between user and server (over IMAP, POP, SMTP or a Webmail session) and between servers. Confidentiality (C) and integrity (I) are ensured under the trust assumption (Tr) that the whole delivery process is secured by TLS and that the servers are trustworthy. It could also be used to authenticate the user with TLS client authentication (therefore offering strong authentication - A.2), but that is not common.

5   Analysis of existing secure email providers

In this section, we analyse five types of email providers according to our criteria while focusing on one representative of each; namely standard (in-secure) email providers, very popular email providers providing some security (Gmail), a combination of the previous and the different PKI approaches from Section 4, providers offering secure email communication in a closed system (DE-Mail/E-Postbrief), and providers offering secure email communication in an open system (Hushmail). The results of the comparison are summarized in Tables 1, 2 and 3.

	A.1	A.2	A.3	I	C
Gmail	Partially (see U.3 Tr: Gmail/DNS). Detect forged Gmail(Tr: Gmail)	2 factor (not visible to receiver)	No	Yes (Tr: Gmail and DNS)	End to Server and Server to Server (if available)
DE-Mail	Yes (Tr: Provider)	Unknown	Yes (Tr: Provider)	Yes (Tr: Provider)	Yes (Tr: Provider)
E-PostBrief	Yes (Tr: Provider)	SMS TAN (not visib. to receiver)	Yes (Tr: Provider)	Yes (Tr: Provider)	Yes (Tr: Provider)
Hushmail	Yes (Tr: Hushmail)	Password only	No	Yes (Tr: Hushmail/Softw.)	Yes (Tr: Hushmail/Softw.)
Gmail & PGP	Restricted contexts (no U.5)	No change	Restricted contexts (no U.5)	Yes	Yes
Gmail & S/MIME	If CA verifies it (Tr: CA)	No change	If CA verifies it (Tr: CA)	Yes	Yes
Gmail & Opp	If had previous secure comm.	No change	No	No	If receiver key is known

Table 1: E-mail services and security criteria

	U.1	U.2	U.3	U.4	U.5
Gmail	Easy	No metaphors	Decide if domain is trustworthy	No PKI	Domain trustworthiness
DE-Mail	Identification on provider	Unknown	Easy: Trust provider	PKI hidden	No out of bounds data
E-PostBrief	Identification on Post office	Encryption and Signature	Easy: Trust provider	PKI hidden	No out of bounds data
Hushmail	Easy	Encryption and Signature	Easy: Trust provider	PKI hidden	No out of bounds data
Gmail & PGP	Hard: create /publish key, get recipient key	Depends on imple-mentation	Decide trusted keys based on WoT	Understand PGP	Obtain information to trust keys
Gmail & S/MIME	Hard: obtain own/recipient certificate	Depends on imple-mentation	If known CA, easy. If not, hard	If verification fails or CA is untrusted	If verification fails or CA is untrusted
Gmail & Opp	Easy	Not necessary	Only in key conflict	PKI hidden	Only in key conflict

Table 2: E-mail services and usability criteria

	IN.1	IN.2	IN.3	IN.4	IN.5
Gmail	Yes	Yes	Open standards	Open standards	PGP, S/MIME
DE-Mail	Closed environ.	Closed environ.	High cost	High cost	PGP/S/MIME
E-PostBr.	Closed environ.	Closed environ.	Closed environ.	No	PGP/S/MIME
Hushmail	Yes	Yes	Open standards	Open standards	DKIM/SPF/S/MIME

Table 3: E-mail services and interoperability criteria

5.1   Standard email

According to the email standards (RFC5322, RFC5321), standard email services are not required to provide too much security information to the receiver. The only somehow relevant security information is the header of an email which provides information regarding the delivery path of this message, but this information is not authenticated, therefore any decision based on it depends on assuming all the servers on the path trustworthy. However these assumptions are hard to verify and rely on too many out-of-bounds information (conflict with U.5) and hard trust decisions (conflict with U.3), and also are not true for many servers. Many email providers operate using no more security than those offered by these standards.

5.2   Gmail

The most popular email providers usually offer at least some security improvements, even if mainly for spam control. We have chosen to analyse Gmail, which verifies SPF and DKIM for email origin authentication, and adds DKIM signatures for emails delivered. When an email has SPF or DKIM authentication but the domain in the address ("from" field) does not match the authenticated origin information, this is shown to the end user as a "via *authenticated origin domain*" after the sender's address. Emails sent from forged Gmail accounts (i.e. from other servers, but with Gmail address on the "from" field), which as a result do not have authenticated information on their origin, are shown to the receiving Gmail user with a warning "*this message may not have been sent by:* email@domain com", in red). This makes impersonating other Gmail accounts difficult.

Emails from domains other than Google and without SPF and without DKIM authentication are shown without any hint or warning. The only difference between a non-authenticated and an authenticated mail is that the authenticated domain is shown as "*mailed-by*" when the user looks at the details of the message header. There is no other visual clue that differentiates an SPF/DKIM authentic message from one without any authentication. Therefore, Gmail only guarantees email proof of possession (A.1) between Gmail users, considering Gmail trustworthy (Tr). When communicating with other service providers, the interface does not show adequate feedback, but even with more information provided it would lead to complex trust decisions (conflicts with U.3), namely deciding if the authenticated domain is trustworthy or not. Gmail supports two-factor authentication (using a smartphone application that generates "One Time Passwords") but this is not enforced (A.2) and not visible to the receiver. Emails originated from Gmail servers are DKIM signed, therefore have their integrity guaranteed (I), considering Gmail trustworthy (Tr). Gmail uses SSL/TLS for end-to-server encryption, and may use it also to communicate with other servers when supported, however even trusting Gmail it is not possible to guarantee confidentiality of messages after they leave Gmail servers. Therefore, (C) is only partially fulfilled. The communication between user and server is encrypted during the authentication process (A.2).

Gmail uses only open standards and is a standard mail provider (IN.1). All the security measures available are also based on open standards and may be used by other providers, so it is possible to have the same level of secure email communication with any other interested provider (IN.2). While there is only one provider of the Gmail solution, we consider IN.4 and IN.5 fulfilled because there is no restriction to operate a similar service once it is based on open standards. It is also possible to integrate PGP and or S/MIME on Gmail (there are even plugins available for that - i.e. *FireGPG* and *Penango*), therefore IN.5 is also fulfilled.

5.3   DE-Mail/E-PostBrief

DE-Mail and E-PostBrief are closed messaging systems, provided by the German government and German postal services. These approaches claim to provide secure email communication and are based on strictly controlled servers that manage the full delivery process. There is also a law regulating DE-Mail. Both systems are closed environments. Thus there is no possibility to forge a message (A.1), if the providers are considered trustworthy (Tr). Users are only allowed to use the system after a personal identification (A.3) at the provider's office (DE-Mail) or at a postal service centre (E-PostBrief). E-PostBrief provides SMS TAN (a one-time-password sent via SMS) as a second factor of authentication, but its use is neither enforced (A.2) nor available to the receiver. There is no information available whether DE-Mail providers will offer this possibility. The communication between different servers of one provider and servers from different providers (in particular within the DE-Mail concept) are secured by TLS. TLS is also used to provide end-to-server security. Correspondingly, integrity (I) and confidentiality (C) are fulfilled based on trust in the provider(s) (Tr). Besides the costs for each email (both services require payment per message sent), interoperability is the greatest disadvantage of these two approaches. Due to their closed environment property, it is only possible to communicate with people who have an account in this environment (IN.1 and IN.2 are not ensured). While there are some providers in DE-Mail, the number is limited number (IN.4 insured) though it is possible to operate your own provider (with high costs involved - IN.3 ensured). It could be possible to use other techniques (IN.5), particularly PGP and S/MIME to provide end-to-end security, using corresponding plugins.

5.4   Hushmail

Hushmail is a web-based solution (It is also possible to use a Java applet to download the encrypted key and process the encryption operations locally. However the same trust assumptions hold for the Java version, since Hushmail provides it. Hushmail is also testing a new interface, but it is not stable. Therefore our evaluation considers the old ("original") interface.). Hushmail calls itself a PGP based secure email system. However, the main characteristic of PGP, namely the WoT model, is not applied. Instead, Hushmail signs all the public keys of the users and publishes them on a key server. Obviously, all keys signed by Hushmail are considered trustworthy. With this approach, it is possible to automate the key trust management process and in particular the user is no longer involved. A Hushmail server generates the user's key pairs and the secret key is encrypted with the user email account password. In addition, everyone is able to publish new PGP keys on the key server, associated to email addresses from other email providers besides Hushmail. In that case, there is a challenge-response mail sent to the email associated with the key to verify the ownership of the account before the key is set as trusted for all Hushmail users. It is also possible to send secure emails to non-Hushmail accounts for which no PGP key is stored on the Hushmail key server, based on Question/Answer that only the receiver should be able to answer.

For all received signed emails for which the corresponding public key is trusted by Hushmail, the signature is verified and if the email is properly signed the email is shown as having valid signatures (*"This message is encrypted, and is digitally signed by Sender Name <username@domain.com>"*), which fulfils A.1. Emails are not verified using DKIM or SPF. There is only a warning if the "return-path" field does not match the sender address. Since this information may be forged, there are no other security indicators of authenticity for non-signed emails that are received. The user's identity is not verified before creating an account (A.3 fails) and the user is authenticated by password.

Email integrity (I) and confidentiality (C) are in general (Due to space constraints we only consider the case where PGP is in place while there are some usability problems with the implementation of the Question/Answer based encryption.) ensured under the assumption that Hushmail is trustworthy (Tr). It is possible for the user to verify message integrity also using its own trusted software and verifying the keys using out-of-bounds data. Since it operates using open standards and can send standard insecure email, all interoperability criteria are fulfilled. The main usability problem is the lack of adequate metaphors for cryptographic operations (U.2) and the communication with users without Hushmail account.

6 Discussion and conclusions

In this paper, we proposed criteria, which a usable and secure email system should ideally ensure. The list only contains the most important security and usability requirements due to space limit, but more should be considered on the development of an ideal solution. We applied these criteria to email security techniques and also to existing email providers while discussing different groups of email providers including a combination with available security techniques as add-on. None of them ensures all the requirements.

Closed and web-based systems like Hushmail are more usable, but they do not provide end-to-end security, as one needs to trust the provider. On the other hand, the consequences of solutions based on security add-on for standard email services are hard trust decisions for the user. It also takes a while to set up these systems. In addition, trust in this security technique is also required, as the average user cannot develop this on its own. The Opportunistic Encryption approach is also more usable, however it does not offer authentication. Approaches similar to Hushmail also have the benefit that secure email can be used from any computer while the PGP/SMIME add-ons require you to carry the key in a secure way. The main disadvantage of DE-Mail/EPostbrief is that these are closed systems, i.e. it is not possible to communicate electronically with people who do not have such an account, and you need to pay for each email. While with Hushmail it is possible to communicate with people who do not have Hushmail both in a secure and insecure way, there are still some security and usability problems in the implementation.

For future work, we propose to merge these approaches. Combine systems like Hushmail with Opportunistic Encryption to hide the PKI and other security trust decisions even more from the user. Registration should be based on in person identification and authentication. Authentication should be based on two-factor authentication at the least. The type of authentication used by the sender should be provided to the receiver. While the key should be generated at the user's side, the email provider could store the encrypted key to make it accessible from any computer. Key management, distribution, and revocation could be based on S/MIME, but operated by the mail servers rather than a third party CA. Communication to users without such an account could be based on an improved implementation of the Hushmail approach.

The biggest challenge seems to be on usability aspects, especially on trust decisions that the receiver needs to take. Future work should consider this carefully and reduce the necessary trust decisions. The software on the client side must be prepared to offer clear information about the security and trustworthiness of an email, so the user can decide how to react to the content of the message. The same applies for sending a message, the sender should be provided with enough information about how secure the delivery process will be.

The proposed criteria focus on aspects that may facilitate the decision of the receiver about the trustworthiness of an email. If we are able to securely authenticate the origin of an email, we can also use this information for spam filtering and also to display more precise and contextualized warnings e.g. regarding phishing emails and dangerous attachments.

7 References

Allman, E., Callas, J., Delany, M., Libbey, M., Fenton, J., Thomas, M.: DomainKeys Identified Mail (DKIM) Signatures. RFC 4871 (Proposed Standard) (May 2007), http://www.ietf.org/rfc/rfc4871.txt, updated by RFC 5672

Alperovitch, D., Judge, P., Krasser, S.: Taxonomy of email reputation systems. In: *Distributed Computing Systems Workshops, 2007. ICDCSW'07. 27th International Conference on. pp. 27. IEEE (2007).*

Butterfield, J., Tracy, M., Jansen, W.: Guidelines on Electronic Mail Security Recommendations of the National Institute of Standards and Technology (2007)

Dusse, S., Hoffman, P., Ramsdell, B., Lundblade, L., Repka, L.: S/MIME Version 2 Message Specification. RFC 2311 (Historic) (Mar 1998)

Elkins, M.: MIME Security with Pretty Good Privacy (PGP). RFC 2015 (Proposed Standard) (Oct 1996)

Garfinkel, S.: Enabling email confidentiality through the use of opportunistic encryption. *In: Proceedings of the 2003 annual national conference on Digital government research. pp. 1-4. Digital Government Society of North America (2003)*

Garfinkel, S., Margrave, D., Schiller, J., Nordlander, E., Miller, R.: How to make secure email easier to use. *In: Proceedings of the SIGCHI conference on human factors in computing systems. pp. 701-710. ACM (2005)*

Garfinkel, S., Miller, R.: Johnny 2: a user test of key continuity management with S/MIME and Outlook Express. *In: Proceedings of the 2005 symposium on Usable privacy and security. pp. 13-24. ACM (2005)*

Klensin, J.: Simple Mail Transfer Protocol. RFC 5321 (Draft Standard) (Oct 2008)

Lyon, J., Wong, M.: Sender ID: Authenticating E-Mail. RFC 4406 (Experimental) (Apr 2006)

Resnick, P.: Internet Message Format. RFC 5322 (Draft Standard) (Oct 2008)

Richardson, M., Redelmeier, D.: Opportunistic Encryption using the Internet Key Exchange (IKE). RFC 4322 (Informational) (Dec 2005)

Santesson, S., Nystrom, M., Polk, T.: Internet X.509 Public Key Infrastructure: Qualified Certificates Profile. RFC 3739 (Proposed Standard) (Mar 2004)

Sheng, S., Broderick, L., Hyland, J., Koranda, C.: Why Johnny still can't encrypt: evaluating the usability of email encryption software. *In: Symposium On Usable Privacy and Security. pp. 3-4 (2006)*

Whitten, A., Tygar, J.: Why Johnny Can't Encrypt. *In: USENIX Security. vol. 1999, p. 1 (1999)*

Wong, M., Schlitt, W.: Sender Policy Framework (SPF) for Authorizing Use of Domains in E-Mail, Version 1. RFC 4408 (Experimental) (Apr 2006)

SecSDM: A Usable Tool to Support IT Undergraduate Students in Secure Software Development

L. Futcher and R. von Solms

Nelson Mandela Metropolitan University, Port Elizabeth, South Africa
e-mail : lynn.futcher@nmmu.ac.za; rossouw.vonsolms@nmmu.ac.za

Abstract

Many IT undergraduate programs neglect to address the importance of integrating information security into the software development lifecycle. SecSDM is an integrated, risk-based methodology for supporting IT undergraduate students in secure software development. A software tool, based on the SecSDM methodology, has been developed to provide a means by which to apply this methodology to software development projects. However, from a developer's perspective, any such software tool needs to be usable. This means that such a tool should have good utility, be effective to use, efficient to use, safe to use, easy to learn, easy to remember and satisfying to use. This paper provides an overview of the SecSDM methodology and presents the results of a user satisfaction survey relating to the SecSDM software tool.

Keywords

SecSDM, secure software development, risk management, user satisfaction

1 Introduction

Technological advancements and the rapid increase in the use of the Internet by organizations and businesses across the globe have had a huge impact on information security. This, in turn, has resulted in major challenges for the software development industry.

Over the past decade there has been an increase in the number of security incidents reported. A substantial percentage of these incidents are the result of inadequate consideration of security during the requirements analysis, the design, implementation and testing of software systems (Walden & Frank, 2006). Conklin and Dietrich (2007) further support this by stating that most cyber vulnerabilities can be traced back to defects in software. These defects are the result of bad design and poor development practices (Conklin & Dietrich, 2007).

Most software development methodologies do not take into consideration the risk issues associated with the information assets implicated, and typically add security as an afterthought, thereby neglecting to integrate security throughout the software development life cycle. This often results in the implementation of inappropriate security controls.

Software engineers need to learn to consider security when writing requirements and design specifications and when developing, testing and deploying software (Pothamsetty, 2005, p. 54). Furthermore, Burley and Bishop (2011) suggest that raising the security implications at each stage of the life cycle would make students more aware of, and more sensitive to, security considerations throughout the software development life cycle (Burley & Bishop, 2011).

Although many researchers are in agreement with this, currently very little has been done to provide a simple, practical, risk-based approach to integrating security into the early stages of the software development life cycle; and that could consistently support students in the development of secure software. For this reason, the secure software development methodology (SecSDM), as described in Section 2, has been developed. SecSDM is an integrated, risk-based approach to support IT undergraduate students in the development of secure software.

This methodology is based on various information security and software development standards, guidelines and best practices. These include ISO/IEC 27002 (2005), the international code of practice for information security management; the various risk-related guidelines, as determined by ISO/IEC 27005 (2008); NIST SP 800-14 (1996), which outlines generally accepted principles and practices for securing information technology systems; and ISO/IEC 7498-2 (1989), which provides the basis of information security in software systems through five basic security services, supported by eight security mechanisms. In addition, the major secure software development contributions of various other key role players were considered including Microsoft, Open Web Application Security Project (OWASP), Oracle and the Software Engineering Institute (SEI).

This paper provides an overview of the SecSDM methodology and presents the results of a user satisfaction survey of the SecSDM software tool which was developed to support IT undergraduate students in the application of this methodology to their software development projects.

2   An overview of SecSDM

This section describes an integrated, risk-based approach to support secure software development. This is achieved by presenting a secure software development methodology, SecSDM, which integrates security aspects throughout the software development life cycle. The following six principles were considered fundamental in the development of this methodology, namely:

- Security must be integrated throughout all phases of the software development life cycle;
- Security aspects need to be considered from the very beginning of the software development life cycle, i.e. from the investigation phase;
- A risk-based approach is required to ensure the implementation of appropriate security controls that are functional, effective, correct and safe to use;

- Any security control implemented must be related to a specified risk identified. Traceability back to such a risk is therefore required;
- A structured approach is required that transparently integrates security aspects, without adding additional overheads with respect to time, cost or expert security skills required; and
- The approach developed must be practical, easy to use and easy to understand.

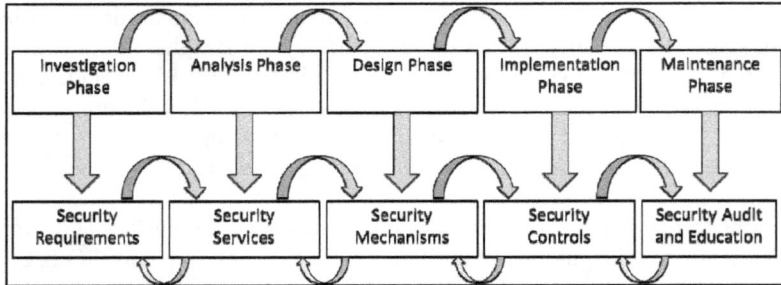

Figure 1: Security in the Software Development Life Cycle

In the literature studied, there exists strong support for integrating security throughout the software development life cycle, in order to minimize the risks associated with the information assets implicated. As depicted in Figure 1, the main security concerns to be addressed at each phase of the software development life cycle, according to SecSDM, are as follows:

- *Investigation Phase*: The output of this initial phase is a set of **security requirements** developed through a simple, structured risk-assessment exercise;
- *Analysis Phase*: During this phase, the **security services** are identified that satisfy the security requirements defined during the investigation phase;
- *Design Phase*: This phase determines how the security services will be implemented, by mapping them to specific **security mechanisms**;
- *Implementation Phase*: This phase identifies and implements the appropriate **security controls and components**; and
- *Maintenance Phase*: During this final phase, users need to be educated in **using the software application in a secure manner**.

SecSDM also ensures that all relevant security-related information is consolidated in a security report. This helps improve the auditability of the software application in question, since security-related decisions are traceable to the appropriate phase, as proposed by this secure software development approach.

A risk management approach, as described by Von Solms and Von Solms (2009) is integral to SecSDM. This approach requires that a detailed risk analysis be performed to identify the potential adverse business impacts of unwanted events, and the likelihood of their occurrence. The outcome of a detailed risk analysis can lead to the effective evaluation of risk, which is necessary in order to identify and implement appropriate security controls and measures. This is essential for the development of secure software applications.

As depicted in Table 1, the ten steps of SecSDM are mapped directly to the risk management approach, as described by Von Solms and Von Solms (2009). From this table it is also clear that Steps 1 to 4 of SecSDM are mapped directly to risk analysis, while Steps 5 and 6 are mapped to risk evaluation. Similarly, Steps 7 to 10 are directly related to the treatment of such risks.

RISK MANAGEMENT	Risk Assessment	Risk Analysis	STEP 3: "Risk" Identification	Assets	Step 1a: Asset identification
					Step 1b: Asset valuation
				Threats	Step 2a: Threat identification
					Step 2b: Threat assessment
			Vulnerabilities		Step 4: Vulnerability assessment
		Risk Evaluation	Step 5: Determine risk value or size		
			Step 6: Prioritize risks		
	Risk Treatment	*Identify suitable controls* Step 7: Identify relevant security services Step 8: Map security services to security mechanisms Step 9: Summarize security services and security mechanisms required			
		Implement identified controls Step 10: Map security mechanisms to appropriate security controls and components			

Table 1: Mapping of SecSDM Steps to Risk Management Approach

An important contribution of this methodology is that it does not simply focus on *'what'* needs to be done to support secure software development, but it also provides valuable guidance in terms of *'how'* this can be achieved. Such a simple, practical approach is always beneficial in the education of IT students. SecSDM provides a simple, easy-to-use and easy-to-understand approach to support secure software development by providing a set of repeatable and systematic steps to ensure that the set of security requirements generated is complete, consistent and easy to understand by all the stakeholders involved in the software development process. In addition, this methodology could help ensure that the security controls implemented will be functional, effective, correct and safe to use.

A further key contribution is the traceability of security requirements throughout the software development life cycle that is provided. This means that any security controls implemented can easily be traced back to a specific security requirement, based on a specific risk identified earlier in the software development life cycle.

3   Using SecSDM

SecSDM was initially implemented as a paper-based tool. However, there are certain drawbacks that are unavoidable when using such a paper-based system, including:

1. Cumbersome and time-consuming to use;
2. Essential steps in the process omitted;
3. Incorrect information captured;
4. Relies on the user recapturing essential information from previous steps;
5. Errors not easily detected;
6. Not easy to go back and make changes;
7. Does not result in a consolidated information security report.

In order to overcome these problems, a software tool, based on the SecSDM methodology was developed. The major goal of the SecSDM software tool is to alleviate all the above-mentioned drawbacks by having the application support the user in a usable and efficient manner.

In designing the software tool, a 'wizard-based' approach was taken to logically progress the user through the ten step process as determined by the SecSDM methodology. In addition, at each step of the application the user is provided with a task pane and an information pane, thereby providing the user with the necessary information relating to the particular step being carried out. A large portion of the interface was translated into background graphics to improve the performance of the application. Only the controls that users need to directly interact with are incorporated as actual controls.

Owing to space limitations, further details of this software tool lie outside the scope of this paper.

4   The User Satisfaction Survey

The usability of interactive products, including software tools and applications, refers to the extent to which such products have good utility and are effective to use, efficient to use, safe to use, easy to learn, easy to remember and satisfying to use - from a user's perspective. In this case, the users of the SecSDM software tool are software developers.

According to Xiao and Dasgupta (2002), *'user satisfaction is regarded as one of the most important measures of Information Systems success'*. The Questionnaire for User Interaction Satisfaction (QUIS) and the Software Usability Measurement Inventory (SUMI) are two well-known usability testing tools that gauge a user's satisfaction with using software applications. Many of the questions addressed by these tools are based on Jakob Nielsen's (1994) design principles, namely: visibility of system status; match between system and the real world; user control and freedom; consistency and standards; error prevention; recognition, rather than recall;

flexibility and efficiency of use; aesthetic and minimalist design; help user's recognize, diagnose and recover from errors; and help and documentation.

A user satisfaction survey was carried out on the SecSDM software tool. The purpose of the survey was to establish the extent to which the IT undergraduate students were satisfied with using the tool, and to gain valuable feedback that could be used to make improvements. The user satisfaction survey took the form of a paper-based questionnaire comprising 19 statements, as shown in Table 2.

Statement
1. Overall, I am satisfied with how easy it is to use this system.
2. It was simple to use this system.
3. I can effectively complete the assigned tasks using this system.
4. I am able to complete the assigned tasks quickly using this system.
5. I am able to efficiently complete the assigned tasks using this system.
6. I feel comfortable using this system.
7. It was easy to learn to use this system.
8. I believe I became productive quickly using this system.
9. The system gives error messages that clearly tell me how to fix problems.
10. Whenever I make a mistake using the system, I recovered easily and quickly.
11. The information (such as online help, on screen messages, and other documentation) provided with this system is clear.
12. It is easy to find the information I needed.
13. The help provided by the system is easy to understand.
14. The information is effective in helping me complete the tasks and scenarios.
15. The organisation of information on the system screens is clear.
16. The interface of this system is pleasant.
17. I like using the interface of this system.
18. This system has all the functions and capabilities I expect it to have.
19. Overall, I am satisfied with this system.

Table 2: SecSDM User Satisfaction Survey

Whereas statements 1 to 8 related to *'ease of use'*, statements 9 and 10 related to *'error messages'* and *'recovery from problems'*. Similarly, statements 11 to 15 related to *'online help and information provided',* and statements 16 to 19 referred to the *'general interface', 'system capabilities'* and *'overall user satisfaction'.*

The IT undergraduate project students were required to rate the extent to which they agreed to each of the 19 statements. A 5-point Likert scale was used for the ratings, where a rating of *'1'* indicated *'disagree'* and a rating of *'5'* indicated *'fully agree'*. A rating of *'3'* indicated that the students *'neither agreed nor disagreed'* with the statement. A *'not applicable'* option was also provided for cases in which students felt they were not in a position to respond to a specific statement.

The user satisfaction questionnaires were distributed amongst IT undergraduate students and completed during a practical class in a computer laboratory where they had further access to the SecSDM software tool. The questionnaires were then collated and the results captured in a Microsoft Excel spreadsheet. These were then analyzed and interpreted. A total of 41 students, of the 56 registered for the software development project module, completed the user satisfaction survey, thereby representing a response rate of 73%. The results of the SecSDM user satisfaction survey and the associated interpretations are presented in the following section.

5   Results of User Satisfaction Survey

The results of the SecSDM user satisfaction survey are depicted in Table 3. From these results it is evident that the majority of respondents indicated that they either *'fully agreed'* (indicated by a *'5'*) or *'partially agreed'* (indicated by a *'4'*) with the 19 statements, as listed in Table 2. Statements 15, 16 and 17, which related primarily to the interface, measured the highest level of agreement with percentages of 78%, 90% and 95%, respectively.

This resulted in a high level of overall satisfaction with using SecSDM, as indicated for Statement 19, which recorded 80% of respondents in agreement with this statement. A further 73% of respondents were in agreement with Statement 3, which related to the effectiveness of SecSDM in completing the assigned tasks.

According to these results, the main areas of the SecSDM software tool requiring attention relate to error detection and recovery (Statements 9 and 10) and help and documentation (Statements 11, 12 and 13).   Between 40% and 50% of the respondents were in full or partial agreement with these particular statements.

The average results indicate that the majority of the respondents were satisfied with the SecSDM software tool, with an average of 26% being in *'full agreement'*, having indicated a *'5'* on the Likert scale, and 37% being in *'partial agreement'*, having indicated a *'4'*. A further 25% were neither in agreement nor disagreement – being in the middle of the scale. On average, only 12% of the respondents indicated any level of disagreement.

Statement	1 Dis-agree	2	3	4	5 Fully Agree	N/A
1. Overall, I am satisfied with how easy it is to use this system	0%	5%	34%	39%	22%	0%
2. It was simple to use this system	0%	10%	24%	37%	29%	0%
3. I can effectively complete the assigned tasks using this system	0%	2%	22%	39%	34%	2%
4. I am able to complete the assigned tasks quickly using this system	0%	20%	20%	32%	27%	2%
5. I am able to efficiently complete the assigned tasks using this system	0%	7%	29%	27%	37%	0%
6. I feel comfortable using this system	0%	10%	29%	41%	20%	0%
7. It was easy to learn to use this system.	2%	7%	39%	34%	17%	0%
8. I believe I became productive quickly using this system.	2%	7%	27%	41%	20%	2%
9. The system gives error messages that clearly tell me how to fix problems.	12%	12%	29%	20%	22%	5%
10. Whenever I make a mistake using the system, I recovered easily and quickly.	7%	12%	32%	24%	22%	2%
11. The information (such as online help, on screen messages, and other documentation) provided with this system is clear.	12%	7%	37%	34%	7%	2%
12. It is easy to find the information I needed.	5%	15%	32%	29%	17%	2%
13. The help provided by the system is easy to understand.	7%	24%	15%	32%	15%	7%
14. The information is effective in helping me complete the tasks and scenarios.	2%	10%	27%	41%	20%	0%
15. The organisation of information on the system screens is clear.	0%	5%	17%	49%	29%	0%
16. The interface of this system is pleasant.	0%	0%	10%	34%	56%	0%
17. I like using the interface of this system.	0%	0%	5%	46%	49%	0%
18. This system has all the functions and capabilities I expect it to have.	0%	7%	29%	44%	20%	0%
19. Overall, I am satisfied with this system.	0%	2%	17%	56%	24%	0%
Average Percentages	**3%**	**9%**	**25%**	**37%**	**26%**	**1%**

Table 3: SecSDM User Satisfaction Survey Results

1	*'It was easy to identify the problems and risks we have never thought of in our project, so by using this software I am well aware of those risks'*
2	*'I was impressed with how easy they made it to generate a report'*
3	*'I find this system very user friendly and I think everyone can use it'*
4	*'I personally don't have dislikes I was totally impressed'*
5	*'This system was easy to use and understand but there is too much information at the information side'*
6	*'All in all it was excellent'*
7	*'This tool seems to be working pretty well, maybe just a few things to look at but I am totally satisfied'*
8	*'Great system it made our task very easy to finish'*
9	*'The interface looked really nice'*
10	*'Inserting my information and assigning risk values to them was relatively easy'*
11	*'The interface looks good, good colour usage'*
12	*'Overall I am very happy with the system it is better than doing it manually'*
13	*'Well done to the people who designed it'*

Table 4: SecSDM User Satisfaction Survey - Positive Comments

Tables 4 and 5 indicate the positive and negative comments recorded from the SecSDM user satisfaction survey carried out, respectively. The positive comments reflected in Table 4 reinforce the high level of satisfaction the students experienced in using the SecSDM software tool. Many of these comments related to the ease with which one could carry out the task of risk identification, and the general appeal of the interface.

An interesting observation is that 27% of the negative comments, as indicated in Table 5, related to a lack of understanding of the terminology used. This re-emphasizes the fact that the understanding of information security terms and concepts is fundamental to basic education in information security. These terms should be introduced early in the curriculum, and re-addressed throughout all the subsequent years of the CS/IS/IT qualification.

1	*'Key word explanation would be nice'*
2	*'The program should describe in greater detail how to identify your information assets'*
3	*'Check updating of risks if you click previous button'*
4	*'Why after moving past a certain point you can't go back and change certain fields'*
5	*'This system was easy to use and understand but there is too much information at the information side'*
6	*'I thought the security mechanisms for each risk would maybe be different or broken down and explained to us'*
7	*'The terminology is difficult to understand'*
8	*'It is good but must I had the English dictionary a few times as the terms used are not familiar'*
9	*'Had trouble generating a report'*
10	*'The system has too much text, the font is not big enough'*
11	*'Did not like the fact that I could not go back and change the assets'*

Table 5: SecSDM User Satisfaction Survey - Negative Comments

6 Conclusion

From the results of the SecSDM user satisfaction survey conducted, one may conclude that the SecSDM software tool supports the activities involved in developing secure software, by guiding the user through the process of risk identification and the selection of appropriate security mechanisms to help ensure the implementation of security controls that are functional, effective, correct and safe to use.

Although one cannot generalize by stating that SecSDM would guarantee the development of secure software, it is believed that SecSDM and the associated software tool form a good foundation to support further research in secure software development. It is envisaged that SecSDM could be extended to other educational institutions and to the software development industry. Although this methodology was evaluated in an academic environment, it is believed that it could also support the software development industry in the development of secure software. However, this would need to be verified by future research.

7 References

Burley, D., & Bishop, M. (2011). Summit on Education in Secure Software: Final Report. National Science Foundation.

Conklin, W. A., & Dietrich, G. (2007). Secure Software Engineering: A New Paradigm. Proceedings of the 40th Hawaii International Conference on System Sciences (pp. 1-6). IEEE.

ISO/IEC. (1989). ISO/IEC 7498-2. Information Processing Systems - Open Systems Interconnection - Basic Reference Model - Part 2: Security Architecture. Switzerland: ISO/IEC.

ISO/IEC. (2005). ISO/IEC 27002. Information technology - Security techniques - Code of practice for information security management. Switzerland: ISO/IEC.

ISO/IEC. (2008). ISO/IEC 27005. Information technology - Security techniques - Information security risk management. Switzerland: ISO/IEC.

Nielsen, J. (1994). Heuristic Evaluation. New York: John Wiley & Sons.

NIST. (1996, September). SP800-14: Generally Accepted Principles and Practices for Securing Information Technology Systems. Retrieved March 23, 2012, from NIST - Computer Security Division - Computer Security Resource Center - Special Publications: http://csrc.nist.gov/publications/nistpubs/800-14/800-14.pdf

Pothamsetty, V. (2005). Where Security Education is Lacking. Proceedings from Information Security Curriculum Development (InfoSecCD) Conference (pp. 54-58). Kennesaw: ACM.

Von Solms, S., & Von Solms, R. (2009). Information Security Governance. New York: Springer.

Walden, J., & Frank, C. (2006). Secure Software Engineering Teaching Modules. Information Security Curriculum Development Conference (InfoSecCD) (pp. 19-23). Kennesaw: ACM.

Xiao, L., & Dasgupta, S. (2002). Measurement of User Satisfaction with Web-based Information Systems: An Empirical Study. Eighth Americas Conference on Information Systems, 1149-1155.

A Framework for Evaluating Usable Security: The Case of Online Health Social Networks

A. Yeratziotis, D. van Greunen and D. Pottas

Institute for ICT Advancement, Nelson Mandela Metropolitan University, Port
Elizabeth, Eastern Cape, South Africa
e-mail : alexandros.yeratziotis@nmmu.ac.za

Abstract

It is vital that the development of security and privacy features for applications and websites
are assessed for their usability. An assessment of such usability will increase the continuous
and effective utilisation from the user perspective. However, owing to a lack of tools and
methods this is difficult to achieve. There is thus a need for a usable security framework to
facilitate the usability assessment of security and privacy features for applications and
websites. This paper discusses such a framework within the context of online social networks
that are particular to the health domain. The framework consists of three components: a three-
phase process, a validation tool and a usable security heuristic evaluation. The paper begins by
providing an overview of the complete conceptualised framework, which is followed by a
more detailed discussion of the components.

Keywords

Framework, usable security, heuristic evaluation, validation tool, three-phase
process, online health social networks.

1 Introduction

Reality is that current security and privacy features make unreasonable demands on
users, system administrators and developers alike (Sasse and Flechais, 2005).
Accordingly, keeping a system's or users' personal information secure involves an
increasing amount of complexity. Owing to the complexity, users avoid interacting
with the available security and privacy features on websites and applications;
consequently providing attackers with an even greater advantage. Developers
struggle because they are not aware of the security implications of their design
decisions; yet, they are the ones left with the responsibility for making security
decisions and designs for these new applications and websites.

The field that investigates the complexities that users experience when interacting
with security is usable security. It embraces the fact that most applications and
websites have security features that users should interact with. However, due to their
lack of usability, users often avoid and even ignore their security responsibilities
(Furnell, Jusoh and Katsabas, 2006). The non-usable design of security has
contributed to the fact that the human is regarded as the most common cause behind
security configuration errors, which undermine the overall security (Furnell et al.,

2006; Whitten and Tygar, 2005). It is evident that there is a problem in the interaction between the human element and the technology (design of the interface). This problem relates to the research discipline of human-computer interaction as much as it does to the discipline of information security. In essence, developing security that is usable has become a necessity and is well supported (Furnell et al., 2006; Whitten and Tygar, 2005).

Properties that define usable security have been determined based on the cumulative knowledge available in this research space. For an application/website to be usable from a security and privacy perspective, users must be consistently and reliably made aware of the security-related tasks they need to perform, users must be able to easily determine how to accomplish the necessary tasks successfully, users must not be prone to making any dangerous errors and users must be comfortable with the user-interface if they are to continue to use it (Yee, 2002; Whitten and Tygar, 2005).

2 Problem and Research Questions

Theories and evaluation tools for usable security, including guidelines and principles, are limited and those that exist are at an elementary and progressive stage. As a result, developers struggle to design security and privacy that is usable. Moreover, usable security is a relatively immature field that needs further development. Research in this field is critical, considering the fact that security and privacy tools are regarded as too complex for users to understand and apply. The need for a privacy framework in social networking environments has been emphasised, as it is seen as a possible solution to conflicting privacy issues (Hodge, 2006). Taking this into account, the purpose of the study was to develop a framework for evaluating usable security to address the usability and user experience issues that users face with regard to the security and privacy features available to them in these environments.

To develop the usable security framework it was initially required understanding the security and privacy requirements for online social networking environments from a user perspective. In addition, considering the lack of evaluation tools that can assist developers in designing usable security on applications/websites was equally important. Owing to the influence human-computer interaction has on usable security, user-centred design approaches were considered as possible evaluation tools. These are referred to as usability inspection methods and are applied to evaluate the usability of applications/websites in the field of human-computer interaction. This is achieved by identifying usability problems or violations on a user interface.

As highlighted, there is currently a paucity of knowledge and research in the literature pertaining to usable security. Hence, the focus of this study was to address this gap. This study investigated the fields of human-computer interaction, information security and usable security to determine the requirements and components that are needed to develop a conceptual framework for evaluating usable security. This framework will benefit users and developers alike and will it is anticipated prove to be a theoretical guide for developers by providing them with the ability to enhance their designs for the intended users. This will be achieved by ensuring that security and usability form a unified process that is considered in user interface design. As a result, user competencies and preferences will be acknowledged, leading to higher levels of usable security. This will, in turn, assist users in protecting their information more effectively and provide a more positive user experience. On the basis of the problems mentioned, the main research question was to determine the components of a framework to evaluate usable security. The supporting four sub-questions included, determining which usability inspection method can be adapted to evaluate usable security, which approach can be followed to develop the selected usability inspection method, how can the validity and applicability of the method and approach be illustrated, and lastly, how can the method and approach be constituted into a framework.

3   The Framework

Lethbridge and Laganiere (2005) portray the composition of a framework as process that moves between several cycles. The cycles consist of components that are connected via relationships. Together, the components and their relationships comprise one logical unit, the framework. Based on Lethbridge and Laganiere (2005) view regarding the composition of a framework, the three components of the framework to evaluate usable security in online social networks are a usable security heuristic evaluation, a three-phase process to develop heuristics for specific application domains and a validation tool. It must be noted that each phase of the process has a number of tasks. In relation to the research questions, the usable security heuristic evaluation represents the selected usability inspection method and the process to develop heuristics for specific application domains is the approach that will be used to develop the method itself. The validation tool is used to determine the validity and applicability of the method. In addition, a case study on two online health social networks was conducted to determine the validity and applicability of both the approach and the method.

As mentioned, it is required to determine the relationships between the components, before composing the final framework. In the case of the usable security framework, there are three relationships between its components. The first relationship is between the process to develop heuristics for specific application domains and the usable security heuristic evaluation. To develop the usable security heuristic evaluation the process needed to be considered and applied. The second relationship is between the validation tool and the usable security heuristic evaluation. To ensure the applicability and validity of the usable security heuristic evaluation, the validation tool had to be applied in order to assess it. The third relationship is between the process to develop heuristics for specific application domains and the validation tool. The validation tool is applied in task 2 of phase 2 in the process.

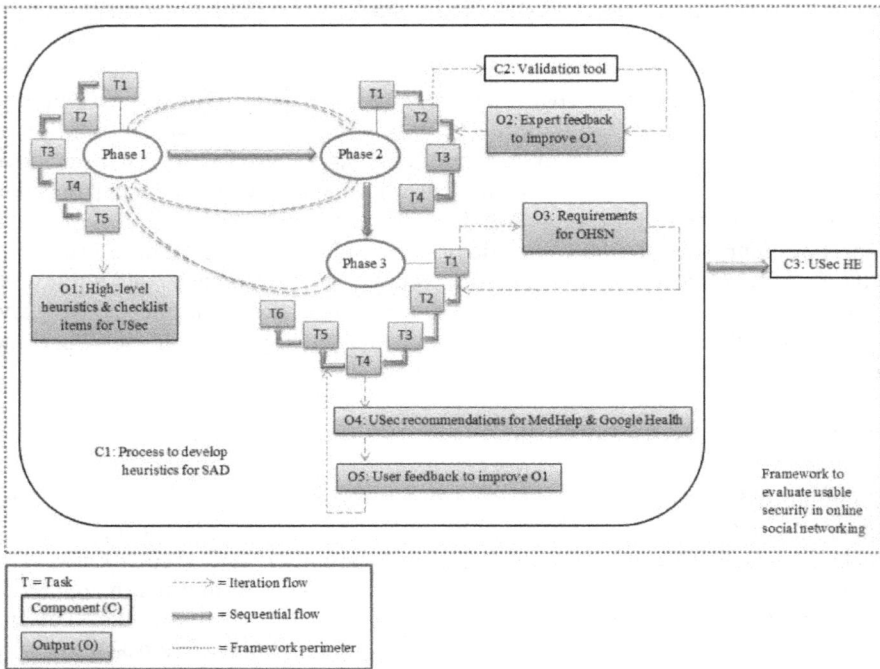

Figure 1: Composition (components, outputs and relationships) of the framework to evaluate usable security in online social networking

The components of the framework and their relationships produce specific outputs. In terms of the framework for evaluating usable security in online social networking, the components are a process to develop heuristics for specific application domains, a validation tool and a usable security heuristic evaluation. The specific outputs that result from the components relationships are high-level heuristics and checklist items for usable security, expert feedback to improve the first output, requirements for online health social networks, usable security recommendations for MedHelp and Google Health (the websites used for the case study) and user feedback to improve the first output again.

Figure 1 illustrates the components, relationships and outputs of the usable security framework. In terms of figure 1, the following abbreviations are used: T = Task; O = Output; C = Component; OHSN = Online Health Social Networks; USec HE = Usable Security Heuristic Evaluation and SAD = Specific Application Domains. From figure 1, the three components can be identified. C1 is the process to develop heuristics for specific application domains. All outputs and C2 (the validation tool) occur within the process. C3 (the usable security heuristic evaluation) is the end result from following the entire process. Together all components, outputs and relationships form the framework to evaluate usable security in online social networks. The three components are discussed in more detail in the following sections.

100

3.1   Component I – Three-Phase Process to Develop Heuristics for Specific Application Domains

The main goal of usability inspection methods is to provide the best possible impact on interactive design at the lowest possible cost (Woolrych and Cockton, 2001). The application of these methods requires the continuous involvement of users in the design and evaluation phases and it must reflect the application of usability practices throughout, in order to meet their needs. In addition to user involvement, expert involvement will complement and enhance the design process. Usability inspection methods are particularly fundamental for data collection and analysis within the human-computer interaction research field. Several prevalent methods include usability evaluations, contextual inquiries and heuristic evaluations. It was stated previously that the selected method was a heuristic evaluation. Research studies show that there is often the need to develop new heuristic sets for a specific application domain, as they will yield more effective results during evaluation. Currently, there is no literature describing a systematic process that can be followed in an attempt to develop new heuristics, even though heuristic evaluations is an area in the human-computer interaction research community that has been well studied. At present, the two main themes within this space is to improve their effectiveness and to develop new heuristic sets for specialised domains (Sim, Read and Cockton, 2009). Considering that there is no systematic process to develop new heuristic sets in combination with the main themes in this research space, the three-phase process to develop heuristics for specific application domains was developed (Yeratziotis, Pottas and van Greunen, 2011a).

The process, which is represented as C1 in figure 1, initiates in phase 1, where the focus is on designing high-level heuristics for the specific application domain. Phase 1 consists of five tasks. By completing phase 1, the first outcome of the framework is achieved, represented as O1 in figure 1. It is the high-level heuristics and checklist items for usable security. The process then continues into phase 2, which consists of four tasks. The validation tool, which is the second component of the framework and discussed in the next section is applied by experts in the second task of this phase. By applying the validation tool, the second outcome of the framework is achieved, represented as O2 in figure 1. It is the feedback that experts provided to improve O1, the high-level heuristics and checklist items for usable security. Once this phase is complete the process continues to the next phase, phase 3, which focuses on applying the high-level heuristics in context. In this research, the context is the online health social networks. Phase 3 consists of six tasks and O3 is achieved by conducting the first task of this phase. It is the requirements for online health social networks. These were subsequently applied to determine the two websites that would be used in a case study, in which users would complete security and privacy tasks and then evaluate the websites with the usable security heuristic evaluation. By completing task four in this phase, O5 and O6 of the framework are achieved. They are usable security recommendations to improve the two online health social networks (Yeratziotis, Pottas and van Greunen, 2011b) and user feedback to improve the high-level heuristics and checklist items for usable security, O1.

All outputs resulting from applying the process, which is the first component of the framework and the validation tool, the second component of the framework, contribute to the third component, the final usable security heuristic evaluation, which is discussed in section 3.3. The three-phase process to develop heuristics for specific application domains is discussed in detail in (Yeratziotis et al., 2011a). This includes a discussion on each phase, its related tasks and iteration cycles that occur between the phases.

3.2   Component II – Validation Tool

The validation tool, which is represented as C2 in figure 1, is applied in task 2 of phase 2 of the process (C1). It was designed in Microsoft Excel and comprised seven sheets (or sections). These included instructions, expert biographical information, heuristics assessments, checklist items assessment, severity ratings, material assessment and a satisfaction questionnaire. The validation tool is customised for usable security; however, it can be used as a template for creating similar validation tools. The tool would be modified to evaluate the heuristics of a specific application domain for which they are being developed. The descriptions of each sheet will follow. The descriptions are based on how each sheet was used to validate the usable security heuristic evaluation.

Sheet I - instructions was used to explain the nature of a heuristic evaluation to the selected experts and how it can be used to evaluate an interface for usability violations. It then mentioned the purpose of the validation tool and the fact that it would be used to assess a new set of usable security heuristics. Additionally, specific instructions were also provided for each sheet. These were available on the actual sheet. *Sheet II - expert biographical information* was used to record the biographical details of the experts and was important to determine the level of expertise that each of the experts possessed in terms of the three fields of usable security, human-computer interaction and information security. This would help measure their comments or feedback for the modifications that are provided in the validation tool and would contribute to understanding the perspective from which they give their opinions and how they rate in terms of their level of skill in the other fields. *Sheet III - heuristics assessments* was used to assess the high-level heuristic names together with their descriptions. These form the "groups" into which relevant checklist items would be categorised. This sheet specifically addressed the importance and clarity of name and description. Experts could also provide optional comments were they felt necessary.

Sheet IV - checklist items assessment was used to assess the checklist items for each high-level usable security heuristic. These items were categorised within one of the high-level heuristics of sheet III. They are supporting and specifying high-level design issues that assist the experts to understand the application of the heuristic in context. The assessments specifically addressed the clarity, grouping and relevance of each checklist item. Measuring the clarity of the wording used for the checklist item will determine whether the terminology is clear and easy to understand or if re-wording is required in the next iteration cycle of the process (C1). Measuring the grouping for a checklist item will determine if it is well categorised under a high-level heuristic. Measuring the relevance of a checklist item will determine whether it is appropriate in identifying a security/privacy usability violation. Experts also provide a verdict on whether or not the checklist item should be included in the final usable security heuristic evaluation (C3). As with the previous sheet, experts could provide optional comments to support their ratings. To conclude their assessments, experts provided their opinions on the completeness of the set of checklist items and could also suggest additional information that should have been considered. The aim was to gain consensus among the experts to ensure that the fields of usable security, human-computer interaction and information security are considered and represented. This can be challenging at times because the fields can offer conflicting views.

Sheet V - severity ratings was used to determine the most effective ratings to be used in the usable security heuristic evaluation. Severity ratings are applied to measure the extent of usability violations in a heuristic evaluation. There are cases however where commonly used severity ratings are insufficient to measure the extent of usability violations in a specific application domain (Sim et al., 2009). In the case of the usable security heuristic evaluation, there was a need to create customised severity ratings that can be more effective in measuring the extent of usable security violations. Jakob Nielsen's acknowledged severity ratings were insufficient to be used alone as they are based solely on a usability perspective, and consequently, they lack a security perspective. Taking into account Nielsen's severity ratings (Nielsen, 1994), and by modifying and adapting them with the standards for security categorisation of federal information and information systems (FIPS PUB 199, 2004), it was possible to include a security perspective in them as well to compliment a usability one. The result was two different sets of usable security severity ratings that experts would assess in order to determine the most effective match for the usable security heuristic evaluation.

Sheet VI - material assessment was used to assess the material that was considered to develop the usable security heuristic evaluation. The assessment examined the usability and usable security material and the security and privacy material separately and specifically addressed the novelty and relevance of the materials. Experts could also provide optional comments were they felt necessary. *Sheet VII - user satisfaction questionnaire* was used to collect the experts overall views regarding the usable security heuristic evaluation as a tool for assessing the level of usable security in online social networking environments.

3.3   Component III – Usable Security Heuristic Evaluation

The usable security heuristic evaluation is the third component of the framework to evaluate usable security in online social networks and is represented as C3 in figure 1. A heuristic evaluation is regarded as an analytical evaluation method, which is undertaken by usability experts. The experts apply a specific set of heuristics to evaluate the usability of a user interface. This provides an immediate analysis of the website/application, which helps to correct confusing elements in the current design and leads to enhanced user experience. The method is widely used because it is an excellent method of diagnostic and perspective analysis for identifying individual problems in a short time period. Specifically, its purpose is to identify problems that are associated with the design of user interfaces. The results are dependent on the experts' broader experience with usability (Nielsen, 2005a; Straub, 2003). Several experts working independently are considered adequate and very effective for identifying usability issues. Nielsen (2005b) is of the opinion that between three to five evaluators are sufficient, as they would be able to discover an average of 75% of usability problems on the user interface.

To reiterate, by completing phase 1 of the process, high-level heuristics and checklist items for usable security (O1) were developed. By completing the entire process (C1), the final usable security heuristic evaluation (C3) is developed. The difference between O1 and C3 is that C3 includes improvements to O1, as were suggested by experts in O2 and users in O5, by applying the validation tool (C2) and conducting the case study respectively. A detailed discussion on how O1 was reached is presented in (Yeratziotis, Pottas and van Greunen, 2012). It includes a discussion on the literature that was considered, how emerging themes from the literature were transformed to high-level heuristics for usable security, how the tailored-method was applied to create the checklist items, and how these were ultimately grouped under corresponding high-level heuristics. The usable security heuristic evaluation (C3) consists of eleven heuristics and seventy checklist items that evaluate the specific application domain of usable security. Table 1 displays the heuristics (with their descriptions) and the number of checklist items within each.

#	Heuristic	Checklist Items
1	Visibility - the system should keep users informed about their security status	6
2	Revocability - the system should allow users to revoke security actions where appropriate	4
3	Clarity - the system should inform users in advance about the consequences of any security actions	4
4	Learnability - the system should ensure that security actions are easy to learn and remember	8
5	Aesthetics and Minimalist Design - the system should apply appropriate visual representation of security elements and not provide irrelevant security information	5
6	Errors - the system should provide users detailed security error messages that they can understand and act upon to recover	5
7	User Suitability - the system should provide options for users with diverse levels of skill and experience in security	4
8	User Language - the system should use plain language that users can understand with regard to security	6
9	User Assistance - the system should make security help relevant and apparent to users	6
10	Identity Signal - the system should use and display information about validated certificates	2
11	Security and Privacy - the system needs to ensure integrity, availability, confidentiality and privacy	20

Table 1: Number of checklist items for each usable security high-level heuristic

4   Practical Applicability of the Framework

The framework outlines the way in which usable security can be evaluated in the context of online social networking. The framework clarifies the components and outputs that are influenced by the relationships that exist between the components themselves and the health online social networking environment. The framework is unique and incorporates three novel components: a process, a validation tool and a heuristic evaluation. From a practical perspective, the framework consists of two reliable measuring instruments in the validation tool and the usable security heuristic evaluation. First, the process was followed to develop a heuristic evaluation for the specific application domain of usable security. The validation tool was then applied by experts in the fields of information security, human-computer interaction and usable security to validate the usable security heuristic evaluation. This was to ensure that it addressed the requirements of all fields. Once improvements were made based on the experts' feedback, participants in a case study applied the heuristic evaluation to evaluate the level of usable security on two online health social networks. The result was usable security recommendations for both online health social networks. The application of each component serves as a proof of concept, illustrating the applicability and use of the entire framework as a unit. Beyond the boundaries of the framework, the process, the usable security heuristic evaluation and the validation tool can be considered as contributions individually. The process can be applied to develop a heuristic evaluation for another specific application domain. The usable security heuristic evaluation can be used to measure the level of usable security on other websites/applications and the validation tool can be used to assess a new set of heuristics and checklist items for another specific application domain, following modifications.

5 Conclusions and the Future

When security compliments usability in online social networks, the interaction between the user and the online environment becomes beneficial. The framework to evaluate usable security in online health social networks contributes to the fields of usable security and human-computer interaction in this sense. The fact that security is a problem area for user interface design contributes to poor usable security. Consequently, developers require tools that can assist them to improve their designs in terms of usable security. Security and privacy design issues can be alleviated with the assistance of the usable security heuristic evaluation, which was used to evaluate security and privacy features of two online health social networks. Future research could be focused on applying it to evaluate another website/application (e.g. Facebook, MS Outlook, e-banking websites). Similarly, the process to develop heuristics for specific application domains was considered to develop a heuristic evaluation for the domain of usable security. Future research could be focused on applying the process to develop heuristics for another specific application domain (e.g. heuristics to evaluate the design of instructional e-learning websites for the Deaf).

6 References

FIPS PUB 199 (2004), "Federal information processing standards publication: Standards for security categorization of federal information and information systems", Department of Commerce: USA.

Furnell, S.M., Jusoh, A. and Katsabas D. (2006), "The challenges of understanding and using security: A survey of end-users, *Computers & Security*, Vol. 25, No. 1, pp27–35.

Hodge, M.J. (2006), "The Fourth Amendment and privacy issues on the "new" Internet: Facebook.com and MySpace.com", *Southern Illinois University Law Journal*, Vol. 31, pp95-122.

Lethbridge, T.C. and Laganiere, R. (2005), *Object-oriented software engineering: Practical software development using UML and Java*, Second edition, McGraw-Hill-Education, Berkshire, England, ISBN: 9780077109080.

Nielsen, J. (1994), "Heuristic evaluation", in Nielsen J. and Mack, R.L. (Ed), *Usability inspection methods*, John Wiley & Sons, New York, ISBN: 0-471-01877-5.

Nielsen, J. (2005a), "Useit.com: Heuristic evaluation", http://www.useit.com/papers/heuristic/, (Accessed 10 October 2010).

Nielsen, J. (2005b), "Useit.com: How to conduct a heuristic evaluation", http://www.useit.com/papers/heuristic/heuristic_evaluation.html, (Accessed October 10 2010).

Sasse, M. and Flechais, I. (2005), "Usable Security Why do we need it? How do we get it?", in Cranor, L.F. and Garfinkel, S. (Ed), *Security and Usability: Designing Secure Systems That People Can Use*, O' Reilly Media Inc., Sebastopol, CA. ISBN: 0-596-00827-9.

Sim, G., Read, J.C. and Cockton, G. (2009), "Evidence based design of heuristics for computer assisted assessment", in *INTERACT '09 proceedings of the 12th IFIP TC 13 International Conference on Human-Computer Interaction: Part I*, Uppsala, Sweden.

Whitten, A. and Tygar, J.D. (2005), "Why Johnny can't encrypt A usability evaluation of PGP 5.0", in Cranor, L.F. and Garfinkel, S. (Ed), *Security and Usability: Designing Secure Systems That People Can Use*, O' Reilly Media Inc., Sebastopol, CA. ISBN: 0-596-00827-9.

Woolrych, A. and Cockton, G. (2001), "Why and when five test users aren't enough", in Vanderdonckt, J., Blandford, A. and Derycke, A. (Ed), in *proceedings of IHM-HCI 2001*, Toulouse, France, Vol. 2, pp105–108.

Yee, K. (2002), "User interaction design for secure systems", in *proceedings of the 4th International Conference on Information and Communications Security, 2002 (ICICS' 02)*, Springer-Verlag, London, UK, pp 278–290.

Yeratziotis, A., Pottas, D. and van Greunen, D. (2011a), "A Three-Phase Process to Develop Heuristics", in *proceedings of the 13th ZA-WWW conference*, 14–16 September 2011, Johannesburg, South Africa.

Yeratziotis, A., Pottas, D. and van Greunen, D. (2011b), "Recommendations for Usable Security in Online Health Social Networks", in *proceedings of the joint conference of the 2011 6th International Conference on Pervasive Computing and Application (ICPCA) and the 2011 3rd International Symposium of Web Society (SWS)*, 26-28 October 2011, Port Elizabeth, South Africa.

Yeratziotis, A., Pottas, D. and van Greunen, D. (2012), "A usable security heuristic evaluation for the online health social networking paradigm", *International Journal of Human-Computer Interaction*, Vol. 29, No. 3.

Proceedings of the Sixth International Symposium on
Human Aspects of Information Security & Assurance (HAISA 2012)

Towards Trust and Reputation for E-Commerce in Collectivist Rural Africa

D. Isherwood[1, 2], M. Coetzee[1] and J.H.P. Eloff[2, 3]

[1]Academy of Computer Science and Software Engineering, University of
Johannesburg, Johannesburg, South Africa
[2]SAP Meraka UTD, CSIR, Pretoria, South Africa
[3]Department of Computer Science, University of Pretoria, Pretoria, South Africa
e-mail: Donovan.isherwood@sap.com

Abstract

Individualistic cultures that prevail in predominantly developed economies thrive on e-commerce environments where consumer trust is facilitated through trust mechanisms such as institutional guarantees, laws and policies, information security mechanisms, and social controls. These trust mechanisms are based on individualist cultural norms of behaviour and values, and are not always relevant to collectivist cultures found in predominantly developing economies such as Africa or South America. The influence of individualist and collectivist culture on consumer trust is discussed in the context of e-commerce. The research aims at providing trust properties that can facilitate consumer trust, required for the success of e-commerce, to rural African environments.

Keywords

Trust, culture, Africa, e-commerce, security

1. Introduction

In emerging economies of rural Africa, very small enterprises (VSEs) such as spaza shops find it challenging to conduct business through e-commerce (Economic Report on Africa, 2011). Spaza shops are informal survivalist businesses in rural townships that are used by residents who cannot travel to formal shopping centres as it is too difficult or expensive (Manana, 2009). Recent research projects have consequently focused on investigating how to support shop owners by means of e-commerce applications backed by mobile and cloud-based technologies (Dörflinger et al., 2009). For such applications to be successful, trust need to be established between spaza shop owners in a single cooperative, as well as between cooperatives and large retail suppliers. Currently, no trust and reputation system exists to solve this problem.

As there are real differences between the environment and cultures of rural Africans and the residents of developed economies in the Western world, the trust mechanisms used by e-commerce environments such as eBay may not be entirely relevant to e-commerce consumers of rural emerging economies (Doney et al., 1998; Zaheer & Zaheer, 2006; Chong, 2003; Botha, 2006). The current research compares the influence of culture on trust from an individualist and collectivist cultural perspective. Hence, three trust properties that can be used by the reputation system of e-commerce applications to support collectivist rural African cultural norms and values are proposed. Section 2 below provides background on trust and the influence culture has on it. Sections 3 and 4 contrast the trusting behaviour of the individualist with that of the collectivist culture. Section 5 identifies three trust properties that are relevant to collectivist cultures in rural Africa. Finally, future research is discussed in Section 6, which also concludes the paper.

2. Trust and Culture

The current research is based on Hofstede's five dimensions of culture that were developed following a survey of 72 countries. Hofstede (1980:5) defines culture as "the collective programming of the mind that distinguishes the members of one group or category of people from another". He identifies the dimensions of power-distance, collectivism vs. individualism, femininity vs. masculinity, uncertainty avoidance and long-term vs. short-term orientation. Next, the influence that culture has on trust is discussed.

2.1. Culture

Westernised American culture adopts a world view that states *I am because I, the individual hero, dream and do* (Mbigi, 2003), whereas the world view in the African culture is *I am because we exist*. These two world views capture the essence of the individualism vs. collectivism dimension defined by Hofstede (1980), and has become the main and most significant difference between cultures (Triandis, 2001). This dimension classifies a culture according to how strong the ties are between individuals in society (Hofstede, 1980).

Individualistic cultures are found mainly in North America and much of Western Europe. Here individuals are responsible for their own welfare and that of their direct family only (Cramer, 2010), and a high value is placed on individual freedom. Westerners tend to be logical and action-oriented. These characteristics determine their behaviour and hence they do not hesitate to criticise an e-commerce website for a failed transaction.

Collectivist cultures are found mainly in much of the Middle East, Asia, Africa and South America. Collectivist cultures integrate individuals as from their birth into tightly knit, cohesive groups (Cramer, 2010). This means that people in these cultures emphasise interpersonal relationships where loyalty is obtained by protecting the group members for life. Individuals see themselves as subordinate to a social collective such as a state, a nation, a race, or a social class. They prefer group harmony and consensus to individual achievement.

Other dimensions of culture also have an impact on trusting behaviour in e-commerce environments. *Power distance* refers to the degree of inequality that exists in society, and the manner in which it is accepted by people with and without power

(Hofstede, 1980). In countries with a high power distance index such as Asian and African countries, subordinates expect to be told what to do, centralisation is seen as popular, and less powerful people are seen as dependent on the more powerful. For most individualistic cultures, a high *masculinity* index means that performance is valued, there is more sympathy for the strong and equality is important. In contrast, in more collectivist cultures a high *femininity* index indicates that people are more generous towards each other; there is sympathy for the weak and intuition is used to strive for consensus (Hofstede, 1980). Finally, *uncertainty avoidance* relates to the degree of anxiety people experience when in uncertain or unknown situations (Hofstede, 1980). People from cultures with a high uncertainty avoidance index have a need for rules and predictability and they consider anything that is different as dangerous. There is an inherent fear of uncertain situations and unfamiliar risks, and a high premium is placed on belief in experts and specialisation.

Since these cultural differences influence the trust building mechanism of members of a cultural group, trust and its components are next described in terms of culture.

2.2. Trust

Mayer et al. (1995:5) define trust as "the willingness of a party to be vulnerable to the actions of another party, based on the expectation that the other will perform a particular action important to the trustor, irrespective of the ability to monitor or control that other party". McKnight and Chervany (1996) identify six trust constructs that illustrate how trust is formed. Figure 1 shows four trust concepts namely 'trusting beliefs', 'system trust', 'dispositional trust' and 'situational decision to trust' that together support the construct 'trusting intentions', and eventually result in establishing 'trusting behaviour'. As the differences in cultural dimensions directly influence these constructs (as shown below), they are now described in more detail.

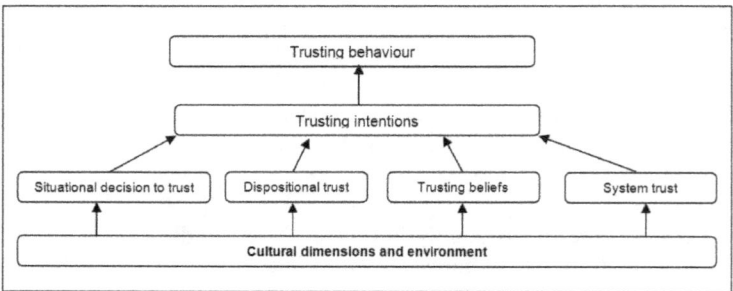

Figure 1: Trust formation

i.   *Situational decision to trust* denotes the readiness to trust other parties in general in a given situation.
ii. *Dispositional trust* is a general inclination to trust others. In task-oriented cultures such as individualistic Western cultures there is a higher initial trust in strangers. In contrast, relationship-oriented cultures such as collectivist

African cultures have lower initial trust in strangers and a personal relationship is required to develop first (Hofstede, 1980).

iii. *Trusting beliefs* define the perception of an e-commerce consumer that the e-commerce website will provide goods and services as it has promised. These beliefs are mainly categorised as ability, integrity and benevolence.

iv. *System trust* refers to one's sense of security from guarantees, assurances or other impersonal structures inherent in a specific context. If a consumer understands how SSL encryption works and experiences a sense of normality when a transaction happens securely, his/her system trust increases.

Given the set of trust constructs for e-commerce, their influence on the individualist and collectivist cultures are explored in more detail next.

3. Consumer trust in individualistic cultures

eBay is considered here as an example of an e-commerce website that has been developed in the environment of an individualist culture in the USA. When transacting on eBay, buyers and sellers sign up for an account and are provided with a comprehensive set of rules and policies that must be followed. They are advised to take note of a seller's feedback rating (eBay website, 2012). If the rating is high, the seller is presumed to be honest. Buyers are further advised to only deal with sellers via the eBay site. There is a feedback system to provide buyers and sellers with the opportunity and a method of evaluating each other. For each transaction, only the buyer and seller can rate each other by leaving feedback. Each feedback left consists of a positive (+1), negative (-1), or neutral (0) rating, and a short comment. It is vital that community members provide honest ratings and comments about a particular eBay member, as eBay stars represent the trustworthiness, reputation and community standing of buyers and sellers. The trust mechanisms used by eBay are defined at numerous layers, which will be described next.

3.1. eBay trust mechanisms

Trust starts with an individualist buyer accessing the eBay website. As the *dispositional trust* of such a buyer is generally higher than that of a collectivist buyer, a basic level of trust exists that enables the buyer to investigate the possibilities that eBay presents. As this buyer is more of a risk taker, acting as an individualist, this may happen without recommendations from friends about the trustworthiness of eBay (Chong, 2003; Huff & Kelley, 2003). The success of eBay supports the notion that people from individualistic cultures tend to trust strangers with more ease. The buyer follows the process to create an account and reads all rules and policies. These safeguards increase the trust of the buyer, as he/she prefers a rules-based environment (Chong, 2003).

System trust in eBay is formed when the buyer observes the institutional guarantees, laws and policies, as well as information security mechanisms that are provided. For example, the buyer understands the meaning of sophisticated mechanisms such as certificates and third party assurances, which increases his/her trust in eBay.

The buyer proceeds to transact successfully with sellers, thereby forming his/her own *trusting beliefs*. If goods are received as promised, the ability belief characteristic increases. In the same way, integrity and benevolence increase and lead to a higher trust in eBay. To enable buyers to avoid untrustworthy sellers, a feedback system is implemented that provides a calculated numeric score indicating the reputation of each seller. This is ideal for individualist buyers who prefer to make trust decisions based on analytical means. Individualist buyers are more willing to share information with the public compared to collectivist consumers (Hofstede, 1980). Their communication style is more expressive and explicit and they are likely to voice their dissatisfaction if necessary. Due to the masculine nature of individualist cultures, individualist buyers behave judgementally and are less concerned about the feelings of others (Hofstede, 1980). This reflects on their consumer satisfaction scores. eBay's feedback system provides buyers and sellers with the opportunity to freely and honestly express their opinion of others. This makes eBay reliable and appropriate to the individualist buyer or seller, leading to its success in Western cultures.

An e-commerce system such as eBay clearly caters for the individualist consumer (Chong, 2003). The collectivist consumer requires a different approach to e-commerce, which should be based on his/her characteristics relating to collectivist norms of behaviour and values, as will be discussed next.

4. Consumer trust in collectivist cultures

A major research focus in rural Africa is to develop e-commerce systems to support economic development. An e-commerce system needs to be created to allow spaza shops to place orders directly with suppliers. They should be supported to cooperate with one another by forming cooperatives (Chebelyon-Dalizu et al., 2010) so as to enable discounts on bulk buying and goods delivery costs. For any system supporting this scenario, cooperative members must trust one another, cooperatives must be trusted by suppliers, and suppliers must trust cooperatives (Tadelis, 2001). The collectivist consumer's approach to conducting business is described next in an attempt to demonstrate the collectivist consumer's behaviour to trust.

4.1. Trust mechanisms of the spaza shop e-commerce system

Trust starts with the collectivist buyer encountering the e-commerce mobile website on his/her cell phone. This system allows the buyer to form a cooperative with other spaza shops and place orders with suppliers that are supported by cloud technology. As the *dispositional trust* of the collectivist buyer is generally lower than that of the individualist buyer (Hofstede, 1980), he/she may choose simply not to investigate the possibilities posed by the e-commerce system any further. Collectivist buyers are risk-averse as they have a high *uncertainty avoidance.* Any unfamiliar situation may be seen as dangerous (Hofstede, 1980) and initial trust will need to be formed using other means. Collectivist buyers are more willing to commit to their existing group relationship, rather than consider forming a relationship with others outside the group. This minimises the perceived risk and collectivist buyers therefore form new relationships only if strong institutional safeguards are present. As a high premium is placed on belief in experts, a recommendation from a well-respected person may be required to ensure a basic level of trust in the system.

System trust in the spaza shop e-commerce system can be formed when the spaza shop owner observes the institutional guarantees, rules and policies, as well as information security mechanisms that are provided. As the spaza shop owner may be unaware of the meaning of features such as certificates and third party assurances, it would not affect his/her trust in the system considerably. Even if the owner proceeds to transact successfully with the supplier, his/her *trusting beliefs* are increased marginally when goods are received as promised, as he/she does not place a high value on the ability belief characteristic. On the other hand, if asked by a leader in the community to use the system, his/her benevolence towards the system may increase, leading to a higher level of *trusting beliefs*. For the collectivist spaza shop owner the stages of trust formation may consequently not be the same as for the individualist consumer.

If a similar feedback system as eBay's is implemented to increase trust, the results may not be able to reflect the true trustworthiness of cooperative members, cooperatives and suppliers. Collectivist consumers are more likely to share their information within the group and be less expressive and explicit when providing an opinion about another (Chong, 2003). Suppliers would be able to rely on the loyalty of cooperatives and need not be too concerned about specific spaza shops badmouthing the supplier publically. This is very different to the individualist consumer, who would easily give negative ratings and comments for poor performance. A collectivist consumer would be more lenient towards a bad experience (Chong, 2003) and would rather discuss this experience within the group than make a public statement. This ensures that any relationship between the group (or a group member) and the entity responsible for the bad experience is not jeopardised. Collectivist consumers are more likely to subordinate their individual goals to the goals of the group (Hofstede, 1980). This approach leads to strong trust communities, where the members of the community are more concerned about the reputation of the community as a whole than about their individual reputations. Such behaviour is not facilitated by current reputation systems where public expressions and ratings are actually encouraged.

Research indicates that trust, in general, is influenced by similarity (Ziegler & Golbeck, 2007). This is especially the case in collectivist cultures where groups form based on shared goals, demographics and personal interests. Shared similarities in a group provide an initial understanding that can influence the trust and provide initial trust among group members.

When cooperatives are formed, new members are generally included only if they are personal friends of existing members (Moliea, 2007). Since the existing member is held responsible to a certain degree for the new member's behaviour, it is vitally important that any new member should be highly trustworthy. The social position of new members relative to the group can indicate an initial trust level assigned to the new member when joining the group. In African cultures, social hierarchies have an influence on trust (Botha, 2006). The collectivist consumer in rural Africa will trust another more if he/she has a higher social standing. Collectivist cultures therefore encourage individuals to trust more in groups and rely less on others outside the group (Yamagishi, 1988; Triandis 2001). This instils strong loyalty towards the group (Huff & Kelley, 2003).

With this being said, collectivist consumers take a longer time to trust outsiders, but once this trust is developed it can be stronger and more enduring (Huff & Kelley, 2003). When spaza shops partake in group buying, a relationship is required between the spaza shops and the suppliers. A new supplier introduced into such an ecosystem would find it challenging to establish initial trust with the spaza shops. However, if the supplier manages to establish a trusting relationship with the group of spaza shops, the supplier would benefit.

In the next section, collectivist trust properties for rural Africa are identified according to the collectivist consumer characteristics discussed so far.

5. Collectivist trust properties for trust and reputation in rural Africa

Since trust properties are derived from the definition of trust and social aspects of trust, they are the basis on which trust can be modelled. Culture has an impact on trust and therefore has an effect on trust properties. Although most of these properties are relevant in both African and Western cultures, the degree to which they are relevant may differ. A number of general trust properties have been defined in trust literature and are used by trust models and mechanisms (Hardin, 2001; Yamagishi, 1988). The properties of trust are as follows (Abdul-Rahman & Hailes, 2000; Josang & Pope, 2005)

a) *Trust is context dependent.* This means that trust associated with someone is relative to that context and the trust may not be the same in another context. For collectivist cultures, this may be more relevant to consider as context is seen as very important when a decision to trust is made.
b) *Trust is transitive.* Transitive involves the notion that trust can be passed on between people to some degree (Matsuo & Yamamoto, 2009). For collectivist cultures, this trust property is influenced by the importance that is placed on relationships and social standing. If the recommendation comes from a person with high social standing, a high transfer of trust will be made.
c) *Trust is subjective.* Trust is a personal opinion and cannot be assumed to be mutual (McKnight & Chervany, 1996). In collectivist cultures, this property is influenced by the effect of the group opinion.

d) *Trust is dynamic and non-monotonic.* This means that trust does not always remain the same and, based on experiences at a later stage, the degree of trust in another may increase or decrease.

e) *Trust is based on prior experiences.* Experience and knowledge of another's previous behaviour provide a basis for trust in future situations that are familiar in terms of context (Luhmann, 1979).

For an e-commerce environment to be successful in a collectivist culture in rural Africa, additional trust properties need to be defined to address the cultural importance that is placed on groups and related behaviour. Next, three trust properties are proposed that need to be considered by the trust and reputation systems to facilitate consumer trust for the collectivist culture that characterises rural Africa.

5.1. Trust is influenced by social position in the community

In individualist cultures, social position is not a defining factor in facilitating consumer trust. Individualist consumers are risk takers who establish initial trust relatively easily with strangers. In contrast, collectivist consumers are risk adverse and they avoid situations where there is a high uncertainty. They rely on group members with higher social standing to make informed decisions. A group leader is highly trusted by its group members and the social position of group leaders can increase or decrease their trust. Those leaders who are well connected and in good standing with others are generally viewed as more trustworthy by members of the group. The group has access to a wider range of resources (such as other potential collaboration groups and suppliers) due to the social connectivity of the group leader. An e-commerce system that attempts to implement this property would need to make better use of information relating to social position in a community.

5.2. Trust is influenced by similarity between members of the group

Collectivist consumers establish groups based on shared similarities. The similarities of group members infer some initial trust within the group. Individualist consumers, in contrast, are not as concerned with similarities since they do not need to form groups in order to facilitate consumer trust. Similarities between members of the collectivist groups provide a common purpose or shared identity that influences trust in a positive manner. Therefore similarity in the formation of buying groups needs to be considered. This can reduce the risk associated with online buying by increasing the consumer trust in groups that consist of members with shared similarities.

5.3. Group reputation facilitates trust between members of the group

Collectivist consumers have the group's best interests in mind and decisions that could influence the group's reputation need to be considered in a collective manner. In an e-commerce environment, a trust mechanism is required to facilitate group reputation. This increases the trust among group members in their group. Others are able to determine the level of trust associated with this group and with each of its members. Members of a group with a good reputation will each ensure they behave in a manner that will maintain this high reputation.

The three properties mentioned above – all influenced by collectivist culture – need to be implemented by a trust model to facilitate e-commerce trust in collectivist rural Africa.

6. Conclusion

Individualist consumers find the use of eBay's trust mechanisms natural to use. Collectivist consumers, on the other hand, may require a different approach to e-commerce since eBay's trust mechanisms are not entirely relevant to them. This paper proposes three additional trust properties to support a trust model for collectivist rural Africa. Future research aims to investigate how these properties can be implemented by a trust model. Recent work of the researchers in which an emphasis is placed on defining and identifying strong trust communities by means of social network centrality measures is to be considered too.

7. Acknowledgement

The support of SAP Research Pretoria/Meraka Unit of Technology Development and the National Research Foundation (NRF) under Grant number 66302 towards this research is hereby acknowledged. Options expressed and conclusions arrive at are solely those of the authors and cannot necessarily be attributed to SAP Research/Meraka UTD or the NRF.

8. References

Abdul-Rahman, A. and Hailes, S. (2000), "Supporting trust in virtual communities", *Proceedings of the 33rd Annual Hawaii International Conference on System Sciences*, Vol. 1, p. 9.

Botha, F. (2006), "The influence of the rural survivalist culture on corporate image", Department of Human Resources Management Faculty of Economics and Management Science, University of Pretoria, Pretoria, South Africa.

Chebelyon-Dalizu, L., Garbowitz, Z., Hause, A. and Thomas, D. (2010), "Strengthening spaza shops in Monwabisi Park, Cape Town", Worcester Polytechnic Institute, Massachusetts, USA.

Chong, B. (2003), "Why culture matters for the formation of consumer trust? A conceptual study of barriers for realizing real global exchange in Hong Kong", *Asia Pacific Management Review*, Vol. 8, No. 2, pp. 217-240.

Cramer, M. (2010), "Trust development and the influence of the individualist/collectivist paradigm", Gordon Institute of Business Science, University of Pretoria, Pretoria, South Africa.

Doney, P.M., Cannon, J.P. and Mullen, M.R. (1998), "Understanding the influence of national culture on the development of trust", *Academy of Management Review*, Vol. 23, No. 3, pp. 601-620.

Dörflinger, J., Friedland, C., Mengistu, M., Merz, C., Stadtrecher, S., Pabst, K. and de Louw, R. (2009), Mobile commerce in rural South Africa – Proof of concept of mobile solutions for the next billion mobile consumers. In *Proceedings of the 10th IEEE International Symposium on a World of Wireless, Mobile and Multimedia Networks – WOWMOM 2009* (June 15-19, Kos Island, Greece).

eBay website. (2011), http://www.ebay.com/ (Accessed 6 February 2012).

e-spaza. (2011), http://www.e-spaza.com/?p=251 *(Accessed 9 February 2012).*

Economic Report on Africa. (2011), "Governing development in Africa – the role of the state in economic transactions", Available from *www.uneca.org/era2011/ (Accessed 8 February 2012).*

Hardin, R. (1993), "The street level epistemology of trust", *Politics and Society*, Vol. 21, pp. 505-531.

Hofstede, G. (1980), "Culture's consequences", Beverly Hills, Sage.

Huff, L. and Kelley, L. (2003), "Levels of organizational trust in individualist versus collectivist societies: A seven-nation study", *Organisation Science*, Vol. 14, No. 1, pp. 81-90.

Josang, S. and Pope, S. (2005), "Semantic constraints for trust transitivity", *Proceedings of the 2nd Asia-Pacific Conference on conceptual modelling.* Vol. 4, pp. 59-68.

Lane, C. (1997), "The social regulation of inter-firm relations in Britain and Germany: market rules, legal norms and technical standards", *Cambridge Journal of Economics*, Vol. 21, No. 2, pp. 197-215.

Luhmann, N. (1979), "Trust and power", John Wiley & Sons Inc., Chichester.

Manana, Z. (2009), "Antecedents of store patronage and cross-shopping: The case for increasing grocery spend in Soweto", Dissertation, South Africa.

Matsuo, Y. and Yamamoto, H. (2009), "Community gravity: Measuring bidirectional effects by trust and rating on online social networks", *18th International World Wide Web Conference*, Madrid, Spain, pp. 751-760.

Mayer, R., Davis, J. and Schoorman, F. (1995), "An integrative model of organizational trust", *Academy of Management Review*, Vol. 20, No. 3, pp. 709-734.

Mayer, R., Davis, J. and Schoorman, F. (2007), "An integrative model of organizational trust: Past, present, future", *Academy of Management Review*, Vol. 32, No. 2, pp. 344-354.

Mbigi, L. (2003), "Leveraging emotional and spiritual resources to increase brand equity", *People Dynamics*, Vol. 21, No. 3, pp. 10-16.

McKnight, D. and Chervany, N. (1996), "The meanings of trust", University of Minnesota, Management Information Systems Research Center, MISRC Working Paper Series, pp. 96-104.

Moliea, H. (2007), "Stokvels as alternative microfinance institutions: Conversations with women from Venda", Gordon Institute of Business Science, University of Pretoria, Pretoria, South Africa.

PayPal. 2012, www.paypal.com (Accessed: 11 February 2012).

Ratnasingam P.P. (2001), Interorganizational trust in business to business e-commerce, PhD thesis, Erasmus University, Rotterdam.

Schlägel, C. and Wolff, B. (2007), "Country-specific effects of reputation and information: A comparison of online auctions in Germany, the UK, and the US", *FEMM Working Papers*.

Tadelis, S. (2001), "Firm reputation with hidden information", *Journal of Economic Theory*, Vol. 2, No. 1, pp. 635-651.

Triandis, H.C. (2001), "Individualism-collectivism and personality", *Journal of Personality*, Vol. 69, No. 6, pp. 907-924.

Tsai, W. (2000), "Social capital, strategic relatedness and the formation of intraorganizational linkages", *Strategic Management Journal*, Vol. 21, No. 9, pp. 925-939.

Yamagishi, T. (1988), "Seriousness of social dilemmas and the provision of a sanctioning system", Social Psychology Quarterly, Vol. 51, No. 1, pp. 32-42.

Zaheer, S. and Zaheer, A. (2006), "Trust across borders", *Journal of International Business Studies*, Vol. 37, No. 1, pp. 21-29.

Ziegler, L. and Golbeck, J. (2007), "Investigating interactions of trust and interest similarity", *Decision Support Systems*, Vol. 43, No. 2, pp. 460-475.

An Evaluation of Linux Cybercrime Forensics Courses for European Law Enforcement

P. Stephens

Department of Computing (Academic), Canterbury Christ Church University,
Canterbury, Kent, CT1 1QU, United Kingdom
e-mail: paul.stephens@canterbury.ac.uk

Abstract

This paper outlines models for the process of course selection and the development process used for producing the Linux as an Investigative Tool and Forensic Scripting Using Bash courses. These modules were developed as part of the ISEC 2008 Project, titled: "Developing and disseminating an accredited international training programme for the future". The two courses are part of an MSc accredited by University College Dublin. The evaluations of the two courses are included showing that the models presented for the course selection and development processes seem to be extremely helpful.

Keywords

Police, Linux, Cybercrime, Forensics, Courses, Evaluation

1   Introduction

This paper outlines a unique development of Linux cybercrime forensics courses for law enforcement practitioners. The design, delivery and evaluation of these courses was carried out by academics and forensic computing professionals from across the European Union with funding from the European Commission (2008a), Microsoft, An Garda Siochana, Landesamt für Ausbildung, Fortbildung und Personalangelegenheiten der Polizei NRW, and the National Policing Improvement Agency. The developers comprised law enforcement personnel from 18 member states, CEPOL, Europol, Interpol, and the UN ODC. In addition, developers from academia included lecturers from Canterbury Christ Church University, University College Dublin, and Universite de Technologie de Troyes. The process of course selection is highlighted in Figure 1, where project participants suggest and discuss new courses culminating in a vote for the most suitable suggestions. This ensures that both professional and academically relevant content is produced leading to accredited courses that are fit-for-purpose. The structure suggested is a modular one with courses at basic, intermediate, advanced and CPD levels.

These courses were part of an MSc in Forensic Computing and Cybercrime Investigation accredited by University College Dublin. This paper discusses two courses for which the author was the course manager and lead trainer: *Linux as an Investigative Tool* and *Forensic Scripting Using Bash*. Before the evaluations of these courses are discussed however it is worth noting how the courses were developed.

Figure 1: Process of course selection

2   Development Process for the Linux Cybercrime Forensics Courses

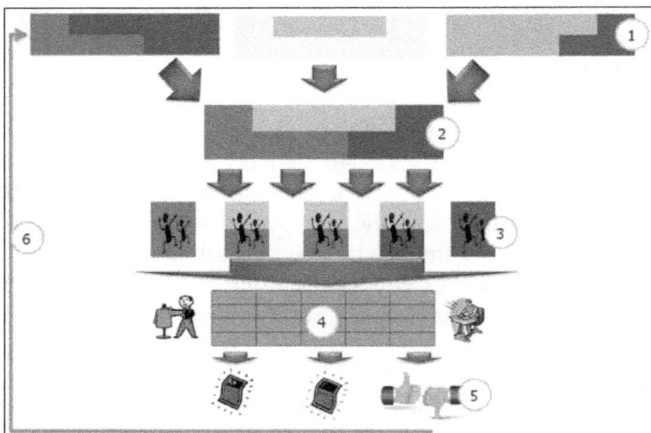

Figure 2: Management Process for Individual Course Development

Figure 2 shows how the development process was managed. **1** Shows how individuals come to the planning meetings with their own courses, ideas for courses and preparatory work. **2** Shows how the courses, ideas and preparatory work are combined to make a coherent timetable. **3** Shows how the content is then given to a presenter to develop and a seconder for checking. Presenters are responsible for content but the syllabus has already been defined in **1** and **2**. At **4** the training designer and course manager okay the final timetable for presentation to students and then the course is run. **5** The course is assessed and evaluated. **6** These outcomes are fed back into future runs and/or upgrades of the course. This model evolved over a number of years through a number of similar development projects funded mainly by the Agis Programme (European Commission, 2008b). One of the elements that was added following the pilot run of the Linux as an Investigative Tool course was the addition of the seconder, not only to check over materials developed by a presenter, but also to support the students in the classroom. Up until this point the other three or four trainers who were not presenting were expected to support students, however, due to the complexity of the subject not all trainers were familiar enough with the content to do this in any meaningful way.

The Linux as an Investigative Tool course was piloted in April 2007 at The Garda College, Templemore, Co. Tipperary, Ireland as a one-week course. Following evaluations by the students, trainers, training designer, and quality assurance experts it was decided that the course be split into a two week course due to its complexity (see Carthy et al. (2007)). The first week would cover the basics of Linux in a forensic computing context. Week two would cover the more in depth forensic features of Linux and the associated tools. The timetable for the first week of the course is shown in Figure 3.

Monday	1.1 Course Opening	1.2 Introduction and installation of Linux	L	1.2 (cont'd) Introduction and installation of Linux	1.3 Self reflection
Tuesday	2.1 Review of previous day	2.2 Basic Linux commands	U	2.2 (cont'd) Basic Linux commands	2.3 Self reflection
Wednesday	3.1 Review of previous day	3.2 Standard Linux Tools	N	3.3 Standard Linux Tools - System Admin Perspective	3.4 Self reflection
Thursday	4.1 Review of previous day	4.2 Standard Linux Tools - Working with Hashes	C	4.3 Week 1 Course Review	4.4 Self reflection
Friday	5.1 Assessment	5.2 Course Evaluation and Next Steps	H	5.3 Tutorials	

Figure 3: Timetable for week one of Linux as an Investigative Tool Course following evaluations

Following this week the recommendation was that students of the course would need one to two months for the material to sink in and to work on related tasks. Therefore the following tasks were outlined as homework:

- Step One: Work through week one's materials and exercises;

- Step Two: Work through tutorial material; and

- Step Three: Brush up on file systems knowledge.

This would be followed by week two of the course as outline in Figure 4.

Monday	6.1 Course Opening and Assessment	6.2 Forensic file formats			6.3 String search with egrep	6.4 Information gathering and acquisition tools	6.5 Self reflection
				L			
Tuesday	7.1 Review of previous day	7.2 Evidence acquisition tools Keyword search		**U**	7.3 Use of the file system Undelete files	7.4 Timeline File headers Finding pictures Metadata in pictures	7.5 Self reflection
				N			
Wednesday	8.1 Review of previous day	8.2 Scripts basics Thumbnails Video analysing	8.3 Salvage - carving Windows registry	**C**	8.4 NTFS compression and encryption MS Office documents Windows password cracking	8.5 Anti-Forensics	8.6 Self reflection
Thursday	9.1 Course Review	9.2 Assessment	9.3 Course Evaluation and Closure	**H**	9.4 Tutorials		

Figure 4: Timetable for week two of Linux as an Investigative Tool Course following evaluations

3 Linux as an Investigative Tool Evaluation

The online element of the course (the development of which is discussed in more detail in Stephens (2009)) was carried out between March and May 2010 and the class-based part was delivered at the Hellenic Police Academy, Veria, Greece in June 2010. There were 28 students from law enforcement agencies across the European Union enrolled on the MSc in Forensic Computing and Cybercrime Investigation accredited by University College Dublin. The students had a range of experience from less than two years to more than fifteen, however all students had attended the previous MSc level courses on Introductory IT Forensics and Network Investigations, Applied NTFS Forensics, Intermediate Internet Investigations, and Intermediate Network Investigations. Less than half the class had any experience of using Linux and less than 20% had used Linux for forensic investigations. All courses on the MSc dealt with differences in practice between member states by focussing on the IOCE (2012) G8 Proposed Principles For The Procedures Relating To Digital Evidence. Provision was also made for students to discuss local variations in practice and legislation in classes with other students and trainers.

Formal evaluation of the MSc run of the Linux as an Investigative Tool took place using the Kirkpatrick Model (Kirkpatrick and Kirkpatrick, 2006) Level 1, Level 2 and Level 3 (previously a pilot of this course had run and was evaluated in Carthy et al. (2007)). Level 1 involves gauging student reaction to the course using student feedback (commonly referred to as 'happy sheets'). In the case of the online element of the course participants completed an end of online course questionnaire on the SurveyMonkey website (SurveyMonkey, 2011). For the in class element of the course, participants completed daily questionnaires on SurveyMonkey. The SurveyMonkey questionnaires provided qualitative and quantitative data. The frequency of feedback made it easier for the trainers to react to any problems that were identified. For example, if students experienced difficulties with a particular element then during recaps more time could be spent on this area. Exercises were also adjusted in line with feedback. Kirkpatrick Model Level 2 involves attempting to assess the extent to which student learning has taken place. The course knowledge assessment/examination acted as this Level 2 independent evaluation of the extent to which course learning objectives were met by the students. The Level 3 evaluation involves asking managers of the students on the MSc to comment on how the programme has affected their working capability and practice. In addition to these Kirkpatrick evaluations, students completed a learning journal for the MSc and an exit interview was conducted by members of the project team.

Student feedback was generally very positive (see Figure 5 for the Aggregate Rating for Overall Session Grading); however, some students struggled with the content including two students, out of the 28 that sat the course, failing the assessed elements. This was despite adding an extra day at the beginning to the class-based part of the course to review work covered by an online part of the module. Overall the student average was 80%. All students passed the assessed elements on resit.

As can be seen from Figure 5, approximately 1% of participants rated any of the sessions as very poor. This equates to only three out of 520 responses overall, restricted to only three sessions. Approximately 1% of participants rated any of the sessions poor. This equates to only eight out of 520 responses overall, restricted to six sessions. Interestingly there is only an overlap between poor and very poor responses for two sessions. Where sessions were rated poor or very poor, comments indicate that students found it difficult to keep up as there seemed to be a lot of material in these sessions. For future runs of the course the materials and the evaluations will be available to trainers so that they can make changes, if they deem it necessary.

Some students believed that the standard of the training equipment could have been improved but on the whole comments were positive. Particular highlights for the students included conversion between forensic file formats, regular expressions and the level of detail covered in describing commands and their switches.

Student quotes directly related to this course include:

> "The course itself was excellently presented, I found the subject matter fascinating, and I am utilising my knowledge in the workplace already. I have spent the last few days stripping out IP/time data from a 900MB text document containing compromised data using Linux, ... it is most definitely not something I could have achieved prior to this course."

and

> "I have learned to convert a DD image to another evidence file format to suit the tools I'm using such as EnCase. This is only one example of how what I have learned can be used to my advantage, other examples include extracting metadata from images and using the file system to undelete files."

These are encouraging as both examples point to ways in which their investigative practice has been improved carrying out tasks that would not have been possible without this training. Managers' feedback for the MSc as a whole was also positive and encouraging.

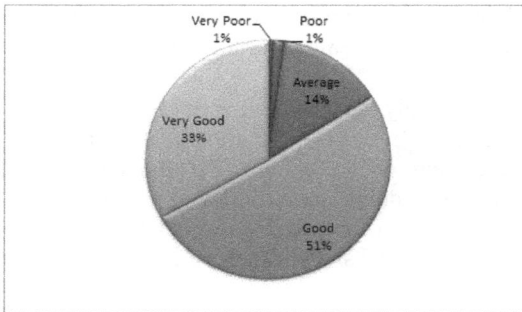

Figure 5: Aggregate Rating for Overall Session Grading for MSc run of Linux as an Investigative Tool

4 Forensic Scripting Using Bash Evaluation

The pilot of the Forensic Scripting Using Bash course ran in April 2010 at the National Police Training Centre, Madrid, Spain. Students for this course were again drawn from the European Union law enforcement community but were not studying on the full MSc programme. There was a pre-course assessment that all students had to take to test their knowledge of Linux before the course. This was necessary as the module was meant to fit into a master's degree program where students had studied Linux forensics to sufficient depth. None of the students on the course in Madrid had previously studied the Linux as an Investigative Tool course and therefore the test was used as a way of judging whether or not students had the equivalent knowledge required. Approximately one-third of students failed the pre-course assessment and five (out of 20) students went on to fail the course assessment at the end. The pre-course assessment was therefore indicative of the number of students that would fail the course. The ISEC 2008 MSc Programme Evaluation Report makes it clear that the pilot of the Forensic Scripting Using Bash course suffered due to some of the students not meeting the pre-requisites specified. In the future students should have either passed the Linux as an Investigative Tool module first or must pass a pre-course assessment. Student feedback was generally very positive (see Figure 6 for the Aggregate Rating for Overall Session Grading); however, there

124

was a recommendation that the session at the end of the course be made optional or removed as students found it difficult to concentrate following a test. Overall the student average was 58%. Figure 6 As shows that no participant rated the sessions very poor and the poor ratings refer to only six out of 329 responses overall, restricted to only four sessions. One of these sessions (Beyond Bash) was removed due to this feedback. The other sessions either did not receive any relevant comments or referred to difficulties in understanding language or the session being 'slow'. The timetable in Figure 7 gives an indication of the content of the course.

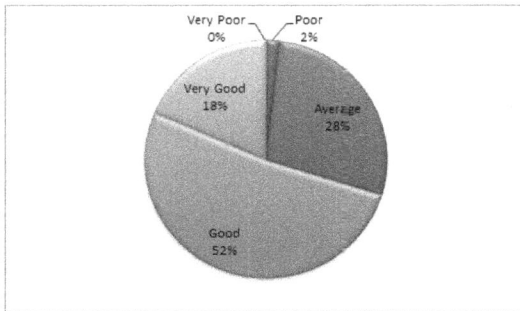

Figure 6: Aggregate Rating for Overall Session Grading for Pilot of Forensic Scripting Using Bash

Monday	1.1 Course Opening	1.2 Introduction to Developing Software and Shell Scripting	L	1.3 Making Decisions (if and case constructs)	1.4 Self reflection
Tuesday	2.1 Review of previous day	2.2 Repeating Sequences (while, until, and for constructs)	U	2.3 Utilities, Functions, Testing, and Debugging	2.4 Self reflection
Wednesday	3.1 Review of previous day	3.2 Forensic Case Studies using the Linux as a Forensic Tool Course examples	N C	3.3 Forensic Case Studies using Grundy examples	3.4 Self reflection
Thursday	4.1 Review of previous day	4.2 Enhancing the User Interface and Improving Output	H	4.3 Further Forensic Scripting (using Linux as a Forensic Tool Course examples?)	4.4 Self reflection
Friday	5.1 Course Review	5.2 **Assessment** / 5.3 Course Evaluation and Closure		5.4 Beyond bash (not assessed)	

Figure 7: Timetable for Forensic Scripting Using Bash Course

The course ran as part of the MSc (with the same students as outlined in section 3 above) in September 2010 at University College Dublin, Ireland. All students on this course had sat the Linux as an Investigative Tool Course (although two had failed the final assessment). Again student feedback was very positive (see Figure 8 for the Aggregate Rating for the Structure and Method of Delivery for the MSc Run of Forensic Scripting Using Bash and Figure 9 for the Aggregate Rating for the Level of Student Understanding for the MSc Run of Forensic Scripting Using Bash), however five students out of 28 failed the end of course assessment worth 50%, however, these students have since passed on resit. The overall student average for the test element was 68%. All students passed the other 50% element for which the average mark was 78%.

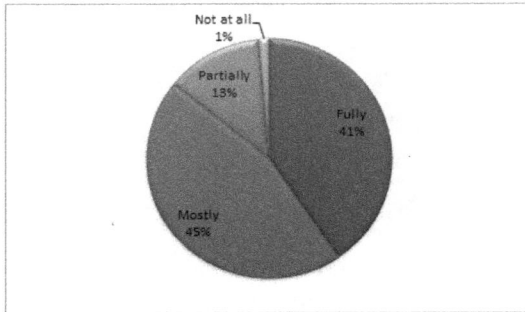

Figure 8: Aggregate Rating for the Structure and Method of Delivery for the MSc Run of Forensic Scripting Using Bash

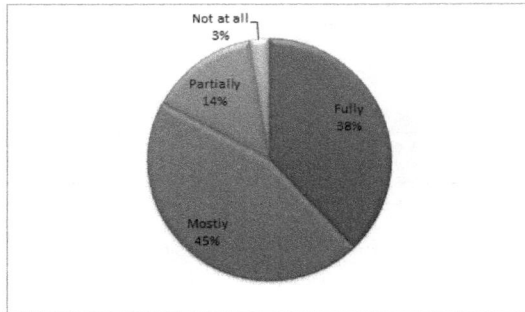

Figure 9: Aggregate Rating for the Level of Student Understanding for the MSc Run of Forensic Scripting Using Bash

Some students were concerned about the difficulty of the subject matter. It is worth noting that trainers put a lot of work into the course including outside of the classroom as shown by the following comment:

> "Working through the exercises in the evening is very beneficial as is the availability of the trainers for that time. Much appreciated."

Student quotes from the learning journals that are particularly relevant to the Forensic Scripting Using Bash course are:

> "The web spider we have learnt is incredibly valuable for our work of monitoring…websites. We were highly surprised when we saw how easy is with a non very long script, to have a real time monitoring system to display all the changes in a website"

and:

> "From a confidence point of view, the last few 'Linux' months, and in particular the scripting course and post-course assignment, having proven to be invaluable. … Over the last three years, I have been constantly mindful of the expertise that surrounds me, the knowledge that my colleagues have acquired over many years of hard work, and for which I feel I can only ever aspire to. Having completed my script, I was asked by two of the most experienced colleagues if I would provide them with a copy of my script, as they wished to look at it and learn from it. I am still in shock that I am seen as somewhat of a relative 'expert' on this subject!"

Again, these are encouraging as both examples point to ways in which their investigative practice has been improved carrying out tasks that would not have been possible without this training. One particularly pertinent manager's response is:

> "has also developed different useful forensics tools and software packages that are used by all members of the unit."

This response shows that the programming elements have really paid off for this particular student and their workplace. For future runs of the course the materials and the evaluations will be available to trainers so that they can make changes, if they deem it necessary.

5 Conclusions

This paper has presented models for the processes of course selection and management for a pan-European, joint venture between law enforcement and academia that may be useful for other professional and academic course development collaborations. In addition, two courses have been evaluated using the Kirkpatrick Model, student learning journals and course exit interviews. The results of these evaluations were highly encouraging, suggesting that the process and management models could be reused in the future.

6   References

Carthy, J., O'Reilly, D., Gillen, P., and Stevens, T. (Eds.) (2007) *Cybercrime Investigation – Developing an international training programme for the future (Phase 4)*, AGIS PROGRAMME JLS/2006/AGIS/010. Wyboston: National Policing Improvement Agency (NPIA).

European Commission (2008a) *Prevention of and Fight against Crime* [online]. Available at: http://ec.europa.eu/justice_home/funding/isec/funding_isec_en.htm [Last accessed 21 June 2008].

European Commission (2008b) *AGIS was a framework programme to help police, the judiciary and professionals from the EU Member States and candidate countries co-operate in criminal matters and in the fight against crime* [online]. Available at: http://ec.europa.eu/justice_home/funding/2004_2007/agis/funding_agis_en.htm [Last accessed 21 June 2008].

IOCE (2012) *G8 Proposed Principles For The Procedures Relating To Digital Evidence* [online]. Available at: http://www.ioce.org/core.php?ID=5 [Last accessed 27 April 2012].

Kirkpatrick, D.L. and Kirkpatrick, J.D. (2006). *Evaluating Training Programs: The Four Levels (3rd Edition)*. San Francisco, CA: Berrett-Koehler.

Stephens, P. (2009) 'Teaching 'Linux as a Forensic Tool' (Online) to European Law Enforcement'. *Readings in Technology and Education: Proceedings of ICICTE 2009*, Corfu, Greece, July 9-11, 2009. ISBN: 1-895802-42-3.

SurveyMonkey (2011) *SurveyMonkey: Free online survey software & questionnaire tool* [online]. Available at: http://www.surveymonkey.com/ [Last accessed: 7 February 2011].

Intrusion Detection and the Role of the System Administrator

T. Sommestad and A. Hunstad

Swedish Defence Research Agency (FOI), Sweden
e-mail: Teodor.Sommestad@foi.se; Amund.Hunstad@foi.se

Abstract

The expertise of a system administrator is believed to be important for effective use of intrusion detection systems (IDS). This paper examines two hypotheses concerning the system administrators' ability to filter alarms produced by an IDS by comparing the performance of an IDS to the performance of a system administrator using the IDS. The comparison was made through an experiment where five computer networks are attacked during four days. The experiment shows that the system administrator significantly improves the system's Bayesian detection rate, without significantly decreasing the probability that an attack is detected. Also, an analysis is made of the types of expertise that is used when output from the intrusion detection system is processed by the administrator.

Keywords

Intrusion detection systems, intrusion detection, system administrator, system administration

1. Introduction

When system administrators monitor the security of computer network(s) they often use an intrusion detection system (IDS). The IDS examines events (in network traffic, operating systems etc.) and raises an alarm if the events are believed to be symptoms of an intrusion. A number of studies investigate IDSs from a technical perspective. These studies typically investigate the technical quality of different solutions in terms of variables such as the probability of attack detection, probability of false alarm, performance constraints, and attack coverage (Mell et al. 2003; Biermann 2001). In practice, however, the IDS is not a standalone entity which makes decisions, but a tool for system administrators. The IDS administrator monitors the IDS output to filter out false alarms and attempts to verify if compromise has occurred, for example by investigating the affected system directly (Werlinger et al. 2010). Hence, in operational environments the output of an IDS is processed by an administrator who tries to detect and respond to attacks.

IDSs used in practice are tools to support system administrators. However, there are few research efforts that investigate intrusion detection that include system administrators in the investigation. Branlat (2011) studied system administrators under attack during a security exercise and identified a number of issues concerning attack detection in this context, e.g., to identify or guess the intentions of the attackers. Werlinger et al. (2008, 2009, 2010) have acknowledged the important role of administrators and have through interviews explored both usability issues and the need of expertise and human interaction qualitatively. Similar research has been performed by Goodall et al (2004, 2009). The findings in Goodall et al. (2009) are that the work of administrators of IDSs require expertise in computer networks and security as well as a high degree of situated expertise and problem solving ability.

For an intrusion detection solution to be effective, it is of course important that it detects attacks that are made, i.e. it should have a high *P(Alarm=True | Attack=True)*. However, it is also important that it has a usable *Bayesian detection rate*. The Bayesian detection rate is the probability that an alarm which is raised corresponds to an actual attack (Axelsson 2000), i.e. *P(Attack=True | Alarm=True)*. False alarms will introduce costs (e.g., due to unnecessary actions taken by IDS administrators) and reduce the faith in that the alarms raised are worth further investigation (which might lead to real attacks being overlooked). Hence, the Bayesian detection rate cannot be too low for an effective detection processes.

The high ratio of false positives is a problem with IDSs available today and several ideas that are aimed at reducing the false alarm rate have been presented, e.g., (Sourour et al. 2009) and (Spathoulas & Katsikas 2010). However, the effectiveness of such solutions in operational scenarios remains unclear. Werlinger et al. (2008, 2009, 2010) and Goodall et al. (2004, 2009) have through qualitative studies found that the expertise of system administrators play an important role for the effectiveness of an IDS when they are used in operational settings. In other words, it is believed that a substantial amount of human involvement and expertise is required to produce a high detection rate and at the same time keep the Bayesian detection rate at acceptable levels. Thompson et al. (2007) has assessed how different types of visualisation support a system administrator. However, the authors of this paper are not aware of any quantitative results that test if a system administrator who use and interpret the output of an IDS will produce a higher Bayesian detection rate. Additionally, no previous work has been found concerning the influence a system administrator's filtering and analysis have on the probability of detection. This paper examines two hypotheses concerning the effectiveness of an IDS in comparison to an IDS plus an administrator:

Hypothesis one: *A competent administrator using an IDS will have a significantly higher Bayesian detection rate than the IDS that is used.*

Hypothesis two: *A competent administrator using an IDS will have a significantly lower probability of detection than the IDS that is used.*

The first hypothesis is based on the idea that administrators will use their expertise to filter the output of the IDS. The second hypothesis is an expected consequence of the filtering process. In other words, when the administrator filters alarms, a portion of the true alarms will be incorrectly dismissed as false alarms.

The research question investigated in this paper stems from the qualitative studies of Goodall et al. (2009) and concern the type of expertise required to use IDSs effectively. It is: *Which types of expertise does the administrator use when correct respectively incorrect judgments are made*? Of particular interest is the use of domain expertise (in intrusion detection, security, and computer networking) and situated expertise (i.e. local knowledge grounded in the analyst's environment).

Data for this study was obtained through a four-day-long experiment where a system administrator used an IDS to monitor a set of computer networks under attack by security professionals. From this test it was possible to assess and compare the effectiveness of a system administrator analysing the IDS output to the raw output of the IDS.Section 2 describes the experiment setup in more detail. Section 3 describes the result. In section 4 the result is discussed. Finally, in section 5 conclusions are drawn.

2. Data collection and analysis

2.1. Target system

The experiment was conducted using a cluster of 160 computers held by the Swedish Defence Research Agency (FOI). In this cluster, virtual machines were installed and configured to represent computer networks of five organizations in the electric power industry. Each organisation's computer network comprised some 30 machines, of which about half were server machines and half were client machines. The five organisations' computer systems were connected to each other through an internet-like infrastructure containing 44 external servers, primarily web servers.

For all organisations the machines were divided into network zones in a manner representative for a small industrial organization with a demilitarized zone, an office network, and an internal "back office" network. The computers within these five organizations' networks differed significantly, both in terms of software products used and the versions of these software products. The target systems were constructed so that security vulnerabilities varied both between organisations and between the machines within each organisation. This was accomplished by randomizing the software versions to install and the security patches to apply. Variation was also introduced in terms of memory protection mechanisms used on the different machines. The purpose of this variation was to decrease the probability that a single vulnerability could be exploited on all systems and thus force attackers to use a wider range of attack-methods.

Realistic background traffic and activity is essential when the effectiveness of IDSs is tested (Mell et al. 2003; McHugh 2000; Ranum 2001), but also difficult to produce. In an attempt to create realistic background traffic, user behaviour was simulated on the client machines. This behaviour was emulated using scripts that generated keystroke-combinations that used software installed on the client machines (e.g., the web browser) to perform predefined tasks randomly in time according to a predefined scheme. Within the organisation's networks the client machines surfed internal and external websites, read email and opened attachments, sent email to other users within and outside the organisation, and accessed and copied shared network files.

2.2. Attackers and their attacks

The attacks in this experiment were performed by staff at the Swedish Armed Forces Network and Telecommunications Unit. The attackers had the broad objective of disturbing the technical infrastructure of the five organisations. They worked on this endeavour during office hours for four days in October 2011. They primarily used the publicly available tool BackTrack 5 as when attacks were executed. They had no prior knowledge of how the five organizations' computer networks were designed, or where they were placed in the network infrastructure.

The attacks started with a reconnaissance phase where the target systems were identified and probed for vulnerabilities. Attacks and reconnaissance were thereafter performed iteratively during the four days. In total the attackers performed 63 attack actions (including network scans, password guessing, exploitation of configuration flaws, software vulnerability exploitation). On the fourth day the attackers had managed to penetrate machines in the computer networks of two organisations and severely decreased the security of all the networks by compromising their network firewalls.

2.3. Intrusion detection solution

The IDS used in this experiment was an integration of the host-based IDS OSSEC and the network-based IDS Snort. Both are public available, open source products commonly used in operational environments. They were installed in the organisations' computer networks and configured by the administrator who monitored them during the exercise. The administrator spent approximately one week to tune the intrusion detection solution in a manner seen as appropriate. Tuning in this context means to define rules that filter alarms in order to lower the number of false alarms and defining environment-specific signatures (Goodall et al. 2009) . The administrator had also been involved in designing and configuring the five organisations computer networks and had a considerable situated expertise of this environment.

Monitoring was performed via a web-based user interface built in Zabbix, a solution for monitoring the availability and performance of computer systems. The administrator received alarms live via a number of predefined views focusing on systems at varying levels of abstraction. In addition to the possibility of viewing these alarms the administrator also had administrative rights on the attacked systems. As the focus of this experiment was the system administrator's analysis of alarms produced by an IDS, no attempts were made to prevent any of the attacks.

2.4. Measurement instrument

Both the attackers and the administrator maintained logs during the experiment. The attackers logged the attacks performed together with their success and outcome. The administrator logged anomalies which the administrator believed were related to attacks. The administrator also entered records in the log if he believed that a host had been compromised. The output of the IDS alarms was also saved. All logs were time synchronized. The data set, as well as other data collected during the exercise (e.g.., raw network traffic), are can be obtained from the authors on request.

2.5. Comparison of detection rates

Hypothesis one concerns the Bayesian detection rate of the IDS alone compared to the IDS administrator. The Bayesian detection rate is the probability that an alarm is raised because of an actual attack. In this study the attackers documented all attacks they performed and the Bayesian detection rate is assessed as the portion of all alarms which can be connected to any of these attacks. An experienced network security expert was used to judge whether this was the case, based on all information available in the logs.

Hypothesis two concerns the probability of detection, i.e., the probability that an attack will cause an alarm. As for the Bayesian detection rate the attackers' log was used to compare the performance of the IDS and its administrator. For each entry in the attackers' log book it was identified if an alarm had been produced because of the actions associated with the attack. The criterion was that at least one alarm should have been raised which could be tied to the actions taken by the attackers. Hence, it was not required that an alarm described everything the attackers did (e.g., all ports that was scanned) in order for the attack to be considered detected.

For both the IDS and the system administrator Bayesian detection rate was obtained as the ratio between the number of alarms raised because of the actions of the attackers and the number of alarms raised in total. The probability of detection was obtained as the ratio between the number of attacks with an alarm tied to it and the number of attacks performed in total.

Fisher's exact test (Fisher 1922) tests if there are non-random associations between two categorical variables. In other words, it can be used to tests if categorical variables have distributions that are different. In this paper it is used to test hypotheses one and two by comparing the result of the IDS and its administrator. A significance level of 0.05 is used in this experiment.

2.6. Interviews concerning the use of expertise

To obtain knowledge of the role of expertise in intrusion detection, an interview with the administrator monitoring the IDS during the experiment, was performed. Due to the large amount of data collected it was necessary to choose a small data subset to focus on for the interview. For each alarm/decision category a number of cases were identified as of special interest to consider. These cases included scenarios where the IDS and/or administrator made correct as well as incorrect judgments. In particular, the interview identified three scenarios for each of the following cases: the system produced several alarms and the administrator made a correct decision; the system produced several alarms and the administrator made an incorrect decision; the system produced few or no alarms and the administrator made a correct decision; the system produced few or no alarms and the administrator made an incorrect decision.

The interview was semi-structured in the sense that the categorization and cases guided the interview, but apart from that no formal interview guide with pre-defined questions was used. The interview was documented with notes which were later confirmed by the respondent.

3. Results

3.1. The performance of the administrator and IDS

During the experiment the administrator produced 70 alarms and the IDS produced 2107 alarms. Meanwhile, the attackers performed 63 actions involving reconnaissance (often network scans) or direct attack (e.g., password guessing). The alarms raised by the IDS pointed to 44 of these actions (i.e., 19 were missed); the alarms raised by the administrator pointed to 37 of these actions (i.e. 26 were missed). The IDS thus outperforms the administrator with when it comes to the probability that an attack is detected (69% vs. 58%). However, with respect to the Bayesian detection rate the system administrator outperformed the IDS. Of the 70 alarms raised by the administrator 40 (57%) was found to be causes of actual attacks; of the 2107 alarms raised by the IDS only 233 (11%) were due to actual attacks.

Hypothesis one states that the administrator will produce a higher Bayesian detection rate than the IDS. To test if the results can be from the same probability distribution Fisher's exact test (Fisher 1922) is applied on the contingency table. The test shows that the difference is significant (p<0.0001). Hypothesis two states that the administrator will significantly lower probability of detection compared to the IDS. However, Fisher's exact test does show a significant difference (p=0.2645) between the IDS and system administrator with regards to probability of detection.

	IDS	Administrator
Alarms raised	2107	70
Probability of detection	69%	58%
Bayesian detection rate	11%	57%

Table 1: Performance of IDS and the administrator.

3.2. The role of expertise

The interview with the human administrator gave some insight in the reasoning and knowledge that applied when IDS are used.

A number of the analysed cases correspond to when *the administrator was facing several alarms and made a correct decision.* This includes scenarios where the administrator correctly identified that the alarms are caused by attack and when the administrator correctly identifies them as false alarms. When identifying the alarms correctly the primary pieces of information used was: the involvement of an external IP-address and the unusually large number of alarms which matched the typical traces of attack-tools. Thus, both situated expertise and knowledge about security is used. In all cases when *the administrator was facing several alarms and made an incorrect decision* the reason was simply that the alarms were missed by the administrator due to the high amount of alarms.

In many cases the administrator correctly identified a comparable amount of alarms as a false positive. In these cases the administrator correctly identified the alarms as causes of normal network traffic (general network expertise) or hypothesized that it would be unlikely that the attackers had access to the machine involved (situated expertise). In one case the administrator correctly ignored alarms because they would have originated from attacks the administrator considered the attackers incapable of. In other words, based on knowledge of which vulnerabilities that were present and a good idea of which resources the attacker had the alarms could be dismissed.

In other cases *the administrator was facing few or no alarms and makes a correct decision.* When few alarms was correctly associated with an attack the information used to identify maliciousness was the presence of external IP-addresses and the indirect effects of attacks, e.g., when a machine starts to execute strange requests to other machines or extraordinary network loads appear. Thus, situated expertise was the primary input to decisions made in such situations.

In a few cases *the administrator faced few or no alarms and made an incorrect decision.* The reason was that the administrator was misdirected by another, high priority, false alarm. In one case the reason was an incorrect hypothesis concerning the privileges acquired by the attackers

4. Discussion

The primary findings of this experiment are described in section 4.1. This experiment has several limitations and its result should therefore be interpreted with care. Some issues with making broad generalizations from this experiment are described in sections 4.2 and 4.3.

4.1. Primary findings

The primary findings in this experiment is that the IDS administrator produces significantly better filtered output than IDS systems do alone, and the administrator's filtering does not significantly impact the detection rate. As suggested in Goodall et al. (2009), the administrator do so by using situated expertise, general expertise about computer networks, and general expertise about security and attacks. In this experiment the administrator also used knowledge (or guesses) about which attack methods and tools the attackers had access to and would use. Knowledge about the capabilities of the threat agent does not correspond to any of the expertise-types identified by Goodall et al. (2009), but can apparently be effectively used to filter alarm lists.

4.2. Control and sampling of nuisance variables

A number of nuisance variables which can be expected to influence the result are kept constant in this test. This includes variables that are given by the administrator (e.g. the competence), the IDS (e.g. signatures and tuning), and the interface between the administrator and the IDS (e.g. how alarms are visualized). As these are kept constant, the result does not reveal how these influence the result. A reasonable hypothesis is that they all have an impact on the result. For instance, it appears likely that a better tuned IDS would increase the IDS's Bayesian detection rate and decrease the difference between the administrator and system. On the other hand, the result from this setup is so clear that it appears unlikely that the overall conclusion would be different. In particular, it appears unlikely that the Bayesian detection rate of the system would come close to that of a competent administrator monitoring it.

A number of nuisance variables in this environment were sampled to produce meaningful variation. Meaningful in this case means that they are varied to represent conditions which make the result generalizable to a realistic context. Attacks executed by the attackers varied over the experiment, the configuration of attacked networks and computers differed, and background traffic varied in the experiment.

Since the attackers actually performed attacks with an explicit objective it appears likely that they represent a set of steps which resembles those attacks undertaken when a computer network is attacked. Likewise, the systems under attack were designed to resemble those of typical organizations in the electrical power industry, with different network zones and types of computer machines. However, it is unclear if the somewhat artificial variation influences the result.

An important factor for the Bayesian detection rate is the background traffic. Effort was therefore made to produce background traffic which resembles real actions in the sense that real software applications were used and real requests were made to a diverse set of websites, etc. As stated in (Mell et al. 2003), "there is no such thing as a 'standard' network", which makes it difficult to produce background traffic so that the result is generalizable to a wide context. The scripts used in this study to generate user actions (i.e. background traffic) and other records from the experiment can be obtained from the authors.

4.3. The measurement instrument and unit of analysis

The unit of analysis in this study is the entries in the attackers' log book. Alarms which are a causal effect of the entries in this log book are correct alarms (true positives); alarms that do not match an entry in this log book are incorrect alarms (false positives). In conventional tests of IDSs the unit of analysis is the unit which the IDS bases decisions on, typically a network session or operating system event. This study uses a coarser unit of analysis since the more coarse decisions of the administrator is to be compared to those of the IDS. While intrusive actions are intuitively meaningful as a unit to detect, its definition is less rigid than conventional units of analysis. For instance, some entries in the log book involves hundreds of network sessions (e.g. a network scan) while other only involve one (e.g. a software vulnerability exploitation attempt).

While it is possible that another set of attackers (with other opinions on what intrusive behaviour is) would have produced a different log book, it appears unlikely that it would result in a dramatically different result. Manual inspections of a subset of the alarms marked as "false positives" strengthen this belief – no apparent traces could be found to actions taken by the attacker (e.g., to machines they had control over).

5. Conclusions

This experiment confirms earlier findings concerning the importance of expertise in the use of intrusion detection systems. In this experiment the intrusion detection system administrator achieves a significantly better Bayesian detection rate than the intrusion detection system, and the administrator's detection rate is not significantly different from the intrusion detection system. An administrator can achieve this effective filtering by using situated expertise, computer networks expertise, computer security expertise, and knowledge about what the threat agent is capable of.

6. References

Axelsson, S., 2000. The base-rate fallacy and the difficulty of intrusion detection. *ACM Transactions on Information and System Security*, 3(3), pp.186-205.

Biermann, E., 2001. A comparison of Intrusion Detection systems. *Computers & Security*, 20(8), pp.676-683.

Branlat, M., 2011. *Challenges to Adversarial Interplay Under High Uncertainty: Staged-World Study of a Cyber Security Event*. The Ohio State University.

Fisher, R.A., 1922. On the interpretation of chi2 from contingency tables, and the calculation of P. *Journal of the Royal Statistical Society*, 85(1), pp.87–94.

Goodall, J.R., Lutters, W.G. & Komlodi, A., 2009. Developing expertise for network intrusion detection. *Information Technology & People*, 22(2), pp.92–108.

Goodall, J.R., Lutters, W.G. & Komlodi, Anita, 2004. I know my network: collaboration and expertise in intrusion detection. In *Proceedings of the 2004 ACM conference on Computer supported cooperative work*. ACM, pp. 342–345.

McHugh, J., 2000. Testing Intrusion detection systems: a critique of the 1998 and 1999 DARPA intrusion detection system evaluations as performed by Lincoln Laboratory. *ACM Transactions on Information and System Security*, 3(4), pp.262-294.

Mell, P. et al., 2003. *An overview of issues in testing intrusion detection systems, (NIST IR 7007)*, National Institute of Standard and Technology.

Ranum, M.J., 2001. Experiences Benchmarking Intrusion Detection Systems. *Security*, NFR Security, pp.1-10.

Sourour, M., Adel, B. & Tarek, A., 2009. Environmental awareness intrusion detection and prevention system toward reducing false positives and false negatives. In *2009 IEEE Symposium on Computational Intelligence in Cyber Security*. IEEE, pp. 107-114.

Spathoulas, G.P. & Katsikas, S.K., 2010. Reducing false positives in intrusion detection systems. *Computers & Security*, 29(1), pp.35-44.

Thompson, R.S. et al., 2007. Command line or pretty lines?: comparing textual and visual interfaces for intrusion detection. In *Proceedings of the SIGCHI conference on Human factors in computing systems*. ACM, p. 1205.

Werlinger, R. et al., 2010. Preparation, detection, and analysis: the diagnostic work of IT security incident response. *Information Management & Computer Security*, 18(1), pp.26–42.

Werlinger, R. et al., 2009. Towards Understanding Diagnostic Work During the Detection and Investigation of Security Incidents. In *Proceedings of the Third International Symposium on Human Aspects of Information Security & Assurance (HAISA 2009)*. Lulu.

Werlinger, R., Hawkey, K. & Muldner, K., 2008. The challenges of using an intrusion detection system: is it worth the effort? *SOUPS '08 Proceedings of the 4th symposium on Usable privacy and security*, (1).

User-centric, Privacy-Preserving Adaptation for VoIP CAPTCHA Challenges

A. Tasidou[1], P.S. Efraimidis[1], Y. Soupionis[2], L. Mitrou[3,2] and V. Katos[1]

[1]Democritus University of Thrace, Dept. of Electrical and Computer Engineering
[2] Information Security and Critical Infrastructure Protection Research Group, Dept. of Informatics, Athens University of Economics & Business (AUEB)
[3]University of the Aegean, Dept. of Information and Communication Systems Engineering
e-mail: {atasidou, pefraimi, vkatos}@ee.duth.gr; jsoup@aueb.gr; l.mitrou@aegean.gr

Abstract

The effectiveness of CAPTCHA challenges largely depends on being simultaneously easier to solve for humans and harder to solve for bots. In this work we argue that it is possible to enhance the effectiveness of audio CAPTCHA challenges by adapting the challenge to the users' characteristics. We propose a method for achieving this adaptation while protecting users' privacy. Moreover, our approach allows us to address discrimination issues that naturally arise in contemporary audio CAPTCHA challenges. Utilizing modern cryptographic techniques we design a privacy-preserving system, called PrivCAPTCHA, which offers customized CAPTCHA challenges.

Keywords

Privacy Enhancing Technologies, Audio CAPTCHA, SPIT, Discrimination, Legal Aspects of Privacy, Incident Response.

1   Introduction

The Internet Telephony (Voice over IP) is a developing technology that promises a low-cost and high-quality and availability service of multimedia data transmission. Inevitably though, VoIP "inherited" not only these positive features of Internet services, but also some obvious disadvantages (Walsh and Kuhn, 2005). One of the main disadvantages is Spam over Internet Telephony (SPIT) (El Sawda and Urien, 2006), which is the popular expression of Spam in VoIP network environments.

A CAPTCHA (Ahn et al., 2004) is a method that is widely used to counter automated SPAM attacks. The same technique can be used to mitigate SPIT. A CAPTCHA is a Reverse Turing Test where a machine tries to identify whether the incoming session is initiated by a software application or a human. The three major categories of CAPTCHA are a) visual CAPTCHA, where the user tries to recognize characters or words in malformed pictures, b) audio CAPTCHA, where the characters or words to be recognized are in an audio file, and c) logic CAPTCHA, where the user tries to answer specific questions. This paper is focused on audio

CAPTCHA. The reason is that visual CAPTCHA are hard to apply in VoIP systems, mainly due to the limitations of end-user devices. Logic CAPTCHAs are well suited for the VoIP context and are appropriate for adaptive challenges, but one should not neglect the practical difficulties of applying logic CAPTCHAs (Hernández-Castro et al., 2011).

The audio CAPTCHA challenges used today to prevent automated SPIT attacks do not take into account the characteristics of the caller or the callee. Therefore, they need to be easy enough for the average user to solve, making them often easy for automated attacks as well. The fact that these challenges are generic, does not allow for the process to take into consideration the cognitive abilities of human users, while at the same time discriminates against users that have difficulties solving the generic challenges. The ability to use information about the caller or the callee opens up new opportunities for creating more effective and fair CAPTCHA challenges. However, the required information about the caller will probably be sensitive personal information, and thus it is important that a privacy-preserving method of achieving adaptation of CAPTCHA challenges is used.

This work proposes a user-centric, privacy-preserving VoIP CAPTCHA adaptation mechanism , which offers a new paradigm for VoIP CAPTCHA systems aiming at increasing the CAPTCHA effectiveness. We consider this mechanism within the framework of the SPHINX project (Distinguishing Human or Machine with Interactive Media Audio, http://sphinx.vtrip.net). According to the SPHINX architecture, VoIP calls are redirected to an audio CAPTCHA server for evaluation. This work proposes a prototype that could be introduced to the SPHINX architecture. However, there should be no serious difficulties in combining our approach with other audio CAPTCHA systems or even conventional CAPTCHA systems.

1.1 Related work

Existing audio CAPTCHAs are proven more difficult to use for visually impaired than non-visually impaired people (Bigham and Cavender, 2009). For their research they used 162 persons, of whom 89 were visually impaired, and popular website audio CAPTCHA implementations. Their research illustrated that audio CAPTCHAs are difficult to solve. Only 43% of users with visual impairments were able to answer an audio CAPTCHA at the first attempt and only 39% of other users. Moreover, it should be noted that visually impaired users took at least twice as long. Yet nearly half of users (47%) failed to respond correctly to an audio CAPTCHA after 3 attempts. This is a somewhat unexpected result, since one would anticipate that audio CAPTCHA challenges would be more appropriate for visually impaired persons.

E. Bursztein et. al. (Bursztein et al., 2010) conducted an extensive study on the ability of people to solve existing CAPTCHAs, as well. Regarding audio CAPTCHAs, they studied eight of the most popular implementations. The conclusions that emerged from their study were a) the period for listening and solving a CAPTCHA is certainly excessive (averaged over 25 seconds), b) the percentage of users who took second or third attempts, because the previous attempt was wrong, it exceeded 50%, and c) people who were not native English speakers had major problems in solving the CAPTCHA and therefore the success rate was reduced by more than 20%.

Y. Soupionis and D. Gritzalis (Soupionis and Gritzalis, 2010) classified the audio CAPTCHA attributes, evaluated the current popular audio CAPTCHA implementations and developed a new audio CAPTCHA for VoIP environments. The CAPTCHA were classified based on their attributes into four categories: (a) vocabulary, (b) background noise, (c) time, and (d) audio production. Afterwards, the evaluation took place where the CAPTCHAs were utilized on the above mentioned attributes. The evaluation process was based on the fact that CAPTCHAs must be easy for human users to solve, easy for a tester machine to generate and grade, and hard for a software bot to solve. Therefore, the final evaluation was made by two means; namely, by user tests (~60 persons) and by two bots configured to solve audio CAPTCHAs. The evaluation process proved that a) the current CAPTCHA implementations are not adequate, meaning that every implementation is either too easy or too difficult to be solved by both users and bots, and b) the implementation attributes of some CAPTCHAs, like long vocabulary (> 8 characters) and language requirements (native vs. non-native English speakers), affects negatively the users' success rate (~40%) in most cases.

In conclusion, these experimental studies present that solving audio CAPTCHA is particularly problematic. The above results indicate that there is a need and the potential to create more appropriate challenges that will allow for fewer problems in solving the CAPTCHA challenges. In order to achieve more efficient CAPTCHA challenges, one needs to remove the connection between the difficulty of CAPTCHA solving for humans and for bots respectively. This disconnection will allow for the creation of challenges that are more appropriate and consequently easy for humans to solve, without reducing the difficulty for bots.

In this work, we propose adapting the CAPTCHA challenges to the person's characteristics. Utilizing these characteristics we expect to provide challenges that are easier to solve for humans, without aiding the bots at the same time, or even making the challenges harder for bots. The focus of this work is to provide the mechanism that will choose and deploy adaptive audio CAPTCHAs. This presupposes that it is feasible to generate such audio challenges. We consider this task of generating the adaptive audio CAPTCHAs an interesting but also viable requirement, which however is outside of the scope of this work.

Taking into account the person's characteristics during CAPTCHA generation, brings about privacy concerns that need to be addressed. There has been significant progress on the subject of accountable privacy preserving services during the past decade. The privacy-preserving techniques used in the proposed system are closely related to accountable anonymous communication systems (Diaz and Preneel, 2007), anonymous credential systems (Camenisch and Pfitzmann, 2007) and electronic identity cards (Poller et al., 2012, Deswarte and Gambs, 2010). Using cryptographic tools, all these systems aim at providing their functionality while protecting users' privacy. Similarly, we utilize existing cryptographic primitives to create a privacy-preserving personalized CAPTCHA system. Using certificates, the system allows users to prove attributes about themselves, without revealing their identity.

2 Concepts and Architecture

2.1 Problem Statement and solution overview

The selection of an appropriate CAPTCHA challenge that successfully distinguishes between human users and bots is a challenging task, since generic challenges often pose difficulties to human users as well. Lowering the difficulty level of the challenges consequently allows for bots to solve them as well. Therefore, we believe that a method is needed to tailor CAPTCHA challenges closer to the human user, without lowering the difficulty level for bots. The goal of this work is offering such customized CAPTCHA challenges. Overall, this work does not aim at making CAPTCHA challenges generally easier, rather, it aims at proposing a method to create more appropriate, effective and fair challenges for the users.

The ability for challenge adaptation protects the users from unauthorized use of their accounts (hijacking) and attempts to impersonate them. Additionally, the combination of certificates and the CAPTCHA test, protects the VoIP system from the use of stolen certificates and from users that misuse their certificates for making SPIT calls. Therefore, this work does not aim at making the CAPTCHA test obsolete by using the user certificates. Using the certificates, callers can assert that they have certain characteristics, but this is also verified during the CAPTCHA test.

2.2 Discrimination issues concerning CAPTCHA challenges

Traditionally, problems of accessibility to IT applications and services were addressed by adapting their design to the so-called "average or typical user", a feature that actually does not exist. CAPTCHAs had been initially recommended and implemented without taking user needs and (dis)abilities as well as accessibility issues into consideration. However usability and accessibility are seriously affected by currently most used visual CAPTCHAs as they pose problems to blind, visually impaired or dyslexic users and, in general, users with disabilities (May, 2005).

Indeed, a CAPTCHA test, which cannot be solved due to the mental or physical disabilities, language, genre, age or even cultural differentiation of the challenged user, interferes with her communication rights (access to and use of IT means) and raises significant discrimination issues (Basso and Bergadano, 2010). A person who cannot respond to a CAPTCHA test on the ground of a disability is discriminated both as subscriber/user of a communication service and as personality, who faces barriers to her communicative interaction with other persons. The use of such a SPIT detection mechanism impairs her right to free communication and consequently the legally embedded right to receive and impart information (Marias et al., 2007).

The United Nations Convention on the Rights of Persons with Disabilities identifies accessibility as one of its general principles and states that States Parties shall take appropriate measures to promote access for persons with disabilities to new information and communications technologies and systems. In many countries including US and the EU countries, legislation in place has to ensure that products and services are accessible and usable by as many users as possible, including people with disabilities and aged persons.

In order to face and/or limit the discriminatory effect of CAPTCHA tests, they should be accessible and usable by all human users, regardless of their cognitive, physical, sensory or cultural characteristics (Fritsch et al., 2010). Apart from having the possibility to switch to a new challenge involving different sensory abilities, the introduction of personalized profiles that take into account the users' diversity, needs and preferences is not only at the core of the inclusive design approach (Fritsch et al., 2010) but seems to be an appropriate response to discrimination concerns.

This approach engages the user in the definition of challenges and tests and considers her needs and abilities. At the very centre of personalized services is the user profile or personal profile, which is a collection of the user preferences and data. However the personalized CAPTCHA service must be designed in a way that allows the user to use and have access to it, while determining when and who should get knowledge about her preferences and /or disability status (Fuglerud et al., 2009). This requirement derives both from the dignity principle and the privacy rights of individuals.

By definition personalized profiles, i.e. in our case personalized CAPTCHAs, require collection and use of personal data (age, education level etc) that may also be sensitive (medical data, disabilities, cultural/religion), affecting the privacy rights of the concerned users. By referring to privacy in this paper we focus on the right of the individual to be in control of the information concerning her so as to formulate conceptions of self, values, preferences, goals and to protect her life choices from public control, social disgrace or objectification.

2.3   PrivCAPTCHA Architecture

In this Section the components of the proposed architecture are described.

2.3.1   Cryptographic Building Blocks

In order to achieve the privacy-preserving attributes of the proposed system (PrivCAPTCHA), we use the cryptographic building blocks presented in the following paragraphs. These building blocks are used as high-level components of our architecture and therefore it is not needed to examine closely the internals of their functions.

2.3.1.1   Anonymous Credentials

Anonymous credentials (Camenisch et al., 2011) allow users to acquire credentials and demonstrate them without revealing their identity. Using the private credential system described in (Camenisch and Pfitzmann, 2007), individuals can use different unlinkable pseudonyms, based on the same credential issued by an identity provider. The private credential system can also provide certified attributes by the identity provider, for the individual to selectively reveal attributes (e.g. their age range, based on their date of birth).

2.3.1.2   Portfolio: a data structure where certified user data is stored.

The user's certificates are stored in a personal portfolio that resides at the owner's side, similar to the one proposed in (Tasidou and Efraimidis, 2012). The contents of a user's portfolio include:

- Certificates of demographic data and personal characteristics, e.g., age, education level, disabilities.

- Certificates of successful CAPTCHA tests issued by the CAPTCHA service. This transaction history can be used to provide further evidence to the CAPTCHA server that the user is human and non-malicious.

2.3.2   Entities

The entities that participate in the proposed system are the following:

The Identity Provider (IDP). Users obtain their credentials by the IDP, by registering an identifier (e.g. their social security number) and a pseudonym P. The IDP is considered a trusted third party (like a passport authority) that retains the user information together with their pseudonym. The IDP does not need to be a single entity, but can be a distributed service, to achieve better service availability and enhanced security.

The User (U). In our system the users are considered the VoIP service users. All can act both as callers and callees. When acting as callers, their portfolio information can be used to receive personalized CAPTCHA challenges as illustrated in Figure 1.

The CAPTCHA server, that also acts as a verifier for the Anonymous Credential System. Moreover, the CAPTCHA server automatically generates the CAPTCHA challenge, evaluates the provided answer and sends back whether the answer is correct or not.

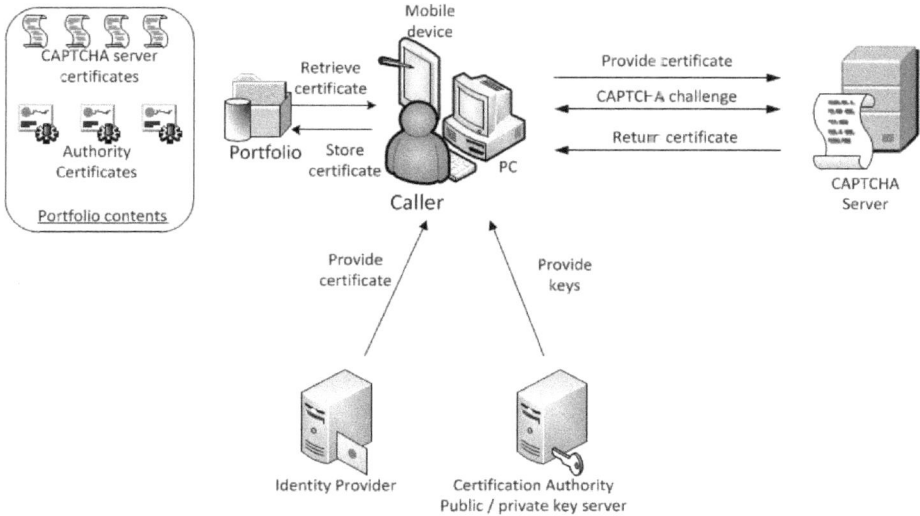

Figure 1: PrivCAPTCHA architecture

The entities of the PrivCaptcha system and their interactions are shown in Figure 1. The user's profile is stored at the personal portfolio residing at the user's side. After registering with an IDP and obtaining her certificates, the caller can prove some attributes to the CAPTCHA server and receive personalized CAPTCHA challenges.

According to the proportionality principle the IDP retains no more data than that strictly required to serve the personalized CAPTCHA service. The IDP entity combines the retained data with a pseudonym in order to protect the identity of the user and it is not allowed to reveal or to use this data for any other purpose , with the exception of law enforcement purposes if and to the extent that is provided by the respective law. The proposed architecture provides personalized and effective VoIP CAPTCHAs while preserving the privacy and communication rights of the user.

2.4   System Functionality

In this section we will describe the general functionalities of the system. Due to lack of space we will not describe the use of the cryptographic tools in detail. Besides, we adhere to the descriptions of the primitives as proposed by their authors.

The main functions of the system are the following:

1. Providing certificates and proving attributes to the CAPTCHA system. After acquiring her credentials by the IDP the user (U) can begin using them to prove attributes to CAPTCHA services in order to receive personalized challenges. U needs to prove to the CAPTCHA service that she has a valid credential C, which verifies that U has a certain attribute.

The verification mechanism is based on efficient zero knowledge proofs, like the ones used in (Camenisch and Pfitzmann, 2007).

2. CAPTCHA generation and outcome. After receiving and verifying the user's certificate, the CAPTCHA service generates the appropriate CAPTCHA challenge, according to the user characteristics. The main two characteristics that the CAPTCHA server takes into account are:

   Language requirements. Based on the users' native language, the CAPTCHA server can provide the appropriate challenge. A certificate on the user's ethnicity can be used to determine the language parameter. As the language itself is not as sensitive as the ethnicity information, language selection can be supported without the need for a certificate, allowing users to select languages other than their native. We believe that the language choice will not diminish the system's effectiveness regarding false positives (i.e., bots will not be able to solve the tests more easily).

   Age. The age of the user affects his ability to answer correctly difficult challenges. If the user is too young or too old, then the CAPTCHA challenge should be adapted to contain less characters or words to be recognized.

   Additional user characteristics that can be considered are mental and physical disabilities (e,g, mobility issues, visual impairment), education level (e.g, literacy) and learning disabilities (e.g. dyslexia).

3. CAPTCHA server certificates. Upon successful completion of a CAPTCHA challenge, the CAPTCHA server sends the user a certificate, attesting that this user did make a legitimate communication. This certificate is inserted into the portfolio and can be used later from U to prove that she is a previous legitimate user to the CAPTCHA service.

The above functionalities are prone to misuse and malicious behavior on the part of the user. In the following Section we address the main issues that have been identified for the system.

2.5 Incident response requirements

Designing a system on a user-centric driven security basis requires that the system is robust in a sense that the user is not significantly exposed during a security failure. In the proposed system we have identified the following aspects and requirements for incident response and escalation procedures in an event of a security failure.

Tolerance to false positives. We can in principle consider that false positives carry a minor security impact. The event of the case of a bot answering successfully the audio CAPTCHA challenge will be detected by the destination/callee and the service should maintain the facility for the callee to report/redirect the call for further logging and analysis. Responding to false positives is a good example of active user participation in the security process. Regarding CAPTCHA server certificates, in case of false positives, a revocation procedure can be followed upon receipt of the callee report.

Tolerance to false negatives. Rejecting a legitimate call request after a failed audio CAPTCHA attempt is an event of major significance. Therefore the underlying security parameters are expected to be set on a level where the false negatives are minimised despite the drop in security. Besides, giving priority to user acceptance over security is part of the user-centric system design practice. In addition, there needs to be a continuous evaluation similar to vulnerability assessment practices. More specifically, as a security administrator must be informed and proactively search for new vulnerabilities affecting the system she is responsible to manage, the audio CAPTCHA engineer must keep the system up to date with the state of the art research in order to maintain the optimum level of security versus user acceptance.

Tolerance to CAPTCHA server certificate misuse. The certificates provided by the CAPTCHA server can be (un)intentionally misused by users to exploit the system. In case of reported malicious use of these certificates, revocation methods (Camenisch et al., 2011) can be examined.

Correlate system failures with SPIT results. A threat management system should be implemented and the audio CAPTCHA service should be placed in the wider system security context in order to identify threat vectors that may target the CAPTCHA but also to exploit the system as a whole.

Reputation management. Reputation mechanisms introduce a number of security issues and should these become part of the audio CAPTCHA service, reputation misuse should be addressed with well defined escalation procedures. The proposed system can adopt published procedures and controls for reputation management.

3   Discussion and Conclusions

In this work, we propose a user-centric, privacy-preserving VoIP CAPTCHA adaptation method. The PrivCAPTCHA architecture combines existing cryptographic technologies, which provide strong privacy guarantees, utilized under a new context. The proposed system aims at providing an improved CAPTCHA service that is more appropriate for and fair to the human users and overall more effective. Although high-level descriptions of the system functionalities are provided in this work, it would be interesting to implement them within the VoIP protocol. The introduction of cryptographic tools is expected to introduce a computational overhead into the audio CAPTCHA application. We expect this overhead to be tolerable for modern computational platforms possibly combined with appropriate performance optimization techniques. Moreover, although we mainly consider CAPTCHA challenges for VoIP calls in this work, we believe that this idea can be useful for providing a general mechanism for CAPTCHA adaptation according to the users' characteristics.

4   Acknowledgements

This work was performed in the framework of and funded by the GSRT/CO-OPERATION/SPHINX Project (09SYN-72-419) (http://sphinx.vtrip.net). A. Tasidou   P.   S.   Efraimidis   and   V.   Katos   are partially supported by national (ETAA) funds.

5   References

Ahn, L. v., Blum, M. and Langford, J. (2004), "Telling humans and computers apart automatically", Communications of the ACM, Volume 47, Number 2, pp. 56-60, ISSN: 0001-0782.

Basso, A. and Bergadano, F. (2010), "Anti-bot Strategies Based on Human Interactive Proofs", in Stavroulakis, P. and Stamp, M. (Eds.) Handbook of Information and Communication Security, Springer, Berlin / Heidelberg, ISBN: 978-3-642-04117-4.

Bigham, J. P. and Cavender, A. C. (2009), "Evaluating existing audio CAPTCHAs and an interface optimized for non-visual use", Proceedings of the 27th international conference on Human factors in computing systems, Boston, MA, USA, 2009, pp. 1829-1838.

Bursztein, E., Bethard, S., Fabry, C., Mitchell, J. C. and Jurafsky, D. (2010), "How good are humans at solving CAPTCHAs? a large scale evaluation", Proceedings of the 2010 IEEE Symposium on Security and Privacy, Oakland, California, USA, 2010, pp. 399-413.

Camenisch, J., Dubovitskaya, M., Kohlweiss, M., Lapon, J. and Neven, G. (2011), "Cryptographic Mechanisms for Privacy", in Camenisch, J., Fischer-Hübner, S. and Rannenberg, K. (Eds.) Privacy and Identity Management for Life, Springer, Berlin / Heidelberg, ISBN: 978-3-642-20317-6.

Camenisch, J. and Pfitzmann, B. (2007), "Federated Identity Management", in Petković, M. and Jonker, W. (Eds.) Security, Privacy, and Trust in Modern Data Management, Springer, Berlin / Heidelberg, ISBN: 978-3-540-69861-6.

Deswarte, Y. and Gambs, S. (2010), "A Proposal for a Privacy-preserving National Identity Card", Transactions on Data Privacy, Volume 3, Number 3, pp. 253-276, ISSN: 1888-5063.

Diaz, C. and Preneel, B. (2007), "Accountable Anonymous Communication", in Petković, M. and Jonker, W. (Eds.) Security, Privacy, and Trust in Modern Data Management, Springer, Berlin / Heidelberg, ISBN: 978-3-540-69861-6.

El Sawda, S. and Urien, P. (2006), "SIP Security Attacks and Solutions: A state-of-the-art review", Proceedings of the 2nd International Conference on Information & Communication Technologies: From Theory to Applications, Damascus, Syria, 2006, pp. 3187-3191.

Fritsch, L., Fuglerud, K. and Solheim, I. (2010), "Towards inclusive identity management", Identity in the Information Society, Volume 3, Number 3, pp. 515-538, ISSN: 1876-0678.

Fuglerud, K., Reinertsen, A., Fritsch, L. and Dale, Ø. (2009), "Universal design of IT-based solutions for registration and authentication", Tech. report: DART/02/09, Norwegian Computing Center, Oslo, 2009.

Hernández-Castro, C. J., Ribagorda, A. and Hernández-Castro, J. C. (2011), "On the Strength of Egglue and Other Logic CAPTCHAs", Proceedings of the International Conference on Security and Cryptography (SECRYPT), Seville, Spain, 2011, pp. 157-167.

Marias, G. F., Dritsas, S., Theoharidou, M., Mallios, J. and Gritzalis, D. (2007), "SIP Vulnerabilities and Anti-SPIT Mechanisms Assessment", Proceedings of 16th International Conference on Computer Communications and Networks, Honolulu, Hawaii, USA, 2007, pp. 597-604.

May, M. (2005), "Inaccessibility of CAPTCHA. Alternatives to visual Turing tests on the Web.", http://www.w3.org/TR/turingtest/, (Accessed November 2005).

Poller, A., Waldmann, U., Vowe, S. and Turpe, S. (2012), "Electronic Identity Cards for User Authentication; Promise and Practice", IEEE Security & Privacy, Volume 10, Number 1, pp. 46-54, ISSN: 1540-7993.

Soupionis, Y. and Gritzalis, D. (2010), "Audio CAPTCHA: Existing solutions assessment and a new implementation for VoIP telephony", Computers & Security, Volume 29, Number 5, pp. 603-618, ISSN: 0167-4048.

Tasidou, A. and Efraimidis, P. S. (2012), "Using Personal Portfolios to Manage Customer Data", in Garcia-Alfaro, J., Navarro-Arribas, G., Cuppens-Boulahia, N. and De Capitani di Vimercati, S. (Eds.) Data Privacy Management and Autonomous Spontaneous Security, Springer, Berlin / Heidelberg, ISBN: 978-3-642-28878-4.

Walsh, T. J. and Kuhn, D. R. (2005), "Challenges in securing voice over IP", IEEE Security & Privacy, Volume 3, Number 3, pp. 44-49, ISSN: 1540-7993.

On the User Acceptance of Graphical Passwords

A.M. Varka and V. Katos

Information Security and Incident Response Unit, Department of Electrical and
Computer Engineering, Democritus University of Thrace, Greece
e-mail : a.varka@ihu.edu.gr; vkatos@ee.duth.gr

Abstract

In this paper we investigate options for improving the user acceptance of graphical passwords.
We conducted a survey with a dual purpose. Firstly, we explored the users' reluctance to adopt
graphical passwords. Secondly, we treated the graphical password authentication process as a
biometric. By doing this, we proposed a distance metric to compare the user authentication
response with the right answer. Although we inherited some drawbacks of biometric
authentication, we established that this tradeoff in security can result in higher user acceptance
and therefore can be used in contexts and environments with flexible security policies.

Keywords

Picture password, ANOVA tests.

1   Introduction and motivation

With the prevalence of smart phones and pervasive, portable computing devices in
general, a wide range of user authentication technologies has been proposed, most of
them relating to knowledge-based authentication, with biometrics (Clarke and
Furnell, 2007; Furnell et al. 2008) being the runner up. The constraints on the user
interface especially in the earlier portable devices encouraged the research in novel
knowledge based authentication technologies such as graphical passwords, which
encompass a wide variety of approaches (Suo et al., 2005).

Although there is some level of consensus in the literature that graphical passwords
may exhibit high usability and user acceptance (Eljetlawi and Ithnin, 2008), the
claim is based upon the hypothesis that users are more effective in memorizing
pictures over numbers. However if we also consider the order/sequence of images
against the sequence of numbers as part of the correct answer, we intuitively may
agree that sequence of numbers are easier to remember than sequence of pictures. As
there is no evidence to our knowledge that specifically puts this hypothesis into test,
the objectives of this paper are twofold. First, we confirm by empirical means that
the sequence of pictures accounts for the first level of mistakes a user may make
during a user authentication process. Second, in order to improve user acceptance we
propose the adoption of authentication practices inspired by biometric based
approaches, and more specifically to introduce tolerance sensitivity levels to
potential failures and reduce false negatives. In addition we present some side
conclusions and findings relating to general behavioural aspects on graphical

passwords future graphical authentication design initiatives may take into consideration.

2 Related work and methodology

A direct consequence of treating graphical authentication by biometric terms is the need to establish a distance metric between an observed (or a user provided) value and the correct data. The metric would need to maintain properties that are desirable and suitable for the underlying context. In the case of picture based authentication, we considered a number of published distance metrics, used in string and number comparison. The rationale behind this is the fact that the user's answer is encoded as a number sequence and comparison is performed on this basis. Candidate distance metrics involved the Levenshtein distance (Levenshtein, 1966) and the Jaro–Winkler distance (Winkler, 1990). Considering that the hypothesis required testing must differentiate between (a) the right answer, (b) correct identification of all pictures but in a wrong order, and (c) a wrong answer, we can see that the published distances are not suitable, as there can be distance collisions between cases (b) and (c). Consider for example the answer strings *abced* and *abcef*. If the right answer is *abcde* then for both cases the Levenshtein distance will be equal to 2. Therefore the need to construct a suitable distance capable of not only discriminating between the two cases above, but also consider (b) *closer* to the right answer arose.

The requirement for considering case (b) close to the right answer can be captured in the following proposed metric. Let *a* be the answer during the user's registration and *b* the answer provided during the user's authentication attempt. Then we define the distance from the correct answer, the nominal metric $d(\cdot,\cdot)$ such that:

$$d(a,b) = \begin{cases} 0, \text{iff } a = b \\ 1, \text{for correct pictures, mistake in order} \\ k+1, \text{for } k \text{ mistakes} \end{cases}$$

The validation of the metric was performed with the following hypothesis:

H_{10}: *Users who have a positive attitude toward graphical passwords make fewer mistakes.*

More specifically, assuming that users behave rationally we intuitively expect that when exposing users to a picture based authentication test, those users who are more positively positioned toward this technology will make fewer mistakes, or alternatively, the users that make more mistakes will be in principle more frustrated by the technology.

3   Empirical work and findings

We conducted a survey consisting of a graphical/picture password simulation at log-in devices, in order to measure user's experience on graphical password usage, and a questionnaire, to assess the acceptance of graphical passwords.

Initially the participants were requested to create and register their own passwords. For that reason, a registration environment was simulated. The simulation was written in PHP programming language and was hosted on a publicly available site, for the period the survey was running. The picture options were based on Jansen's (2004) technique 'picture password 1' – individual selection. This approach results to a password space of S possible combinations where

$$S = A \cdot (M \cdot N)^X$$

and A denotes the number of different thematic categories, M,N the table (grid) dimensions, and X the number of password digits (pictures). Jansen used a password space of $A \cdot (5 \cdot 6)^5$. In our example, for usability reasons we made the following changes:

- 4x5 templates (20 pictures in total per category) were used instead of 5x6 (30 pictures in total per category)

- Only 5 thematic categories were available to the participants: sea, flowers, animals, art, faces.

This yielded a password space of 16 million passwords. All pictures were retrieved through Google, by using various key words, related to the thematic categories, such as sea, flowers, cats, dogs etc. Every picture corresponded to a number (from 1-20), so a 5-picture password was stored in the equivalent "passwords" database as a 5 digit password.

The questionnaire consisted of 21 questions and the duration of the survey was 16 days, from 10/5/2010 to 26/5/2010. The users were informed for this survey via a personal Facebook account and emails, with the exhortation to forward this survey. There was an explanatory message that accompanied the site address, containing information about text, pin and graphical passwords, the advantages and the problems of each method and a brief explanation of the procedure that users should follow. The instructions also brought to the users' attention that the order of the selection is also important. This message was sent to approximately 1300 people, from 16 to 55 years old, and about 270 valid results were collected and used in the analysis.

3.1   The survey and test

Figure 1 shows the first form of the registration phase where the users were requested to submit their thematic preference.

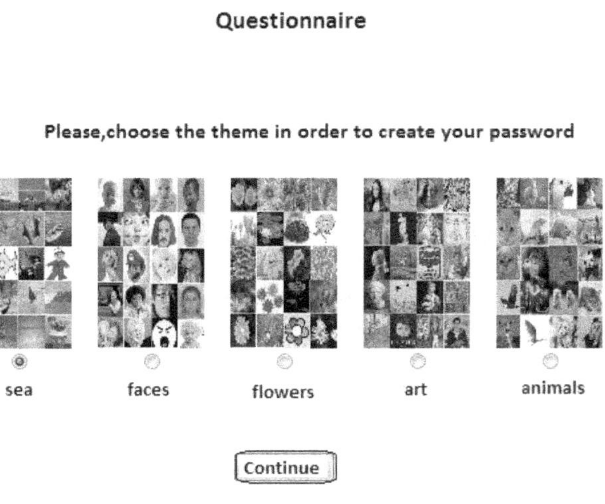

Questionnaire

Please,choose the theme in order to create your password

sea   faces   flowers   art   animals

Continue

Figure 1: The initial registration screen

Upon submission, the registration proceeded by presenting a 4x5 template (Figure 2)and the users were asked to create their own graphical password. It was mentioned that they should pay attention to the password selection and try to memorize not only the pictures, but the sequence as well.

Choose password

Please choose 5 pictures, which will be your personal password.After that,press the button continue

Continue

Figure 2: The specific theme selection

Upon completion of the registration, the user was directed to the questionnaire procedure, at first with some demographic questions and then generic questions on text, pin and graphical passwords, the usage of them in their daily routine and their awareness on graphical passwords.

Approximately halfway through the procedure, the participants were requested to authenticate with their password. They were presented with the 5x4 template with the same thematic category they choose during the first step. In order to be more accurate and realistic and to avoid any shoulder surfing problems at this stage, the pictures were in a different order.

Repeat the password

Try to repeat the password you created, by picking the right pictures at the **exact** order

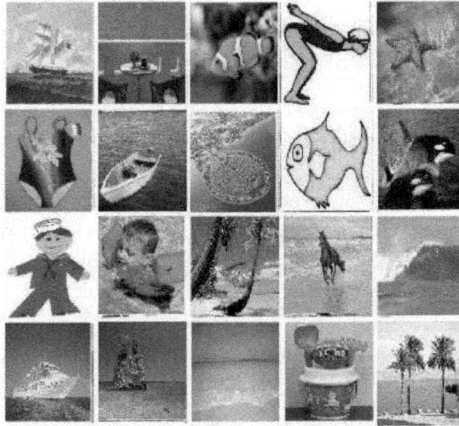

Continue

Irrespectively of their answer (correct or not), users continued and completed the questionnaire.

All passwords (both those created at the first step and the authentication attempts of), were stored in the database as 5 digit representation together with the questionnaire answers and were compared, correlated and analysed.

3.2   Demographics and user profile

The 270 valid questionnaires corresponded to persons of whom 57% were women and 43% men, whose majority (84%) was between 21-30 years old.

The majority of participants have 1-3 passwords (49%), and they use passwords consisted of numbers and letters (66%).

They are wary of the security of their passwords, so the majority create passwords of more than 7 digits that consist mostly of letters and characters. The users do not reveal their passwords, although they do not change them often.

In Figure 3 we show the breakdown of the users ways of memorising their passwords and their intention to use graphical passwords instead of text passwords.

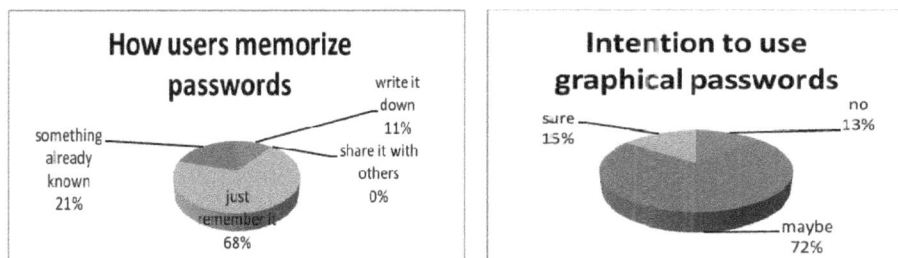

Figure 3: User practices on text passwords and intention to use graphical passwords

Lastly, Figure 4 summarizes the comparative evaluation and ranking of the three types of passwords (text, PIN, graphical). The 3 methods were evaluated and ranked in terms of aesthetics, security, time consumption, ease of memorizing and friendliness. We initially performed χ^2 homogeneity test in order to determine whether the five distributions were the same (H_0). The result was $\chi^2(4)=27.864[p=0.000]$ revealing that the distributions were not the same (hence rejecting H_0).

We also performed z-tests to identify whether there are statistically significant differences in the preferences for the attributes with close answers. For a 5% significance level (a=0.05), we obtained that there is no difference between the friendliness of text and graphical passwords (z=1.07<1.96), no difference between the security of text and graphical passwords (z=1.85) and no difference between graphical and text passwords with respect to time consumption. However, although the friendliness is higher for graphical passwords compared to pins (z=2.78), there is no differentiation between text passwords and pins (z=1.81) in terms of friendliness.

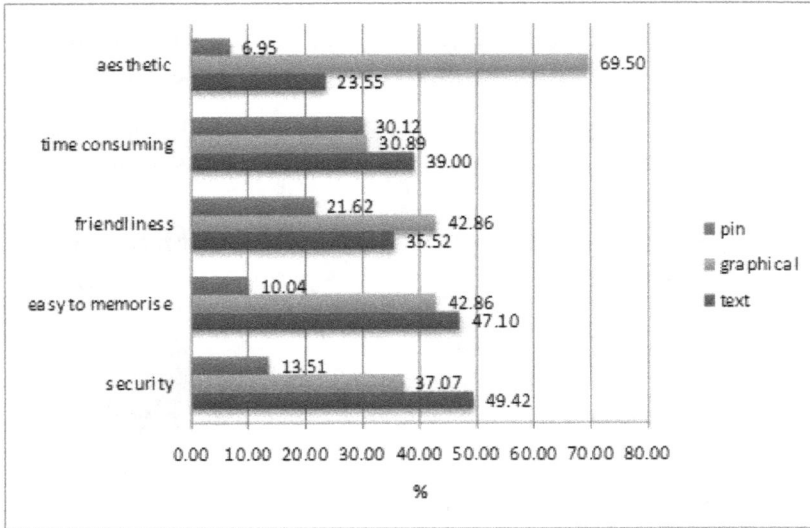

Figure 4: User evaluation of text, graphical passwords and PINs

3.3   Results

With a high degree of confidence, we see that users who had positive attitude to graphical passwords or they probably use them in the future, had also less mistakes comparing to them who had a negative attitude or were negative to future use (Table 1). Hence, the H_{10} hypothesis which we intuitively expect to hold is also statistically confirmed. We use these result as a basis for validating and consequently accepting the proposed distance metric.

Position_gp	N	Subset for alpha= 0.05	
		1	2
Positive	117	.8291	
Skeptical	135	1.1481	1.8750
Negative	16		
Sig.		**.247**	**1.000**

Use_of_gp	N	Subset for alpha= 0.05	
		1	2
Yes	40	.6000	
Maybe	187		1.1123
No	35		1.2571
Sig.		**1.000**	**.548**

Table 1: Anova grouping results for H_{10} (1=right answer(low d), 2=wrong answer(high d)).

Another test reinforcing H_{10} was on the ability to remember graphical and text passwords (Table 2). Nonsurprisingly, those who find difficult or more difficult to remember graphical passwords, made more mistakes. In addition, participants who write down their passwords in order to remember them made more mistakes than the others.

remembering _gp	N	Subset for alpha= 0.05	
		1	2
Very easy	35	.4857	
Easy	92	.7717	
Neutral	84	1.3214	1.3214
Difficult	41	1.4146	1.4146
Very difficult	14		1.7143
Sig.		.053	.392

remembering	N	Subset for alpha= 0.05	
		1	2
Something known	56	.8036	
Just remember it	184	1.0380	
Write it down	30		1.6000
Sig.		.319	1.000

Table 2: Anova grouping results: ease of remembering graphical passwords and practice of remembering text passwords (1=no or less mistakes, 2=more mistakes).

Having confidence on the distance d meeting the representation condition, we run some further tests with the results captured in Table 3. There is differentiation on mistakes by education level. Quite surprisingly, although younger participants were expected to make fewer mistakes, in fact they made most of them. There was also significance on the differentiation of mistakes by theme. Users who choose art and faces made fewer mistakes than the others.

education	N	Subset for alpha = 0.05	
		1	2
High School	80	,8250	
Master	59	1,0508	
Bachelor	124	1,1532	1,1532
Student	7		1,8571
Sig.		,401	,055

theme	N	Subset for alpha = 0.05	
		1	2
Art	55	,8545	
Faces	87	,9080	
Animals	74	1,0541	1,0541
Flowers	13	1,3077	1,3077
Sea	41		1,5366
Sig.		,159	,119

Table 3: Anova grouping results: education and theme discrimination (1=no or less mistakes, 2=more mistakes).

4   Conclusions and future work.

We argue that user acceptance of graphical passwords can be improved if these are treated as biometric type of passwords. This is because although there is a positive attitude toward using graphic passwords, people tend to get the order of pictures wrong, rather than the actual pictures themselves. We defined a distance metric which considers the event *<right answer, wrong order>* to be closer to the *<right answer>*, whereas *<one mistake>* or higher number of mistakes are further away from the right answer. This convention was tested against user's attitude, expectations and behaviour and provided statistically significant results. As such, in applications where the authentication level can be decreased within acceptable levels, the optimum trade-off between security and user acceptance would prioritize to accept the right selection of passwords irrespective of order, as opposed to one or more mistakes. This will have a significant impact on false negatives, whereas the false positives can be filtered out or further reduced by adding a second layer of authentication, depending on the policy.

The distance metric can be further refined by increasing the granularity in the order of the pictures selection. Provided that the user responds with the right pictures but in the wrong order, distances like number of permutations needed to get to the right answer can be considered. However, these will also need to be validated to get the most suitable metric.

As for the survey results, a number of interesting conclusions were reached. The majority of participants realize the importance of having a strong password, with more than 7 digits and combining letters and numbers. Also, none of them reveal or share their passwords to others. However, they do not change them often and have the same passwords for different applications. In addition, it was clear that there is a strong correlation between the successful application of graphical passwords and users' attitude on remembering passwords. Those who found difficulties in memorizing them, made more mistakes. More mistakes were also made by the users who use ways to remember their passwords other than learning them by heart. Nevertheless, the majority of them have a positive attitude toward graphical passwords and they will probably use them in future.

For future research a better security level assessment model is considered. It was noticed that some categories and pictures were more popular than others, creating the so-called hotspots, resulting to a non-uniform distribution of graphical password selection. This means that the effective password search space can be smaller than the actual space. Research on factors leading to a distribution closer to the uniform distribution is also planned for future work.

5   References

Clarke, N., Furnell, S. (2007). "Advanced user authentication for mobile devices", *Computers & Security*, 26, pp. 109-119

Eljetlawi, A. M., Ithnin, N. (2008). "Graphical Password: Comprehensive study of the usability features of the Recognition Base Graphical Password methods". *Third 2008 International Conference on Convergence and Hybrid Information Technology*, pp. 1137-1143.

Furnell, S., Clarke, N., Karatzouni, S. (2008). "Beyond the PIN: Enhancing user authentication for mobile devices". *Computer Fraud & Security*, August, pp.12-17.

Jansen, W. (2004). "Authenticating Mobile Device Users Through Image Selection". *Data Security*.

Levenshtein, V. 1966, Binary codes capable of correcting deletions, insertions and reversals. In Soviet Physics Doklady, Vol. 10.

Suo, X., Zhu, Y., Owen, S. (2005). "Graphical Passwords: A Survey". *Proceedings of Annual Computer Security Applications Conference*, pp. 463-472.

Winkler, W. E. (1990). "String Comparator Metrics and Enhanced Decision Rules in the Fellegi-Sunter Model of Record Linkage". *Proceedings of the Section on Survey Research Methods*, pp. 354–359.

Multi-Factor Authentication Using Hardware Information and User Profiling Techniques

A. Alnajjar and H. Janicke

Software Technology Research Laboratory, Faculty of Technology, De Montfort University, Leicester, UK
e-mail: P08041453@myemail.dmu.ac.uk, heljanic@dmu.ac.uk

Abstract

This paper presents a multi-factor authentication approach that extends traditional username-password authentication with hardware and user behaviour profiling techniques. The aim of the approach is to improve the reliability of authentication by computing trust and confidence scores against user profiles. Based on the level of trust, the access control mechanisms may then choose to (un-)lock certain functions or even classify the access as an attack and redirect the user to a honey-pot to gather additional information about the attacker that can be used for a trace-back. The novelty of the approach is that it observes the correlation between users' behaviours and their hardware usage as implicit verification procedures to discriminate the usage of the user-name and password entry.

Keywords

Authentication, Profiling, Multi Factor Authentication, Keystroke Recognition.

1   Introduction

In this paper, we present a simple password mechanism that is augmented with additional profiling techniques to create a form of multi-factor authentication. Using password keys in authentication alone is not reliable due to the user's inability to keep them confidential; in addition passwords are often prone to dictionary or rainbow-table attacks as well as the ease with which social engineering techniques can obtain passwords. To address some of these issues our approach integrates with the traditional password authentication by using Hardware Manufacture Serial Part Numbers (*HMSPNs*) to consider the user environment. This approach can be easily integrated in existing password based authentication schemes. Additional factors that are considered in the authentication process are the users' behaviour in providing the user-name and password and the user-profile in using a variety of hardware. Both factors do not require the user to memorise or otherwise keep additional secret information.

Three widely accepted authentication principles base the identification of a user on a) something the user has, b) something the user knows or c) something the user is or does. Multi-factor Authentication Mechanisms employ various techniques, often drawing on several of the above principles to establish a user's identity. For example the credit card payment system (Kumar et al. 2008) with biometric authentication proposes to employ fingerprint verification with a credit card in a multi factor authentication scheme, combining principles a) the card and c) the fingerprint. However, such an approach would require the installation of additional equipment, thus increasing the cost. The use of additional devices such as fingerprint readers typically also adds to the time taken for authentication which affects the user acceptability for the system. Given that fingerprints can be spoofed with relative ease (Ihmaidi et al. 2006) the overall gain in security is questionable. Indeed most current approaches to multi-factor authentication (Naji et al. 2011, Trevathan et al. 2009) are typically expensive and difficult to deploy and directly affect the usability of the system, as they prolong the authentication process. The approach presented in this paper avoids the impact of the additional authentication procedures on usability and does not require extra devices to be deployed to end-users. The key novelty of the presented approach is that it integrates profiling information with established user-name/password authentication and can be used to discriminate valid use of password credentials against misuse by an attacker, without complicating the authentication process or incurring large extra costs.

This paper is organized as follows. Section 2 reviews related work of authentication techniques, HMSPNs usage in access control and tracking approaches. Section 3 illustrates our authentication approach and the main system activity. Next, the paper provides a sample analysis scenario using our approach to profile hardware and user activity. After that, the paper provides our system architecture and implements a prototype to show a case study. Finally, the paper evaluates the initial results of our technique and presents the conclusion of the paper including achievements and future work.

2   Related works

Naji et al. (2011) enhance the security of an access control system using handwritten signature. Their system employs the static and dynamic features of the signature to make a decision about the identity of the signature through a combination of matching statistical models to analyse them. Handwritten signature processing and extracting their features is time consuming and requires dedicated hardware at the user-end.

Card readers are an additional level of hardware security is using one-time password (*OTP*). The chip on the client "user" card generates the *OTP*, with the caveat that the account is rendered inaccessible if the card is lost or stolen. This additional challenge-response mechanism over a separate channel removes the need for security questions to confirm transactions and helps preventing fraud. However, this mechanism requires additional accessories and increases deployment cost (Ravi et al. 2004). With the ubiquity of mobile phones, sending *SMS* text or voice messages that include one-time password (*OTP*) is in effect extending the card-reader approach. Here the mobile phone is considered a secure channel, albeit with the increasing connectivity of smart-phones this cannot be considered as independent as the original card-reader. Whilst this approach reduces the cost in deploying readers it adds additional costs on the extra communication channel and requires these channels to be accessible to the user (Zomai & Jsang 2010).

Hardware has been used to facilitate authentication for a long time. The idea is that users register devices (e.g. based on their MAC address) so that the devices are authenticated rather than their users. Examples of devices are storage media drivers such as hard disc drives HDDs. Each storage media has a unique HMSPN as an identifier product that can be used in profiling (Patowary 2009). This HMSPNs are already actively used for identification, albeit they can be modified at a firm-ware level and thus are susceptible to spoofing, e.g. Microsoft products send product and hardware identifiers during the activation process (Microsoft Corporation 2010). This hardware information provides the opportunity to profile the users' computing environment.

Based on the hypothesis that different people type in uniquely different typing measure, there are many basic methods (Shanmugapriya & Padmavathi 2009, Attila M 2007, Bergadano et al. 2002, Clarke & Furnell 2007, Yu & Cho 2004, Lee & Cho 2007) used to analyse keystroke typing.

Keystroke dynamics can be used as behavioural biometrics for users. It is an analysing technique for users typing behaviour when keyboard input is monitored (Obaidat & Sadoun 1999). However, if keystroke is not combined with particular keystrokes keys such as the password, it is insufficient to be an objective authentication factor (The et al. 2010). The keystroke approach is mostly characterised by the error rates in these following precision cases based on False Acceptance Rates (FAR), False Rejection Rates (FRR) and Equal Error Rates (EER) (Monrose & Rubin 2000).

Statistical (Bergadano et al. 2002) and *neural network* (Gunetti & Picardi 2005) techniques are the main two analysing keystroke approaches. Additionally, there are some combinations of both approaches (Monrose et al. 1999, Clarke & Furnell 2007). Statistical approaches compare a reference set of typing characteristic of specific user with test set of typing characteristic of the same user. Neural Networks use historical data that come from first usage, and then uses this data model to expect the result of new test or classify a new observation (Yu & Cho 2004, Lee & Cho 2007).

Some drawbacks have been exposed by other research (Lv & Wang 2006) that inhibits keystroke from real word applications. One research experiment provided the possibility of using modified keyboards that were based on a pressure sensor to recognize users keystroke (Lv & Wang 2006). This method requires specific keyboards that thus adding again additional cost to the user. To reduce the environment factor that may affect user behaviour in keystroke, Maxion & Killourhy (2010) explored a number pad input using a single finger. They tried to discriminate users typing style, FAR and FRR scope suggests a low level of surety that authentication using keystroke biometrics might be possible in this particular environment.

162

3   Our Approach

Our approach combines hardware identification with key-stroke biometrics, yielding a multi-factor authentication approach in which user biometrics can be correlated with the hard-ware that is used during the login process. The analysis of user-typing patterns on particular hardware by monitoring the keyboard inputs can visualize the significant pattern difference between the users. This correlation is reducing the FAR and FRR rates and allows the approach to be deployed throughout heterogeneous systems which are comprised of various hardware interfaces.

The key contribution of our approach is to improve the login-procedure by determining the level of trust of the user without additional cost or making the deployment of the solution overly complex. Thus, the key objective of our approach is developing a novel technique for the analysis of HMSPNs properties and patterns that are captured in the computational model. After that, an approach is developed for modelling the dynamic behaviour of the user. Then, user profiles based on analyzing and modelling users' behaviour to develop a new technique for the analysis of Internet services based on these profiles is formulated.

Hardware parts have a particular history in *HMSPNs* usage. Some computer hardware parts have not changed and have been used by the manufacturer for a long time. Therefore, every computer device has a history tracking over the time of its *Life cycle*. Thus, each computer hardware part has a particular track of usage from manufacture phase to destruction. First, if a user has been dealing with a device for every log in procedure for access control applications for a long time, this user will be more familiar with this hardware and has a particular behaviour when using it. Therefore, the user has a particular pattern scope that will be used with this hardware. Consequently, if the number of users of a particular hardware is increased, our authentication approach has to recognize the way these users behave when using this hardware, even if they use the same user-name and password. Of course, the sharing of accounts is bad practice, but still commonly encountered in both domestic and corporate environments over which the service provider has little influence. For example in Figure 1 Bob and Colin used John's hardware, however they have different behaviours in dealing with same hardware. Consequently, our approach has to find the different attribution of users' behaviour when they use the same hardware and the same user-name and password. Ultimately, our authentication technique maps user environment hardware in order to demonstrate the user behaviour in previous pattern usage in particular hardware.

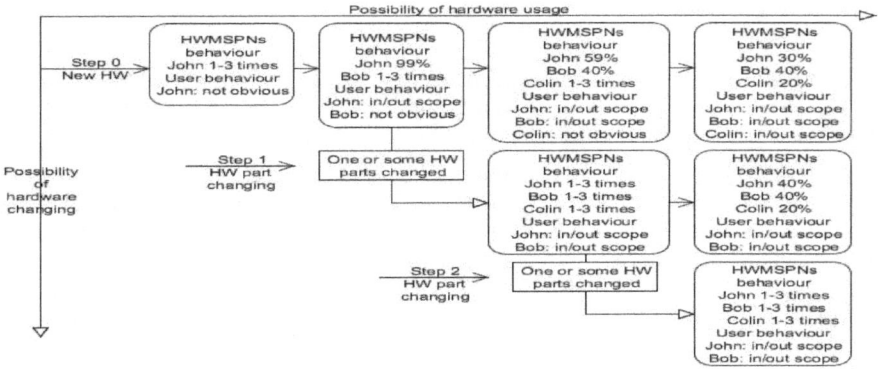

Figure 1: Hardware and users behaviour *Life Cycle*

The hardware *life cycle* in Figure 1 explains conceptually the hardware usage that supports the learning of user behaviour depending on a particular hardware configuration. However, the hardware parts may change over the time, resulting at configuration that is distinct to previous login attempts by their users. One example is the use of a tablet. E.g. the login may be typed on the touch screen or (after attaching the tablet to a docking station) through a physical keyboard. These changes in hardware configurations affect user profiling. \Step 1" and \Step 2" in Figure 1 reflect changing the hardware parts which change user environment. Therefore, the system has to recognise hardware changing and compare user's hardware at every login.

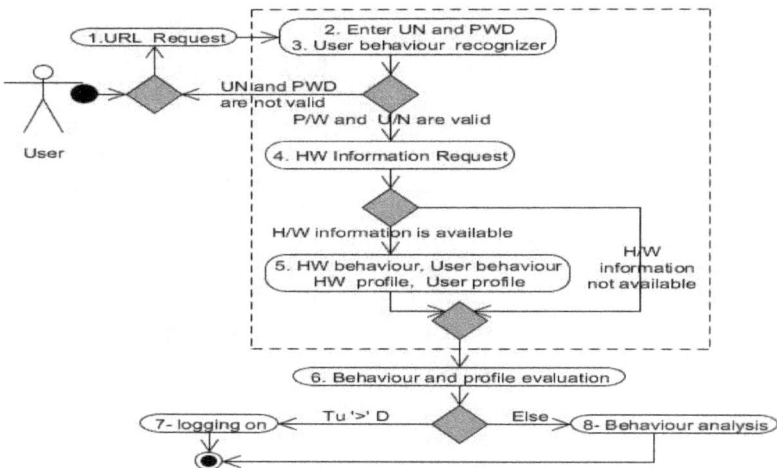

Figure 2: System Overview

3.1 System Overview

Our authentication system uses two components in the login procedure. Whilst the user u is typing his/her user-name and password, our first component captures the current user behaviour (b_u) by calculating the keystroke (both key-press and release) speed when username and password are typed. The second component collects the HMSPNs, which make up the user's current hardware configuration (c_u). As the user or other security software installed on the client machine can prevent the gathering of hardware information, we consider this to be optional information.

However, if this information is not provided it has a detrimental effect on the accuracy of our mechanism, as the hardware profiling information is coupled with the selection of the user-profile for keystroke recognition. If the user provides access to the hardware profile, the system begins to analyse and compare the current hardware configuration (c_u) with the established profile of that user ($\_c_u$) to determine their similarity. If the user has used the current hardware before, the system computes the similarity between the current keystroke behaviour of the user (b_u) and the behaviour that has been recorded against this hard-ware configuration previously ($\_b_{u;cu}$). If the current hardware configuration is not known, the component will try to match bu against all known keystroke behaviours for that user bu; indiscriminate of the hardware configuration, which obviously reduces the effectiveness of this mechanism.

Given that the username and password checks are successfully passed, the system will compute out of the similarity between the hardware configuration and their profiles, and the associated keystroke behaviour similarity to their profiles two levels of trust. If only keystroke information is available, only one level of trust is being used in the following.

Given that usernames and passwords are not very secure, the hardware similarity test reflects the idea that hardware that has been previously used by the same user increases the likelihood of the user being genuine, as this rules out attacks in which passwords have been observed by shoulder surfing or rainbow table attacks. In addition, uncharacteristic use of hardware, e.g. the use of a company PC that has regularly been used during office-hours for 6 month and from which now an access is taking place at 2am in the night, is flagged up by a low trust-level in the hardware.

Similarly the key-stroke behaviour is evaluated, linked against the used hardware configuration (c_u) if available. The system will authenticate normally if the username and password are correct and a threshold in both levels of trust is passed. If the username and password do not match, the authentication is considered failed. If the username and password are correct, and only a low level of trust is established based on the hardware or keystroke behaviour the system can be configured to adapt to the level of trust. E.g. the authentication can be failed; the user can be authenticated with reduced privileges such as only being able to view his account details; the system can increase the threshold for an intrusion detection system that identifies fraudulent activity based on the transactions that are undertaken or even redirect the user to a honey pot trapping system to explore if the user is a hacker using a spoofed user-name and password. In an e-banking context, this could e.g. mean to delay the transactions and attempt to contact the user via a different channel such as email or phone. Figure 2 shows the basic steps in the system operation.

3.2   System Activities

Our technique depends on the matching of the current hardware configuration cu against the users' previous hardware behaviour $\_c_u$ and the associated user behaviour b_u against the previous user behaviour $\_b_u$ as part of the login procedure.

On the client side, the login prompt performs three data-collection functions. Firstly the username and password is collected in the traditional way. Secondly the keystroke behaviour of the user is gathered during the typing of the username and password. Functions like auto completion and provision for copy & paste are turn off, as they would effectively disable the recognition of the keystroke behaviour. Thirdly the login prompt will attempt to collect the hardware configuration from the user's operating system. This may require the user to white list the login software or the server address from which the login prompt is loaded.

On the server side the authentication module will first check the username and password hash against the stored credentials. If this is successful, the additional two components hardware recogniser and keystroke recogniser are invoked to further qualify the login request, thus providing additional scrutiny.

3.2.1   Hardware Recogniser

The hardware trust is computed by the hardware recogniser, which matches the current configuration against previously used hardware configurations for the same user based on the parts' serial numbers. This process takes into account the previous usage patterns of the user over time and also considers other aspects such as concurrent usage of the same hardware configuration or hardware parts in different login processes, which e.g. could indicate a spoofing attack. Essentially there are three key results that can are generated by this component:

1. Trust level based on usage of hardware configuration
2. Known configuration for use in behaviour recognition (or matching configuration)
3. Cross login analysis for attack detection.

The trust level is computed against the history of previous login-attempts and their associated hardware configurations $\_cu$ which is essentially drawn from the sequence of previous successful login attempts by this user.

Figure 3: Hardware history

Figure 3 shows a simplified example. Every node on the timeline represents a successful login by the user in question. The used hardware configuration is depicted by the shape of the node, e.g. the empty circle could be the user's office machine, the square a mobile device, the filled circle a user's home computer. The first step is that the hardware is checked whether it has been used before, ie. it is known to the system, which is important for the keystroke recogniser in subsequent checks. This establishes a baseline trust for the access in case the hardware is known.

Secondly the access is viewed in the context of the other accesses (left neighbours), the time and the day of the access. We chose metrics based on time of day and day in week as these constitute the majority of repetitions we have encountered. We currently do not support more complex analysis of these events in our prototype, but envision the use of neural networks or support vector machines to establish a behaviour baseline against which the check can be performed. Based on the "fit" of the hardware configuration used in the login the trust level is adjusted.

Thirdly, the hardware recogniser maintains a cache of recent and current login activities over the entire user-base. If there is a current login from the same hardware configuration or configurations that share particular hardware components there is a chance that one of the logins is fraudulent and based on spoofed hardware information. It is known that some hardware manufacturers fail to provide unique serial numbers for their components. For the known cases we have a black-list of manufacturer ids which are excluded from this analysis step. A collision here reduces the trust level established by the hardware recogniser.

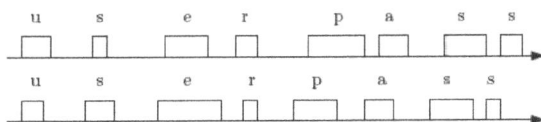

Figure 4: Keystroke patterns

#	1	2	3	4	5	6	7	8	9	10	11
$u\downarrow$	10	8	9	11	15	8	10	8	11	6	12
$u\uparrow$	10	8	9	11	15	8	10	8	11	6	12
$s\downarrow$	6	5	7	8	9	6	7	6	8	5	8
$s\uparrow$	15	10	10	12	20	12	11	10	12	12	10

Table 1: Keystroke profile $\_b_{u;cu}$ against hardware configuration c_u

3.2.2 Keystroke Recogniser

The keystroke recogniser takes the current keystroke pattern entered by the user (b_u) and matches it against the previous recorded keystroke behaviour of that user using that hardware ($\_b_{u;cu}$).

The keystroke pattern is characterised by the press and release times of the keys that are used in entering the username and password and is gathered on the client side. Figure 4 gives an example of such a pattern.

Our current prototype only considers the press and release times as a proof of concept and does not use other correlations between subsequent keypress events that may be further improving the accuracy. As the contribution of this paper is not a novel keystroke recognition scheme, but the integration of multiple approaches this mechanism can be replaced with more sophisticated techniques such as specific keystroke recognition (Shanmugapriya & Padmavathi 2009).

We currently build a trust-metrics based on whether the current keystroke pattern fits the users profile information, where the profile is created based on the previous user inputs. For example with respect to Figure 4 the first keyevent is the time the letter \u" is pressed. Previous logins e.g. recorded the times in Table 1 which forms the user profile, depicted in Figure 5. Currently the system looks at the variance of the data and the percentile into which the current keystroke pattern falls with respect to each of the keypress and release events and computes an accumulated trust level over all events contained in the keystroke pattern. In comparison to e.g. specific keystroke recognition (Obaidat & Sadoun 1999) this is a very simple approach which we plan to refine in the future.

3.3 System analysis

Our technique depends on the matching of the current hardware configuration cu against the user's previous hardware behaviour _cu and the associated user behaviour bu against the previous user behaviour _bu as part of the login procedure. On the client side, the login prompt performs three data-collection functions. Firstly the user-name and password is collected in the traditional way. Secondly the keystroke behaviour of the user is gathered during the typing of the user-name and password. Functions like auto completion and provision for copy & paste are turn off, as they would effectively disable the recognition of the keystroke behaviour. Thirdly the login prompt will attempt to collect the hardware configuration from the user's operating system. This may require the user to white list the login software or the server address from which the login prompt is loaded.

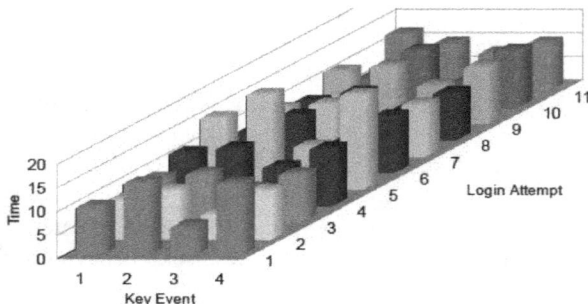

Figure 5: Keystroke Profile

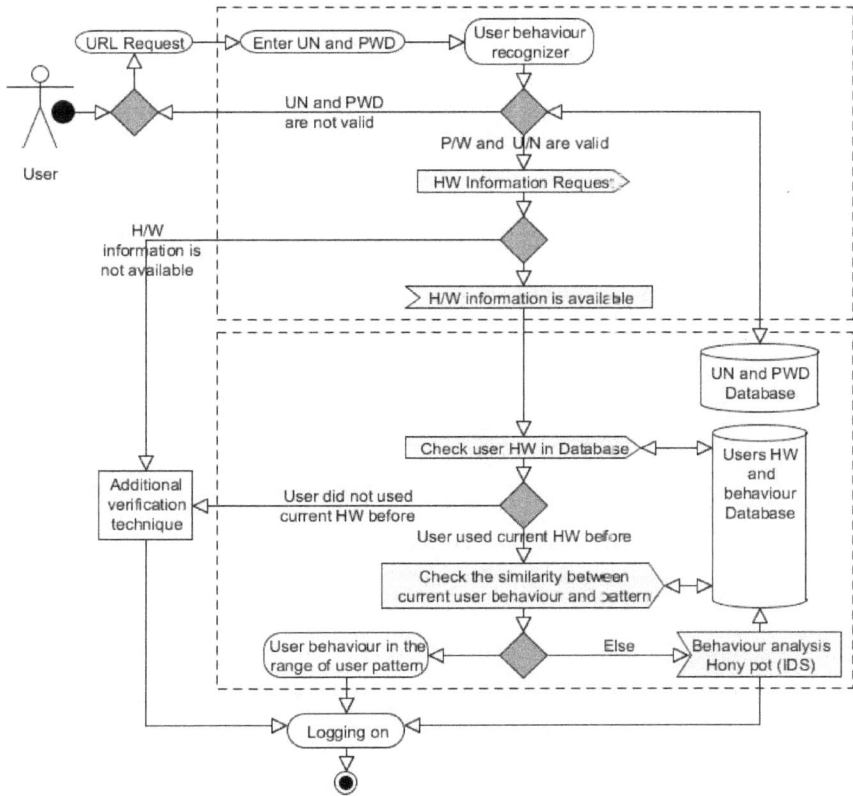

Figure 6: Flow chart

4 Case Study

We developed a simple Java application to apply our approach in the login process as an implicit login procedure. Every log in, our system captures user behaviour using a keystroke function to calculate users typing speed and response time among the keys of the user-name and password. The user-name and password contains characters and number. Then, when the user typed his/her valid user-name and password the system collects three parts of *HMSPNs*. These parts are the BIOS device number, MAC address number and the hard disk drive number. After that, the system recognizes if the user used current hardware before and if and to what extend the hardware was used by other users. Figure 7 shows the percentage of hardware usage and user pattern stamp by determining how the current user behaviour is related to previous usage patterns. In this case study, system improves the ability of observe the levels of trust to reflect the different bu when the user uses different hardware. In this scenario, the user performed 200 succeeded log in using username and password as key to log. However, the user used two devices representing two different hardware environments.

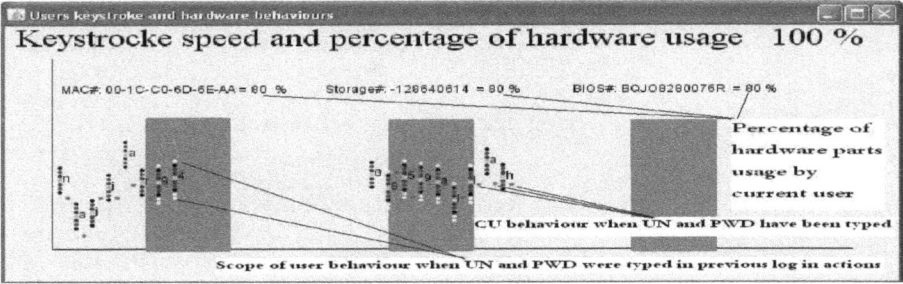

Figure 7: *HMSPNs* usage c_u and profile $\_b_{u;cu}$ against keystroke pattern b_u.

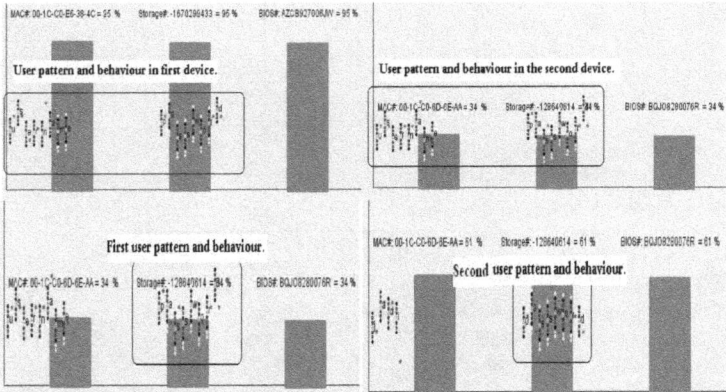

Figure 8: LEFT top: *HMSPNs* usage cu and profile $\_b_{u;cu}$ against one user uses two hardware. RIGHT bottom: HMSPNs usage cu and profile $\_b_{u;cu}$ against two users use same login information (password) in one hardware

In the second scenario, two users used same hardware and a shared password for 100 successful logs in attempts. The system recognised the effect of the hardware in user keystroke behaviour. In addition, the system compared between the users depending on their familiarity with the hardware. This recognition comes from the hardware trust.

4.1 Trust

For all login attempts that provided the correct username and hardware we computed the hardware trust based on the hardware configuration that was used in the login attempt against the previously encountered hardware. We computed the trust-level based on precedences, ie if the hardware was encountered previously we assigned a baseline trust of 40% for previously encountered hardware. Based on whether there was a precedent of that hardware being used on that day in the week, within that hour of the day and after the use of the previously used hardware configuration, we added additional 20% as these occurrences increased our confidence. If the hardware configuration (or part thereof) was used concurrently in another login process we subtracted 60% from the trust-level.

For all three hardware configuration that were used in the case-study, we recorded 100 keystroke patterns to build up the profile. The trust was computed by calculating the deviation from the mean for each key-event (key- press and release) of the profile against the standard deviation as a percentage value. The overall keystroke trust was then computed as the mean of the individual percentage values.

We overall set relatively low thresholds for both trust levels, and proceeded with the authentication when both trust levels exceeded 70%. If only one of the trust-levels exceeded the threshold, an additional verification question was asked from the user. If this was answered correctly the authentication was considered successful. If both trust levels fell below the threshold, the login attempt was considered unsuccessful and the user was returned to the login prompt. We considered a maximum of three unsuccessful login attempts before the account was blocked.

The recorded profile information was only updated after a successful login attempt. This means that even if behaviour or hardware usage changed over time the system was able to adapt, in most cases via the provision of an additional security question. We did not yet integrate actual honey-pots into our system or linked it to the access control system.

5   Conclusion & Future Work

The availability of hardware information can enhance authentication mechanisms. The work presented in this paper shows that by capturing a wide range of statistics it is possible to perform an analysis of hardware and user behaviour. In this paper we considered keystroke as a biometrics. By combining password based authentication with hardware profiling and keystroke recognition we provided a multi-factor authentication scheme that does not require additional devices to be deployed and adds little cost to the deployment of the authentication system.

The paper reviewed related work on authentication approaches and their limitation as a motivation for this approach. We then presented our approach and showed how the additional data can be collected on the client side and what data needs to be collected. We then described in detail the server-side and the functioning of the hardware-recogniser and the keystroke recogniser and how their interaction improves the accuracy of keystroke recognition as a more specific profile can be maintained depending on the hardware that is used.

We implemented our prototype system using basic profiling techniques for the analysis and presented a trust- model that takes into account the hardware usage and the user behaviour when entering his/her username and password. The prototype is of course a proof of concept that shows that the techniques can be combined and that their combination yields a positive influence on the accuracy of the detection. In the future we will refine the individual techniques and adopt e.g. keystroke recognition approaches that have been presented in (Obaidat & Sadoun 1999). We provided a java-based prototype implementation of our authentication system and presented a small case-study as a proof of concept for our work.

In the future we will refine the profiling techniques used in our authentication framework and are looking at implementing techniques based on neural networks or support vector machines. We also investigate the use of the profile information in attack attribution, as the hardware profiles can provide indication about (fraudulent) users.

In addition, we will look at geo-spatial information and its integration in the hardware recogniser. The idea is that successive logins from different geographical areas are not plausible and can indicate fraudulent activity. In this line of investigation we will also actively deploy honey-pots to further identify behavioural traits of the user. This information can then be used two folds: a) to provide additional attribution information about the attacker; b) to retrospectively authorise the actions performed if the user is deemed to be genuine.

6   References

Attila M, Zoltn B, L. C. (2007), `Strengthening passwords by keystroke dynamics', IEEE . www.knt.vein.hu

Bergadano, F., Gunetti, D. & Picardi, C. (2002), `User authentication through keystroke dynamics.' ACM Trans. Inf. Syst. Secur. 5(4), 367-397. http://dblp.unitrier.de/db/journal-s/tissec/tissec5.html/BergadanoGP02

Clarke, N. L. & Furnell, S. (2007), `Authenticating mobile phone users using keystroke analysis.', Int. J. Inf. Sec. 6(1), 1-14. http://dblp.unitrier.de/db/journals/ijisec/ijisec6.-html/ClarkeF07

Gunetti, D. & Picardi, C. (2005), `Keystroke analysis of free text.' ACM Trans. Inf. Syst. Secur. 8(3), 312-347. http://dblp.unitrier.de/db/journals/tissec/tissec8.html/GunettiP05

Ihmaidi, H.-D., Al-Jaber, A. & Hudaib, A. (2006), Securing online shopping using biometric personal authentication and steganography', in `Information and Communication Technologies, 2006. ICTTA '06. 2nd', Vol. 1, pp. 233-238.

Kumar, D., Ryu, Y. & Kwon, D. (2008), A survey on biometric fingerprints: The cordless payment system, in `Biometrics and Security Technologies, 2008. ISBAST 2008. International Symposium on, pp. 1-6.

Lee, H. & Cho, S. (2007), 'Retraining a keystroke dynamics-based authenticator with impostor patterns'. Computers and Security 26(4), 300-310. http://dblp.uni-trier.de/db/journals/compsec/compsec26.html/LeeC07

Lv, H.-R. & Wang, W.-Y. (2006), `Biologic verification based on pressure sensor keyboards and classifier fusion techniques', Consumer Electronics, IEEE Transactions on 52(3), 1057 - 1063.

Maxion, R. & Killourhy, K. (2010), `Keystroke biometrics with number-pad input, in `Dependable Systems and Networks (DSN), 2010 IEEE/IFIP International Conference on', pp. 201-210.

Microsoft Corporation (2010), `Microsoft office activation/registration privacy statement'. http://office.microsoft.com/en-us/help/HP010069531033.aspx

Monrose, F., Reiter, M. K. & Wetzel, S. (1999), `Password hardening based on keystroke dynamics`, in J. Motiwalla & G. Tsudik, eds, `ACM Conference on Computer and Communications Security', ACM, pp. 73-82. http://dblp.uni-trier.de/db/conf/ccs/ccs1999.html/MonroseRW99

Monrose, F. & Rubin, A. D. (2000), `Keystroke dynamics as a biometric for authentication`, Future Gener. Comput. Syst. 16, 351-359. http://dl.acm.crg/citation cfm?id=338350.338359

Naji, A. W., Housain, A. S., Zaidan, B. B., Zaidan, A. A. & Hameed, S. A. (2011), `Security improvement of credit card online purchasing system', Scientific Research and Essays 6(16), 3357-3370.

Obaidat, M. S. & Sadoun, B. (1999), `Keystroke dynamics based authentication, in In &quot; Biometrics`. Personal Identification in Networked Society". A.Jain, R.Bolle, S.Pankanti (Eds', Kluwer Academic Publishers, pp. 213-229.

Patowary, K. (2009), `How to interpret hard disk model numbers'. http://www.instantfundas.com/2009/02/howto-interpret-hard-disk-model.html

Ravi, S., Kocher, P. C., Lee, R. B., McGraw, G. & Raghunathar, A. (2004), `Security as a new dimension in embedded system design`, in S. Malik, L. Fix & A. B. Kahng, eds, `DAC', ACM, pp. 753-760. http://dblp.uni-trier.de/db/conf/dac/dac2004.html/RaviKLMR04

Shanmugapriya, D. & Padmavathi, G. (2009), `A survey of biometric keystroke dynamics: Approaches, security and challenges', CoRR abs/0910.0817. http://dblp.uni-trier.de/db/journals/corr/corr0910.htmlabs-0910-0817

Teh, P. S., Teoh, A. B. J., Tee, C. & Ong, T. S. (2010), `Keystroke dynamics in password authentication enhancement', Expert Syst. Appl. 37, 8618-8627. http://dx.doi.org/10.1016/j.eswa.2010.06.097

Trevathan, J., McCabe, A. & Read, W. (2009), `Online payments using handwritten signature verification`. In S. Lati_, ed., `ITNG', IEEE Computer Society, pp. 901-907. http://dblp.uni-trier.de/db/conf/itng/itng2009.html/TrevathanMR09

Yu, E. & Cho, S. (2004), `Keystroke dynamics identity verification - its problems and practical solutions.' Computers and Security 23(5), 428-440.http://dblp.uni trier.de/db/journals/compsec/compsec23.html/YuC04

Zomai, M. A. & Jsang, A. (2010), `The mobile phone as a multi otp device using trusted computing`, in Y. Xiang, P. Samarati, J. Hu, W. Zhou & A.-R. Sadeghi, eds, `NSS', IEEE Computer Society, pp. 75-82. http://dblp.uni-trier.de/db/conf/nss/nss2010.html/ZomaiJ10

Analysis of Characteristics of Victims in Information Security Incidents: The Case of Japanese Internet Users

K. Hanamura[1], T. Takemura[1,2] and A. Komatsu[1]

[1] Security Economics Laboratory, IT Security Center Information-Technology Promotion Agency, Japan
[2] The Research Institute for Socionetwork Strategies, Kansai University, Japan
e-mail: k-hanamura@ipa.go.jp; a084034@kansai-u.ac.jp; a-koma@ipa.go.jp

Abstract

In this article, we investigate the attributes of victims in information security incidents for the purpose of reducing the damages. Information-Technology Promotion Agency (IPA) conducted the Internet (Web-based) survey titled "Survey of awareness toward information security incidents" whose targets are the Japanese Internet users at October 2010. By using micro data collected from the survey, we employed multinomial logit regression analysis. As a result, we find some common factors affecting the all experience of the incidents, and factors affecting the specified incidents. Accordingly, we suggest some policies for reducing the damages.

Keywords

Information Security Awareness, Security Measures, Behavioral Science, Security Economics

1. Introduction

Among the Internet rapidly spreads in households, the users can enjoy the various Internet service such as online shopping or financial transaction. On the other hand, we have some information security threats such as virus and phishing. Therefore, the situation in which users are complicit in malicious attackers without the recognition is one of problems. For reducing or preventing the damage caused by the threats, it is effective to introduce information security software into their computers as part of information security measure. But, recently it is pointed out that it is fatigued for the Internet users to continue to implement the measure (Japan Information Security Policy Meeting, 2008) Hence, it is expected to clarify what kinds of measures are effective when individuals use the Internet in safety.

In the current article, to tackle the issue, we analyze micro data collected from the survey. We clarify factors affecting the presence or absence of experiencing the information security incident damage and suggest the effective measures and policies.

This article consists of the following sections. Next section introduces some related works. In section 3, we briefly explain our framework, summary of the survey and the data which we use in the analysis. In sections 4, we show the results of our analyses and suggest some measures and policies. Finally, we summarize this article and show the future work.

2. Related works

A research called "Security Economics" has been highlighted as one of solving key problems. Security Economics is a frontier research on information security approaching from combining knowledge from psychology and computer science with framework of traditional economics. Actually, according to the information stored in "Science Direct" of ELSEVIER, the number of articles on information security with keywords such as "economics" and/or "game theory" has been increasing after 2004 (Mochinaga et al, 2009). Hereinafter, we introduce a part of previous works on information security related to Economics and behavioural science. Anderson et al show the details about the research trend of Security Economics (Anderson and Moore, 2009).

From the perspective of economics, we have empirical studies with regarding to incentive to invest in information security (Tanaka et al., 2005), or studies for estimating economic loss caused by information security incidents (Cavusoglu et al., 2004) and some facts are shown. Tanaka et al. confirm that Japanese firms optimally invest in information security according to the middle degree of vulnerability by using optimum information security investment model that Gordon and Loeb suggest. Cavusoglu et al. confirm that stock price had fallen about 2.1% within a couple of days according to data on information security troubles occurred in the period 1996-2001. They mentioned that by clarifying the amount of economic loss caused by the incidents, we can discuss the level of investment in information security and these amounts lead to incentive to implement the measure. Additionally, in some empirical studies with regarding to the effectiveness of investment in information security (Liu et al., 2007; Hagen et al., 2008; Takemura et al., 2009), it is important to not only introduce the information security technologies but also implement management measures including the attention-seeking toward the Internet users, and information security education and training. In these studies from perspective of economics, because the targets of researches are workers, companies and/or countries, home Internet users such as housewives, househusbands and students are not included. However, housewives, house husbands and students have occasion to become victims in information security incidents, too.

On the other hand, various knowledge from behavioural science apply to issues which do not be treated in traditional economics and new facts are discovered. Komatsu et al. have continued to analyze various issues with regarding to information security in Japan since 2008 (Sugiura et al, 2008). For example, about issues on promotion of implementing the information security measures, they regard the gaps with regarding to implementing the measures as a social dilemma, and they build a decision-making model based on game theory (Komatsu et al., 2010). In addition, they challenge to investigate the factors that stimulate to implement the measures by applying persuasion theory in social psychology (Komatsu et al., 2011).

Because these studies relate to individual's decision-making on implementing the information security measures, it is indispensable to capture their characteristics in the analysis. From the perspective of behavioural science, we can clarify the structural relations between their characteristics and the outcome of their behaviours scientifically.

3. Framework

3.1. Multinomial logit regression model

The multinomial logit model is one of the most commonly used methods for analyzing unordered categorical response variables in social science research. In this article, by a multinomial logit regression equation we build our model with regarding to experiencing the information security incident damage. Here, we briefly explain our model according to Powers and Xie (2008).

The multinomial logit model can be viewed as an extension of the binary logit model to situations where the outcome variable has multiple unordered categories. In this article, we assume the case of three categories (1: the individual encounters information security incident, 2: the individual do not encounter the incident, and 3: the individual do not know whether or not he encounters the incident), we can write the probabilities as

$$P_1 = 1/(1 + \exp[\mathbf{xb_2}] + \exp[\mathbf{xb_3}]),$$

$$P_j = \exp[\mathbf{xb_j}]/(1 + \exp[\mathbf{xb_2}] + \exp[\mathbf{xb_3}]), \quad j=2 \text{ and } 3$$

whether $\mathbf{b_2}$ and $\mathbf{b_3}$ denote the covariate effects specific to the second and third response categories with the first category as the reference, and $\mathbf{x}$ is a vector of factors affecting the probability. Note that the equation for P_1 is derived from the constraint that the three probabilities sum to one. That is, $P_1 = 1-(P_2+P_3)$. When the first category is used as the reference category (or baseoutcome), all parameter estimates of $\mathbf{b_j}$ are in reference to it. Changes of the reference category result in apparent changes in normalized parameter estimates but not in substantive results.

Odds and odds-ratios play an important role in multinomial models. In the multinomial logit model framework, the odds between categories j and 1 are simply

$$P_j/P_1 = \exp[\mathbf{xb_j}], \quad j=2, 3.$$

The log-odds, or logit, is then a linear function of $\mathbf{x}$:

$$\log(P_j/P_1) = \mathbf{xb_j}, \quad j=2, 3.$$

A positive coefficient for an explanatory variable (x_k) implies an increased odds of observing an observation in category j rather than category 1 as x_k increases. On the other hand, a negative coefficient implies that the chances of being in the baseline category are higher relative to category j as x_k increases. By using this equation, above mentioned, we can discuss which measures they can use to reduce the risks. At the same time, we can evaluate the risk that each individual faces.

3.2. Design of survey

In Japan, IPA has continued to conduct the survey titled "Survey of Awareness toward Information Security Incidents (IPA survey)" since 2006. Mission of IPA is mainly to provide information regarding information security as public service. So, the purpose of IPA survey is to grasp the PC-users' recognition degree of the Internet threats and their implementation status of the information security measures. This survey includes various question items including recognition degree and understanding of the Internet threats. If you are interested in the survey sheet and outcome of IPA survey, you can access to the IPA's website (http://www.ipa. go.jp/security/products/products.html). In our analysis, we use data collected from IPA survey which conducted at 25 October to 1 November 2010 (abbreviated, IPA survey 2010). The subjects of IPA survey 2010 are Japanese home Internet users who are over 15 years old. In addition, the sample in this survey is arranged by age-group and gender (Internet Association Japan, 2007). The number of the sample is 5,019.

We employ the Internet survey as survey method. This survey method inescapably contains certain weakness of the data collection. The Internet survey is well-used in the field of marketing, but has the statistical bias. Unfortunately, this statistical problem has not been solved yet. It is suggested that it is not necessarily undesirable to use the Internet survey if the aim of the survey is to offer judgmental materials that are useful for individual and organizational decision makings (The Japan Institute for Labour Policy and Training, 2005). Of course, we must discuss the accuracy of the survey. In near future, we will need to expand the scope of the utilization of the data from the Internet survey. Wherein, we interpret and analyze data from population of Japanese registered with the Internet survey company. In addition, we presume that these collected data are useful for reasonable analysis.

3.3. Question items used in analysis and processing data

(1) Experience of Information security incident damage in the past year

We ask questions with regard to whether you experienced information security incident damage in the past one year. As information security incident damages, we pick up 1) the computer virus infection, 2) phishing, 3) billing fraud, and 4) monetary damage by spoofing, shown in Table 1. In addition, we have 899 respondents (about 18% of all respondents) who answer that they do not know whether to experience the damage.

	Experience	Not experience	I do not know
1) Computer virus	572	3,548	899
2) Phishing	131	3,989	899
3) Billing fraud	343	3,777	899
4) Spoofing	89	4,031	899

Table 1: Experience of information security incident damage

(2) Information security awareness

Information security measures are roughly classified by technical and non-technical ones. The former are to install the information security software, update security patch, or use the rooter, and the latter are to relate to promote the moral, or sustain high information security awareness.

We ask questions with regard to implementation of information security measures and information security awareness. Unfortunately, with regarding to implementing information security measures we cannot judge whether the technical measures are implemented before they are victims in information security incidents. On the other hand, information security awareness (non-technical measures) cannot continue to be enhanced at once even if they are victims in information security incidents. Thus, in this article we only focus on information security awareness. By employing the principle component analysis, we create indicator of information security awareness using three question items as follows: 1) I do not open the attached file of suspicious e-mail, 2) I do not access the suspicious website, and 3) I download neither the file nor software from unfamiliar website.

It is said that a first step of implementing information security measure is to collect the information voluntarily and to make a useful choice from the various information. On the contrary, it is not easy to collect the information. We ask questions with regard to the issue on collecting information. In the question has the following options: 1) I have unknown word on information security, 2) the content of information security is difficult, 3) information is too many, 4) it is messy to study information security or to collect information, 5) the update of information is too fast to catch up, 6) I do not know place of the information, and 7) I do not know whether the information have relevance to me. We assume that the respondents have high ability to collect and process the information if they select no ones in this article. In sum, score of the respondent who selects no one is 7 points and reversely score of the respondent who selects all one is 0 point. Figure 1 shows the distribution of the score.

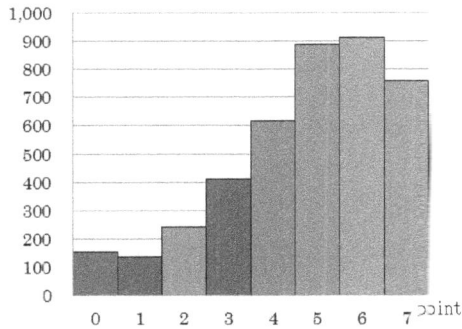

Figure 1: Ability of collecting and processing the information

(3) Overconfidence regarding information security knowledge

Some previous studies point out that it is important to have information security knowledge (Schultz, 2005; Rezgui and Marks, 2008). In this article, we introduce overconfidence with regarding to information security knowledge. This concept represents respondent's gap between knowledge and cognition, and often used in the field of behavioural finance.

This survey has 40 quizzes on eight kinds of information security incidents such as computer virus. Respondents select one of options (1. correct, 2. wrong, and 3. I do not know) for each the statement in questionnaire. If they select right answer, one point would be assigned. If they select all right answers, their points are 40 points. In addition, we ask questions with regard to their cognition on information security incidents. Respondents select one of options (1. I never know it, 2. I hear it once or twice, 3. To some degree, I know it, and 4. I know it in details) for eight incidents. By combining quizzes and question items on the cognition, we calculate the difference of scores. The respondent is regarded as overconfident individual if his score of cognition is higher than quiz (the difference is positive). The distribution of degree of overconfidence regarding information security knowledge is shown in Figure 2.

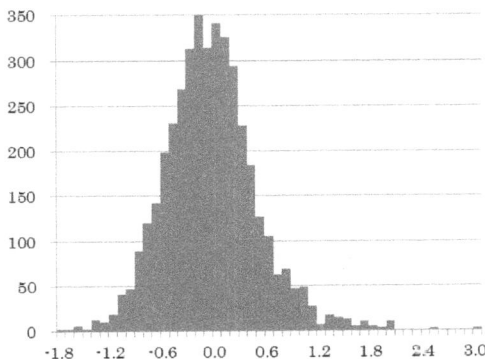

Figure 2: Degree of overconfidence regarding information security knowledge

(4) Individual attributes

This survey has respondent's attributes such as gender, age, the learning level of PC, the time of using the Internet, the place of accessing the Internet and the purpose of using the Internet. With regarding to age, we use the square of age because we assume that young people and elderly people have the same trends. We use the learning level of PC as a proxy of respondent's IT skill. In this survey, the level is scored by four-scales. According to the outcome of IPA survey 2010, with regarding to the correspondence when respondent encounter the damages and troubles, the ratio of answering "I do nothing" differ according to the learning level of PC. Especially, the ratio of starters who answer it tends to be higher. In addition, we ask questions with regard to using at the Internet cafe and the purpose of using the Internet. As the purpose of using the Internet, we pick up 1. online shopping, 2. the Internet auction, 3. SNS, 4. online game, and 5. file-swapping software such as Winny. We assign zero if the respondent uses it. Otherwise, we assign one. The ratio of using the Internet cafe is about 7.4%. Figure 3 shows the distribution of the purpose of using the Internet.

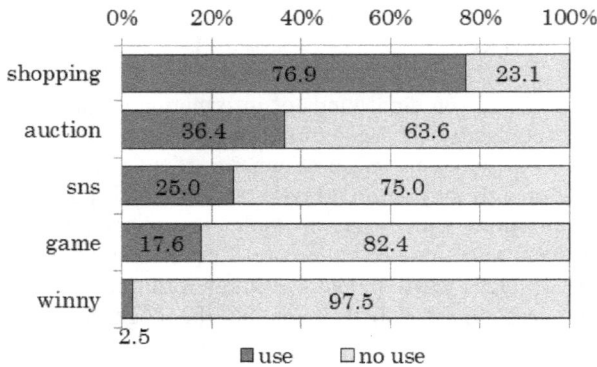

Figure 3: The purpose of using the Internet

4. Results of analyses

4.1. Principal component analysis

Table 3 shows result of principal component analysis with regarding to information security awareness explained in section 3.3. Using this result, information security awareness is scored.

Statement	Eigenvector
1) I do not open the attached file of suspicious e-mail	0.5695
2) I do not access the suspicious website	0.5910
3) I download neither the file nor software from unfamiliar website	0.5714

Table 3: Result of principal component analysis

4.2. Multinomial logit regression analysis

Tables 4 and 5 show statistics and estimated results of multinomial logit regression analysis. Note that in this article Stata 12/SE is used as statistical analysis software.

First of all, for all information security incident damages, the estimated coefficients of information security awareness (X_{aware}) and ability of collecting and processing the information ($X_{ability}$) are statistically significant and these factors affect the probability that individual encounters information security incidents. In addition, for many information security incident damages, the estimated coefficients of the time of using the Internet (X_{time}), age (X_{age} and X_{age}^2), use at the Internet cafe ($X_{netcafe}$) and use of the Internet auction ($X_{auction}$) are statistically significant and these factors

	Statistics
1) Computer virus	LR chi2(28) = 354.81 Prob > chi2 = 0.0000
	Log likelihood = -3841.5146 Pseudo R2 = 0.044
2) Phishing	LR chi2(28) = 364.81 Prob > chi2 = 0.0000
	Log likelihood = -2757.4397 Pseudo R2 = 0.062
3) Billing fraud	LR chi2(28) = 424.81 Prob > chi2 = 0.0000
	Log likelihood = -3327.7672 Pseudo R2 = 0.060
4) Spoofing	LR chi2(28) = 305.95 Prob > chi2 = 0.0000
	Log likelihood = -2635.5767 Pseudo R2 = 0.055

Table 4: Statistics of multinomial logit regression analysis

	Var	Coef.	S.E.	Z		Var	Coef.	S.E.	z
Computer virus	**(1)**				**Phishing**	**(1)**			
	X_{aware}	-0.070**	0.033	-2.090		X_{aware}	-0.236***	0.061	-3.860
	$X_{ability}$	-0.111***	0.025	-4.470		$X_{ability}$	-0.197***	0.046	-4.280
	$X_{overconf}$	-0.003	0.086	-0.040		$X_{overconf}$	0.301**	0.156	1.930
	X_{learn}	0.042	0.073	0.580		X_{learn}	0.105	0.143	0.730
	X_{time}	0.071***	0.041	1.730		X_{time}	0.129*	0.078	1.660
	X_{male}	0.556	0.104	5.370		X_{male}	0.940***	0.218	4.300
	X_{age}	-0.005	0.009	-0.520		X_{age}	-0.035**	0.017	-2.100
	X_{age}^2	0.000*	0.000	0.400		X_{age}^2	0.001**	0.000	2.420
	$X_{netcafe}$	0.284	0.158	1.800		$X_{netcafe}$	0.585**	0.271	2.160
	X_{shop}	-0.045	0.115	-0.390		X_{shop}	-0.049	0.234	-0.210
	$X_{auction}$	0.134	0.099	1.350		$X_{auction}$	0.612***	0.195	3.140
	X_{sns}	0.043**	0.109	0.390		X_{sns}	0.106	0.212	0.500
	X_{Winny}	0.510	0.240	2.120		X_{Winny}	0.067	0.436	0.150
	X_{game}	0.153	0.118	1.290		X_{game}	0.404*	0.216	1.870
	(3)					**(3)**			
	X_{aware}	-0.262***	0.026	-10.18		X_{aware}	-0.261***	0.025	-10.25
	$X_{ability}$	-0.082***	0.021	-3.910		$X_{ability}$	-0.073***	0.021	-3.540
	$X_{overconf}$	0.192***	0.074	2.600		$X_{overconf}$	0.206***	0.073	2.820
	X_{learn}	-0.420***	0.059	-7.090		X_{learn}	-0.421***	0.059	-7.190
	X_{time}	0.043	0.036	1.180		X_{time}	0.037	0.036	1.030
	X_{male}	0.340***	0.085	4.000		X_{male}	0.293***	0.084	3.490
	X_{age}	-0.006	0.007	-0.750		X_{age}	-0.006	0.007	-0.850
	X_{age}^2	0.000	0.000	0.870		X_{age}^2	0.000	0.000	1.010
	$X_{netcafe}$	0.184	0.156	1.180		$X_{netcafe}$	0.163	0.154	1.060
	X_{shop}	-0.176**	0.091	-1.930		X_{shop}	-0.170*	0.090	-1.890
	$X_{auction}$	-0.019	0.087	-0.220		$X_{auction}$	-0.016	0.086	-0.180
	X_{sns}	-0.127	0.100	-1.280		X_{sns}	-0.129	0.099	-1.310
	X_{Winny}	0.017	0.292	0.060		X_{Winny}	-0.084	0.287	-0.290
	X_{game}	-0.259**	0.118	-2.200		X_{game}	-0.266**	0.116	-2.290
Billing fraud	**(1)**				**Phishing**	**(1)**			
	X_{aware}	-0.063***	0.043	-1.470		X_{aware}	-0.152**	0.073	-2.090
	$X_{ability}$	-0.142***	0.031	-4.640		$X_{ability}$	-0.132**	0.057	-2.310
	$X_{overconf}$	-0.062***	0.106	-0.580		$X_{overconf}$	0.809***	0.171	4.730
	X_{learn}	0.122***	0.093	1.310		X_{learn}	0.105	0.143	0.730
	X_{time}	0.118	0.051	2.320		X_{time}	0.238***	0.088	2.700
	X_{male}	1.031***	0.140	7.370		X_{male}	0.880***	0.251	3.510
	X_{age}	-0.031	0.011	-2.790		X_{age}	-0.035*	0.019	-1.890
	X_{age}^2	0.001	0.000	3.380		X_{age}^2	0.000	0.000	1.430
	$X_{netcafe}$	0.529	0.181	2.920		$X_{netcafe}$	-0.244	0.404	-0.600
	X_{shop}	-0.083**	0.145	-0.570		X_{shop}	0.115	0.291	0.400
	$X_{auction}$	0.206	0.125	1.660		$X_{auction}$	0.754***	0.237	3.180
	X_{sns}	0.471	0.132	3.570		X_{sns}	-0.055	0.257	-0.210
	X_{Winny}	0.294	0.290	1.020		X_{Winny}	0.450	0.449	1.000
	X_{game}	0.131**	0.147	0.890		X_{game}	0.346	0.261	1.330
	(3)					**(3)**			
	X_{aware}	-0.258***	0.026	-10.09		X_{aware}	-0.296***	0.025	-11.99
	$X_{ability}$	-0.078***	0.021	-3.750		$X_{ability}$	-0.093***	0.020	-4.590
	$X_{overconf}$	0.187***	0.073	2.550		$X_{overconf}$	0.208***	0.072	2.890
	X_{learn}	-0.416***	0.059	-7.080		X_{learn}	-0.420***	0.059	-7.090
	X_{time}	0.043	0.036	1.180		X_{time}	-0.005	0.035	-0.130
	X_{male}	0.341***	0.084	4.040		X_{male}	0.068	0.078	0.870
	X_{age}	-0.007	0.007	-1.010		X_{age}	-0.008	0.007	-1.160
	X_{age}^2	0.000	0.000	1.220		X_{age}^2	0.000	0.000	1.600
	$X_{netcafe}$	0.197	0.155	1.270		$X_{netcafe}$	0.119	0.153	0.780
	X_{shop}	-0.178**	0.091	-1.960		X_{shop}	-0.239***	0.089	-2.700
	$X_{auction}$	-0.021	0.087	-0.240		$X_{auction}$	-0.051	0.086	-0.600
	X_{sns}	-0.090	0.099	-0.900		X_{sns}	-0.189**	0.098	-1.940
	X_{Winny}	-0.052	0.289	-0.180		X_{Winny}	-0.121	0.284	-0.430
	X_{game}	-0.270**	0.117	-2.310		X_{game}	-0.319***	0.116	-2.760

*: baseoutcome is (2) no experience of encountering the incident

Table 5: Result of multinomial logit regression analysis

affect the probability that individual encounters information security incidents, too. Especially, the sign of estimated coefficients of ability of collecting and processing the information and information security awareness are negative, and these factors decrease the probability that individual encounters information security incidents.

Next, for all information security incident damages excluding computer virus, it is found that young users and elderly users tend to encounter the incident damages. In addition, individuals who use the Internet cafe tend to encounter the incident damages. For the purpose of use the Internet, according to the sign of estimated coefficient of Internet auction, SNS (X_{sns}), and online game (X_{game}), the individual tends to encounter the incident damages. One the other hand, the sign of estimated coefficient of online shopping (X_{shop}) is negative.

Third, for many incidents, the sign of estimated coefficient of overconfidence is statistically significant and positive. This implies that the individuals who are overconfident tend to encounter the incident damages. Because they subjectively mistake for understanding the information security in detail, consequently they may fall for the trap and encounter the incident damages.

Finally, I found that some estimated coefficients of category 1: I encounter the incident and category 3: I do not know whether or not I encounter the incident in Table 5 are the same sign.

5. Concluding remarks

In this article, we analyse the characteristics of the Japanese Internet users by using micro data collected from IPA survey 2010, with regard to the information security incidents such as virus and phishing. As a result, we can obtain the interesting findings. We find the ability of collecting and processing the information and the time of using the Internet are common factors affecting the all experience of the incidents. In addition, information security awareness, age, use at the Internet cafe and use of the Internet auction affect many incidents. Especially, ability of collecting and processing the information and information security awareness decrease the probability that individual encounters information security incidents, but overconfidence regarding information security knowledge increases the probability for phishing and spoofing. In the near future, we hope to implement the information security measures incorporated our results.

6. References

Anderson, R., Moore, T. (2009) Information Security: Where Computer Science, Economics and Psychology Meet. Philosophical Transactions of the Royal Society A, Vol.367, pp.2717-2727

Cavusoglu, H., Mishra, B., Raghunathan, S. (2004) The Effect of Internet Security Breach Announcements on Market Value: Capital Market Reactions for Breached Firms and Internet Security Developers, International Journal of Electronic Commerce, Vol.9, No.1, pp.69-104

Hagen, J.M., Albrechtsen, E. and Hovden, J. (2008) Implementation and effectiveness of organizational information security measures, Information Management & Computer Security, Vol. 16 No. 4, pp. 377-397

Internet Association Japan (2007) White paper of the Internet 2007. Tokyo: Inpress R&D

Japan Information Security Policy Meeting (2008) Secure Japan 2008, 9th June 2008, p.6

Komatsu, A., Takagi, D. and Matsumoto, T. (2010) Experimental Study on Individual Gain and Cognitive Structure in Information Security Measures. Transactions of Information Processing Society of Japan 51(9), 1711-1725

Komatsu, A., Yoshikai, N., Takagi, D., Numata, H., Ueda, M., Inomata, A., Shima, N. (2011) Experiment report on attitudinal change by persuasion communication stimulate to implementing the information security measure. Proc. of SCIS2011

Liu, W., Tanaka, H., Matsuura, K. (2007) Empirical-Analysis Methodology for Information-Security Investment and Its Application to Reliable Survey of Japanese Firms, IPSJ Journal, Vol.48, No.9, pp.3204-3218

Mochinaga, D., Sugiura, M., Komatsu, A., Murano, M. Akai, K. (2009) Research trends in social scientific approach to information security. IPSJ SIG Notes, IPSJ-SIG-SPT-41(109), pp.281-287

Powers D.A. and Xie, Y. (2008) *Statistical Methods for Categorical Data Analysis*, 2nd ed., Bingley: Emerald Group Publishing Limited

Rezgui, Y. and Marks, A. (2008) Information security awareness in higher education: An exploratory study, computers & security, 27, pp.241-253

Schultz, E. (2005) The human factor in security, Computers & Security, 24, pp.425-426

Sugiura, M., Komatsu, A., Ueda, M. and Yamada, Y. (2008) Challenging to Economics of Information Security. Proc. of CSS2008, pp.725-730

Takemura, T., Osajima, M., Kawano, M. (2009) Economic Analysis on Information Security Incidents and the Countermeasures: The Case of Japanese Internet Service Providers, K. Jayanthakumaran (Ed.), Advanced Technologies, INTEH, pp.73-89

Tanaka, H., Matsuura, K. and Sudoh, O. (2005) Vulnerability and information security investment: An empirical analysis of e-local government in Japan, Journal of Accounting and Public Policy 24, pp. 37–59

The Japan Institute for Labour Policy and Training (2005) Can the Internet Survey Be Used for the Social Survey?: A result by Experiment. Reports on Labour Policy, No.17

Dynamic Rights Reallocation in Social Networks

A. Ahmad[1], B. Whitworth[1] and L. Janczewski[2]

[1]Massey University, Auckland, New Zealand
[2]The University of Auckland, Auckland, New Zealand
e-mail : {A.Ahmad, B.Whitworth}@massey.ac.nz; Lech@auckland.ac.nz

Abstract

Access control, as part of every software system, has evolved as computing has evolved. Its original aim was to limit unauthorized access to centralized systems, but the rise of social networks like Facebook has changed that. Now each person wants to control who sees photos or makes comments on their local wall by making and unmaking friends, i.e. dynamic, distributed rights control. Social networks already have access control, but there is currently no agreed logical model for their rights, no consistent scheme for allocating and re-allocating permissions to create, edit, delete and view social objects and entities. A socio-technical approach based on social and technical requirements can give the basics of a model. Various rights reallocations like multiply, divide, transfer and delegate are explored. It suggests a theoretical base for access control beyond its security parent.

Keywords

Social Networks, Rights analysis, Rights reallocation

1   Introduction

The need for access control arose with multi-user computing, as users sharing the same system came into conflict (Karp *et al.* 2009). As computing evolved, access control logic developed to offer domain access control for distributed systems and roles for systems with many users. With variations, the traditional access control approach has worked for military and commercial applications, organizational structures, contextual decisions, distributed applications, medical data, peer-to-peer networks and the grid environment (Lampson, 1969; TCSEC, 1985; Clark and Wilson, 1987; Ferraiolo and Kuhn, 1992).

The last decade has seen extreme multi-user systems emerge – social networks (SNs) where millions of users share billions of resources and grant each other access rights (Carminati *et al.* 2008). As access control now depends on the number of interactions, its complexity increases geometrically with size, not linearly. Mapping millions of subjects directly to billions of resources is unwise, as each account adds hundreds or thousands of photos and comments a year. The world population is at seven billion and growing, if Facebook's current 800 million active accounts is just the beginning, traditional access methods may be ending their useful life.

As social networks are here to stay, and growing in number and size, a logical model of distributed rights reallocation is needed. This includes rights multiplication, division, transfer and delegation. The aim is to identify software patterns that embody social principles as well as technical principles like efficiency (Ahmad and Whitworth, 2011). The result would be a consistent scheme to allocate and reallocate distributed rights in a socially acceptable way. The rest of the paper is organized as follows: Section 2 reviews previous work, Section 3 gives the specifications, Section 4 presents the model, and Section 5 concludes it.

2 Review

Carminati et al. presented a semi-decentralized access control model for social networks (Carminati *et al.* 2008), where users are categorized in terms of relationship type, depth and trust level. Likewise dRBAC manages trust in coalition environments by decentralized access control (Freudenthal *et al.* 2002). Additionally, some other access control solutions use trust (Ali *et al.* 2007), reputation (Carminati *et al.* 2006) and relationships (Tapiador *et al.* 2011) to manage access rights between users. However, there is no access control model for SN that supports rights reallocation.

There are delegation models for traditional access control, but other types of right reallocation, like multiplying and dividing, have received little attention. Existing delegation models can be categorized into machine to machine – one object acting on other's behalf (Varadharajan *et al.* 1991), user to machine – objects acting on user behalf (Gasser and McDermott, 1990), and user to user role delegation – user assigning roles to other users (Barka and Sandhu, 2000).

Traditional models cannot be mapped to current SN for the following reasons:

1. Traditional solutions do not give local control over user contributions like family photos, and so struggle with privacy demands. Central access control gives each user the same policy, so variants must be requested from a central authority who sets system wide roles. The user has no local control over their resources as friends are based on generic roles.

2. The delegation models presented in literature are based on system wide entities and are hard to apply on SN local autonomous domains, where domain based delegation is required rather than role based. Current models provide single user, multi-level delegation, but SN require multiple user, single level delegations to maintain domain accountability.

3. Current access control models for SN do not specify the dynamic reallocation of distributed rights found in social networks (Carminati *et al.* 2008; Simpson, 2008), where everyone can give rights away. In dynamic, distributed control, each person can fully administer their own domain.

The above expands on previous work aimed at developing a general and logical rights framework for online social interactions (Ahmad and Whitworth, 2011; Whitworth, deMoor and Liu, 2006; Whitworth and deMoor, 2003). It addresses rights reallocation because in social networks friends are regularly made and unmade, i.e. managing rights allocations is a critical success criterion.

3   Specifications

A socio-technical system is a social system on a technical case, as a socio-physical system is a social system on a physical base. Socio-technical design involves technical and social requirements, to model not just what can be done but what should be done.

3.1   Overview

An information system has *entities* and *operations*, where:

1. **Entity**. Stored as static information, with properties.

    a. *Actor.* An entity that can participate in a social interaction.

        i.   *Persona*. Represents an accountable offline person or group.

        ii.   *Group*. A set of personae acting as one.

        iii. *Agent*. An actor that represents another actor.

    b. *Object.* Conveys information and meaning.

        i.   *Item*. A simple object with no dependents, e.g. a bulletin board post.

        ii.   *Space*. A complex object with dependents, e.g. a bulletin board.

    c. *Right.* A system permission for an actor to operate on an entity.

        i.   *Simple rights*. Rights to act on object or actor entities.

        ii.   *Meta-rights*. Rights to act on right entities, e.g. transfer.

        iii. *Role*. A variable right (a set of rights).

2. **Operations**. Stored as a program or method that processes entities.

    a. *Null operations* don't change the target entity, e.g. view, enter.

    b. *Use operations* change the target in some way, e.g. edit, create.

    c. *Communication operations* transfer data from sender(s) to receiver(s), e.g. send.

    d. *Social operations* change a right or role, e.g. delegate.

3.2   Reallocating Rights

The ability to reallocate social rights is the key to meeting social requirements. It allows socio-technical systems to evolve from an initial state of one administrator with all rights to a community with delegated rights. Re-allocation can change the actors in a right or role as follows:

1. *Transfer.* Allocate use and meta-rights and is irrevocable.

2. *Delegate.* Allocate use rights only and is revocable.

3. *Divide.* Allocate rights jointly to an actor set.

4. *Multiply.* Allocate rights severally to an actor set.

If a right is owned *jointly,* all must agree to allow the act, while if it is owned *severally,* any party alone can activate it. The above can act in combination, e.g. to transfer joint ownership. Table 1 shows the details, as follows:

1. *Transfer*. Transfer gives all entity rights, including meta-rights (Gaaloul *et al.* 2010). Rights are irrevocably given to the new owner, e.g. after selling a house, the old owner has no rights to it.

2. *Delegate.* Delegate gives use rights but not meta-rights, so can be taken back, e.g. a system administrator who delegates rights can take back the top system priority (Gaaloul *et al.* 2010).

3. *Divide.* Those who divide ownership jointly own an entity, e.g. a couple who jointly own a house must both agree to sell it. In joint ownership, any party can stop an act.

4. *Multiply.* In multiply, the entire right is given completely, so any party can act alone as if they owned it exclusively, e.g. a couple's bank account where both can withdraw all the money.

	Allocated by (Actor)		Allocated to (Actor)	
	Meta	Use	Meta	Use
Transfer			√	√
Delegate	√			√
Divide	√	½√		½√
Divide all	½√	½√	½√	½√
Multiply	√	√		√
Multiply	√	√	√	√

Table 1: Allocating use and meta-rights

For example, a many author paper submitted online can let *one* author alone edit it (transfer), let *one* author edit as allowed by the primary author (delegate), let edits proceed only if confirmed by *all* authors (divide), or let *any* author do any edit (multiply). The model covers all these social options.

If a delegatee gets no meta-rights, they can't pass rights on, e.g. renting an apartment gives no right to sublet. Similarly, lending a book to another doesn't give them the right to on-lend it, though as with all social requirements, it happens. Yet being consistent maintains accountability, e.g. if one loans a book to a person who loans it to another person who then loses it, who is accountable to the original owner? This gives the operational principle:

> *P1. Delegating doesn't give the right to delegate.*

A right reallocation is *revocable* if the initiating party keeps the meta-rights, so delegation is revocable but transfer is not. Dividing use rights is revocable but dividing all rights is not, as reverting would require joint agreement. Multiplying use rights is revocable but multiplying meta-rights is a dictator's dream case as anyone can allocate all rights to anyone, which is likely unstable.

To allocate a right to an existing object makes one accountable for it, so by fairness requires consent, e.g. one doesn't add a paper co-author without their agreement. The principle is:

> *P2. Allocating use rights to existing objects requires consent.*

One can't make someone the owner of something unless they agree. The access control system would have to put a question like: "*Martin wants to transfer edit rights over xyz to you, do you agree?*" In contrast, rights with no accountability for existing objects can be allocated without permission, as the other can use them if they wish, e.g. view and enter. The principle is:

> *P3. Rights that imply no existing objects or null acts can be allocated freely.*

So space owners can delegate entry and view rights without inconsistency. These are social requirements not technical necessities. As technical requirements express technical good practice, so social requirements express social good practice. For best effect, they should be applied consistently.

3.3   Social networks

The model both clarifies how social networks operate and suggests alternatives, e.g. social networks send messages like:

> "*X wants to be friend with you*'

In this model, it is a social trade: X will add you to their friend role if you add them to yours. It can be handled as a two-step social transaction, but the steps need not be linked. A tit-for-tat is assumed, but one can *befriend* another, i.e. add them to a friend role, without their permission (P3). One could make another a friend, with view rights, whether they return the favor or not. So, one could receive messages like:

"X has made you a friend"

This is an offer to *be a friend*, not a request to *be my friend*. As one can love another who doesn't return the favor, so friendship needn't be mutual. Systems that axiomatize friendship as always a duality limit it, as friendship is given as well as received.

4   The formal model

An access control matrix can be expressed using function Grant-Right (A, O, R) which holds whenever the access control matrix gives right R to actor A over object O. So function of the form

Grant-Right (Alice, abc.txt, View)... (i)

states that Alice can view the abc.txt file. This kind of simple function can also be used to assign various rights to roles instead of individual actors, e.g. the function to give edit right to family role over abc.txt will look like

Grant-Right (Family, abc.txt, Edit)... (ii)

Also, some rights can contain others as their subset, e.g. allocating an edit right implies a view right to the same actor:

Grant-Right (A, O, Edit) $\models$ *Grant-Right (A, O, View)... (iii)*

Apart from the basic Grant-Right function, which is a nice way to represent the rights stored in the access control matrix, access control logics also include formulae of the form A says Ω, where A is an actor and Ω is a right statement (Genovese *et al.* 2010). The formula represents that actor A makes statement Ω, which can be a request, assignment of rights to some actor or role, or as a part of the security policy, e.g. the owner of an object grants a friend the right to view it, this assertion can be represented as:

Owner says Grant-Right (Friend, Object, View)... (iv)

The precondition of using this say function is that the authorizing actor holds the meta-right to the right that is given away. In the above statement, the owner is by definition the person with meta-rights to that object, so can re-allocate its rights.

In a typical SN instance, suppose Alice sets David as family, George as a friend and Bob as a colleague, where David has a friend Harry and George has a friend Frank. If Alice posts a photo collage of her family on her wall (space) as entity O1, she may wish to let David view and edit (add a photo to it), George to view it, but to not let Bob see it at all. This can then be done by granting those rights to those roles. Yet David might post his family photos O2 on his wall but not to let his friends view it, as his domain has different rules from Alice. This can be modelled in a consistent way, as shown in Table 2.

This model lets Alice delegate or transfer *view* rights to her family photo. If she delegates view to her friend George, he can't show it to his friend Frank (by P1), but if she transfers view to David, then David can show it to Harry. So delegate means you can't pass it on.

If Alice delegates *edit* rights to David, only he can add photos. If she multiplies edit rights to him, both her and David can add photos. If she divides the rights, photos can only be added if they both approve. If Alice transfers edits rights to David, he can on-delegate, to let his friend Harry add a photo.

Alice can delegate, divide or multiply *delete* rights, but to transfer them would be to give up ownership of her space, e.g. another could post a picture she disapproves of which she could not delete. If the right to delete, or at least to say who can delete, is basic to the ownership of any local domain space, it can't be given away without giving away the space.

This access control model not only supports existing rights, as granted by systems like Facebook, but also suggests new ones, e.g. to let SN actors set their role allocations different from the general template, or create new local roles like colleague. Local domain control involves decentralizing meta-rights, not just rights.

The proposed framework can handle this because it doesn't distinguish the administrative authority. The condition formula *A says Ω* can be used by many as well as by one, as both *A* and Ω are arbitrary. In this approach:

Access Control Model Instance [*]	
Subject (type : subject, identifier : number, name : string)	*User (subject, number, user)*
Right (type : right, identifier : number, name : string)	*Role (subject, number, role)*
Object (type : object, identifier : number, name : string)	
User (subject U, #1, Alice)	*User (subject U, #2, Bob)*
User (subject U, #3, David)	*User (subject U, #4, George)*
Object (object O, #5, O1)	
Right (right R, #6, View)	*Right (right R, #7, Edit)*
UserRoles (subject UR, #8, Family)	*UserRoles (subject UR, #9, Friend)*
UserRoles (subject UR, #10, Colleague)	
ActiveRole (subject AR, ar#11, U : #3 (David), R: #8 (Family))	
ActiveRole (subject AR, ar#12, U : #4 (George), R: #9 (Friend))	
ActiveRole (subject AR, ar#13, U : #2 (Bob), R: #10 (Colleague))	
Auth (S : ar#11 (Family), O : #5(O1), R : #6 (view), Y: +)	*subject (U, #3, David)*
Auth (S : ar#11 (Family), O : #5(O1), R : #7 (edit), Y: +)	*subject (U, #3, David)*
Auth (S : ar#12 (Friend), O : #5(O1), R : #6 (view), Y: +)	*subject (U, #4, George)*

Authorization Set

(ar11, O1, View)	*(UR: #8, O : #5, R: #6, Y:+)*	*(ar11, O1, Edit)*	*(UR: #8, O : #5, R: #7, Y:+)*
(ar12, O1, View)	*(UR: #9, O : #5, R: #6, Y:+)*		
(David, O1, View)	*(U: #3, O : #5, R: #6, Y:+)*	*(David, O1, Edit)*	*(U: #3, O : #5, R: #7, Y:+)*
(George, O1, Edit)	*(U: #4, O : #5, R: #6, Y:+)*		

*Owner has all the rights over the object so owner role is not considered

Table 2: Access control model instance and its authorization set

1. *Transferring* changes the actor property of all rights to an object, including meta-rights. It changes the owner, as formalized by

   OldOwner says Grant-Right (NewOwner, Entity, AllRights) ... (v)

   By this access matrix change, the *NewOwner* has all rights to the object and the *OldOwner* has none. The *says* method is the means by which that occurs. As it is one atomic operation, the rights of the *OldOwner* and the *NewOwner* cannot conflict.

2. *Delegating* a right reallocates all rights except the meta-rights. Again, the *says* operation changes object rights from the delagator to the delegatee in one atomic step, so at each point it is clear who is responsible for acting upon it. In this case, the delegatee is responsible for the object, but the delagator is responsible for the delegatee, and can revoke their permission at any time.

3. *Multiplying* a right replaces its actor by an OR set, where the formula $A \lor B$ *says* Ω to mean that principal A or B says Ω. This explicitly lets any actor execute the given operation on the defined object alone.

4. *Dividing* a right replaces the actor by an AND set, where the formula $A \land B$ *says* Ω to mean that principal A and B jointly says Ω. This would require the consent of both A and B to execute a function Ω, where Ω can be any arbitrary operation legal in the settings of access control model instance.

Note that to automatically make the friends of my friends also my friends is to not recognize the difference between delegate and transfer rights re-allocations. It contradicts P1, that giving a use right doesn't give the meta-right. The attempt to make friends of friends also friends illustrates a technical option that failed because it had no social basis. Designing social interactions without regard to social requirements is how we got the current spam problem (Whitworth and Liu, 2009). It is a social fact that liking someone doesn't guarantee that one will like their friends. In the above, if a role delegates a right, it can't be passed on.

5 Conclusions

This paper suggests how to allocate and reallocate access control rights to satisfy social requirements like local ownership. It arises because those who add photos of their family won't add them if they can't control them. The semantics of this model satisfies social requirements P 1-3 and its formal syntax is consistent (Table 2). It not only defines what SNs like Facebook currently do, and what they should not, but also suggests new options not yet tried (Table 1).

Access control began in the shadow of security but socio-technology will make it a new discipline. While security needs secrecy for obvious reasons, access control today is more about access than control. It is about getting participation rather than stopping it, as a socio-technical system without an active community isn't a socio-technical system at all.

The next phase of this project is to develop a distributed, dynamic access control plug-in for a NSF granted open knowledge exchange (OKE) system and evaluate it with respect to both social criteria like fairness and technical criteria like storage efficiency. This "rights module" will also give human readable reports to actors of granted rights, i.e. be transparent. The goal is that social rights are not only applied but also seen to be applied, as this is critical for trust and synergy.

Online communities today can't survive without participation, so access control is increasingly about letting people in rather than keeping them out. This model follows the socio-technical paradigm: to first define the social requirements then design a technical solution to meet them. It tries to avoid social errors like the unfairness of spam but still addresses technical requirements like consistency and efficiency. The evolution of access control to include social requirements goes beyond the traditional physical security focus, into new research dimensions.

6   Acknowledgment

This work has been sponsored by National Science Foundation (NSF), USA, under award number 0968445. "OKES: An open knowledge exchange system to promote meta-disciplinary collaboration based on socio-technical principles".

7   References

Ahmad, A. and Whitworth, B. (2011), "Distributed Access Control for Social Networks", *International conference of information assurance and security IAS'11.*

Ali, B., Villegas, W., and Maheswaran, M. (2007), "A trust based approach for protecting user data in social networks". *Conference of the Center for Advanced Studies on Collaborative research (CASCON'07),* pages 288–293.

Barka, E. and Sandhu, R. S. (2000), "Framework for role-based delegation models", *16th Annual Computer Security Applications Conference (ACSAC 2000)* New Orleans, La. Dec. 11–15). IEEE Computer Society Press, Los Alamitos, Calif., 168–177.

Carminati, B., Ferrari, E., and Perego, A. (2006), "Rule-based access control for social networks". *On the Move to Meaningful Internet Systems: OTM Workshops.*

Carminati, B., Ferrari, E. and Perego, A. (2008), "Enforcing access control in web-based social networks" *ACM Transactions on Information & System Security.*

Clark, D. D., and Wilson, D. R. (1987), "A Comparison of Commercial and Military Computer Security Policies," *IEEE Symposium of Security and Privacy,* pp. 184–194.

Ferraiolo, D. and Kuhn, D. R. (1992), "Role-Based Access Control," *NIST-NSA National (USA) Computer Security Conference,* pp. 554–563.

Freudenthal, E., Pesin, T., Port, L., Keenan, E., Karamcheti, V. (2002), "dRBAC: Distributed role based access control for dynamic coalition environments" In ICDCS '02: *22nd International Conference on Distributed Computing Systems (ICDCS'02)*.

Gaaloul, K., Zahoor, E., Charoy, F., and Godart, C. (2010) "Dynamic Authorisation Policies for Event-based Task Delegation", *Advanced Information Systems Engineering, 22nd International Conference, CAiSE,* Hammamet, Tunisia.

Gasser, M., and McDermott, E. (1990), "An Architecture for practical Delegation in a Distributed System". *IEEE Computer Society Symposium on Research in Security and Privacy.* Oakland, CA.

Genovese, V., Giordano, L., Gliozzi, V., Pozzato, G. L. (2010), "A constructive conditional logic for access control: a preliminary report". *19th European Conference on Artificial Intelligence.* pp.1073~1074.

Karp, A. H., Haury, H. and Davis, M. H. (2009), "From ABAC to ZBAC: The Evolution of access control models", *Technical Report HPL-2009-30,* HP Labs.

Lampson, B. W. (1969), "Dynamic Protection Structures," *AFIPS Conference Proceedings,* 35, pp. 27–38.

Simpson, A. (2008), "On the need for user-defined fine-grained access control policies for social networking applications," In SOSOC '08: *Workshop on Security in Opportunistic and social networks*, New York, USA, 2008.

Tapiador, A., Carrera, D. and Salvachúa, J. (2011), "Tie-RBAC: an application of RBAC to Social Networks". *Web 2.0 Security and Privacy*, Oakland, California.

TCSEC, Trusted Computer Security Evaluation Criteria (TCSEC) (1985), *DOD 5200.28-STD.* Department of Defense.

Varadharajan, V., Allen, P. and Black, S. (1991), "An Analysis of the Proxy Problem in Distributed systems". *IEEE Symposium on Research in Security and Privacy.* Oakland, CA.

Whitworth, B., and deMoor, A. (2003), "Legitimate by design: Towards trusted virtual community environments". *Behaviour and Information Technology Journal,* 22:1, p31-51.

Whitworth, B., deMoor, A. and Liu, T. (2006), "Towards a Theory of Online Social Rights", in R. Meersman, Z. Tari, P. Herrero et al. (Eds.): *OTM Workshops,* LNCS 4277, pp. 247 – 256, Springer-Verlag Berlin Heidelberg.

Whitworth, B. and Liu, T. (2009), Channel email: Evaluating social communication efficiency, *IEEE Computer,* July, p63-72.

Utilizing Survival Analysis for Modeling Child Hazards of Social Networking

D. Michalopoulos[1] and I. Mavridis

[1] Department of Applied Informatics, University of Macedonia, 156 Egnatia Street
54006 Thessaloniki Greece
e-mail: {dimich,mavridis}@uom.gr

Abstract

Social networks induce several hazards to children, which are correlated with the amount of time that children are exposed to those networks. To this end, this work investigates the relation of the aforementioned hazards with the exposure time. To address this issue, we adopt techniques used in survival analysis. These techniques involve the estimation of certain functions which reflect the relation of a disastrous event with time. In particular, we derive the distribution of the rate at which suspicious activities towards children occur in social networks. This is accomplished through experiments on data sets extracted from Facebook. The results show that the incoming hazards for minor female profiles follow the Logistic distribution, while the corresponding hazards for minor male profiles follow the Normal distribution. This knowledge is then utilized for developing an effective system for automated grooming recognition, by optimizing the detection threshold as a function of time. Thus, the threshold sensitivity can be appropriately adjusted such that lower frequencies of occurrence lead to lower threshold sensitivities, and higher frequencies of occurrence lead to higher threshold sensitivities.

Keywords

Social networks, grooming, sexual exploitation, survival analysis

1 Introduction

The evolution of communication media leads to new forms of experience in our days. Social networks are becoming very popular among teenagers, mainly through Facebook, which is reaching almost 800 million active registered users (Facebook 2012). However, these new forms of communication have raised significant hazards for minor users. Many children and teenagers have become victims of online sexual exploitation attempts (Armagh, Battaglia *et al.* 2006). This phenomenon is generally known as grooming (O'Connell 2003). The consequences for grooming victims are catastrophic and many child victims are harmed for the rest of their lives (Berson 2003). Child grooming occurs in every country, civilization, religion or ethnic group, and incidents are dramatically increasing . Cyber-predators are usually using social networks for communication, as well as searching and attracting new victims. According to experts, predators never before had the opportunity to communicate so directly with their victims as they do online (Olson 2007).

The research work presented in this paper was developed in the context of our general effort that is mainly focused on creating defenses against grooming attacks. For this purpose, the Grooming Attack Recognition System (GARS) has been introduced in (Michalopoulos *et al.* 2010), which is designed to transparently monitor internet communications with full respect in communication privacy. Moreover, we have published research work on privacy and security leaks of social networks (Michalopoulos and Mavridis 2010). This work has revealed that Facebook users tend to make public their personal data and exchange personal information with strangers. As the problem of online grooming is recent, there in not much published related research. In a similar work, Kontostathis et al. have analyzed the challenges of creating effective defenses against child sexual exploitation (Kontostathis 2009). In addition Olson et al. has analyzed the strategies which sexual predators follow to achieve their goals (Olson 2007). Similarly, predators' approaches are studied by O'Connell, revealing the nature of online grooming attacks (O'Connell 2003).

More specifically, we investigated in this work the relation of the hazards in social networks with the time children are exposed to them (exposure time). To address this issue, we adopted techniques used in survival analysis. These techniques involve the estimation of certain functions which reflect the relation of a disastrous event with time. More specifically, we initially extracted an experimental data set from Facebook by creating 10 fake profiles and collecting all data that indicate a potential risk (incoming friend requests, requests to date applications). We then noticed that hazards' occurrence rate varies with time and gender. Utilizing methods used in survival analysis, we made the hypothesis that incoming risks can be modeled for each gender by existing statistical distributions. Using proper tools, we calculated the parameters that optimize the distribution fitting, thereby testing the validity of our hypothesis. The verification of our hypothesis provides us with the ability to calculate the hazards' rate of occurrence as a function of time, for each gender. Subsequently, this knowledge can be used for optimizing the detection threshold (viz. in GARS) as a function of time. For example, the threshold sensitivity can be adjusted such that lower frequencies of occurrence lead to lower threshold sensitivities, and higher frequencies to higher threshold sensitivities.

This paper is structured as follows: Section 2 provides a brief description of survival analysis methods that are utilized in our experimentation scenario described in Section 3. The exercise of various distribution fitting tests is presented in Section 4, and the obtained results are discussed in Section 5. Our conclusions and future work are included in Section 6.

2   Survival Analysis

One of the major research tasks in health sciences is the identification of the risk factors for diseases, as for example the study on the connection between ionizing radiation and leukemia (Le 1997). Such a connection can be verified by performing scientific investigation (Balakrishnan and Rao 2004). The usual steps for investigating the effects of an exposure to a risk factor are (Le 1997):

- Define the hypothesis proposal
- Investigate the hypothesis by testing or experiment
- Make a decision based on collected information, if the hypothesis is supported.

Survival analysis research includes studding of groups of people with similar characteristics exposed to the same risk factor for a dedicated time period (Allison and Books24x7 Inc. 2010). The basic aim of such a research is the identification of a potential statistical relation between the risk factor and the disease. Indeed, the important feature in such research is the time when the catastrophic event happened. This time is commonly named as *survival time T.*

The distribution of the survival time T from the starting point until the catastrophic event is denoted by two functions: the *survival function, S(t)* and the *hazard or risk function $\lambda(t)$*. The survival function is expressed as the probability that the patient survives longer than t time units (Le 1997). Therefore, if T is a continuous random variable, and $F(t)$ is the Cumulative Distribution Function (CDF) on $[0, +\infty)$, then it holds that (Papoulis and Pillai 2002):

$$S(t) = \Pr(T > t) = 1 - F(t) \tag{1}$$

The hazard function denotes the direct failure rate assuming the patient has survived to time t and it is the probability of death in a very small time interval δ (Le 1997):

$$\lambda(t) = \lim_{\delta \to 0} \frac{\Pr(t \leq T \leq t + \delta \mid t \leq T)}{\delta} \tag{2}$$

For a small increment of δ, equation (2) yields (Klein and Moescberger 2003):

$$\lambda(t) = \frac{\left[-\dfrac{d}{dt} S(t) \right]}{S(t)} \tag{3}$$

Consequently, the formula (3) can be written as (Le 1997):

$$S(t) = e^{-\int_0^t \lambda(x)dx} \tag{4}$$

In health science (Miller, Gong *et al.* 1981), the estimation of the survival function and the risk function indicates the calculation of disease's spread as a function of time. The above functions are used for creating medicine treatments dedicated on the specific type of a disease. In addition, the estimation of the above functions of survival analysis can contribute to the comparison of different treatments. For example, when two different treatments are compared, researchers separate patients of the same disease into two groups, where the age composition of these groups is maintained as uniform as possible. The two treatments are implemented into the aforementioned groups such that, after a certain period of time, the survival and risk functions are calculated and compared. This comparison is used for identifying the most effective treatment (Le 1997).

Similarly to the survival analysis in health sciences, where the catastrophic event is death, we define the sexual exploitation of the minor Internet user to be the catastrophic event in our research work. The risk factors where minor users are exposed are online hazards. Cyber-predators follow different strategies on approaching their victims and thereby performing their grooming attacks. Usually, they implement the so-called "hit and run" method, which refers to a vast attack against the minor user (O'Connell 2003). In other cases, they put into practice more sophisticated techniques by spending more time on knowing their victim and learning details for victim's personal life (O'Connell 2003). Therefore, sometimes the catastrophic event of child grooming occurs in a short period of child's exposure time, while other times this event occurs after a longer period of time.

The main purpose of this work is to identify the statistical relation between malicious approaches and the minor's exposure time (Papoulis and Pillai 2002). Similarly to the survival analysis in health sciences, where the estimation of the above functions can be used for improving the medication treatment, such calculation can be used in our research for improving GARS effectiveness with variable detection thresholds.

3 Experimentation scenario

In order to identify the relation between grooming hazards and the exposure time, we made the hypothesis that incoming hazards in social networks follow statistical distributions. In order to collect a data set of hazards related to the time unit, we created 10 Facebook profiles of minor users. As time unit we assumed that of one week and the whole experiment lasted for 24 weeks.

All profiles represent young teenagers aged 13 to 15 years old, half of them for male and the other half for female. Instead of clear face photographs, common images for youth were used. For example, boys used images for cars and famous sport teams, while girls used romantic images, actor and music group images. In all profiles we used the default privacy settings (Facebook 2012), as well as the typical activities for a minor. For example, joining groups of famous sport teams and music stars and registering in social and dating applications, like "Zoosk" and "Speed Dating".

The whole experiment lasted for 24 weeks. In the beginning of this period, our profiles were sending randomly to other profiles with common interests about 10 friend requests per day for the next 5 weeks. After that, our profiles kept going sending only 2 friend requests per week, according to Facebook's suggestions of mutual friends. By the end of experimental time, we collected for further analysis all necessary test data using the Facebook applications "Activity Statistics", "friendstats", "cha.fm" as well as the e-mail accounts connected with our profiles. Surprisingly, we discovered that our profiles had many friends and received friend requests and personal messages from many unknown so far profiles. Summarizing, we collected all suspicious incoming activity for each one profile. As suspicious activity we consider each activity that can lead to child grooming. For example, a message with a link to inappropriate material, or a chat request with date intention. Specifically, as suspicious activity we reflect on personal messages – chat request, incoming friend requests, invitations in dating, posts in profile's Wall and any incoming activity from dating applications (like zoosk).

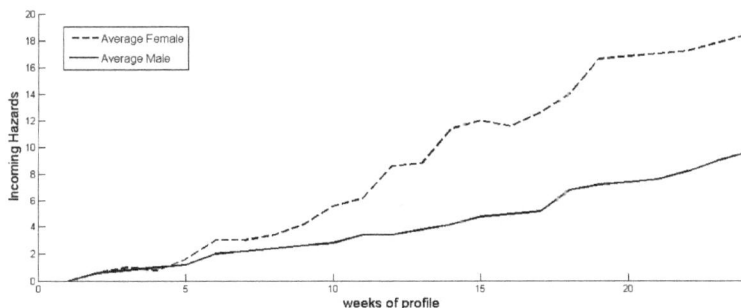

Figure 1: Plotting average incoming hazards

Figure 1 depicts the evolution of the average collected data for each gender as a function of time.

4   Distribution fitting

Having collected the data set from our experimentation scenario, we made the hypothesis that hazards in social networks can be modeled with known statistical distributions. If this hypothesis is true, we can model incoming hazards as function of time and therefore create effective defenses. To verify this hypothesis, we used the Matlab's distribution fitting tool (MathWorks Inc. 2005) and the Kolmogorov-Smirnov tests (Papoulis and Pillai 2002). The former identifies the known distributions which are closer for fitting with the hypothesized which is created by the captured data set, whereas the latter compares the hypothesized with the existing distribution and concludes about their fitting.

The distributions we used for fitting were: Normal (N), Generalized extreme value (GEV), Exponential (E), T location Scale (TLS), Logistic (L), Extreme value (EV), Generalized pareto (GP), Rayleigh (R), Gama (G) and Weibull (W).

4.1   Average data fitting

Figures 2 and 3 represent the female and the male average distribution fittings, respectively. The parameters for standard distributions were extracted from Matlab "dfiittool" for the first seven distributions (MathWorks Inc. 1999; MathWorks Inc. 2005). Similarly, using Matlab's standard functions ("rayfit", "gamfit" and "wblfit"), we calculated the parameters for distributions Rayleigh, Gama and

Weilbull (MathWorks Inc. 1999). These last three functions were not calculated with "dfittool" but with the corresponding Matlab's standard functions.

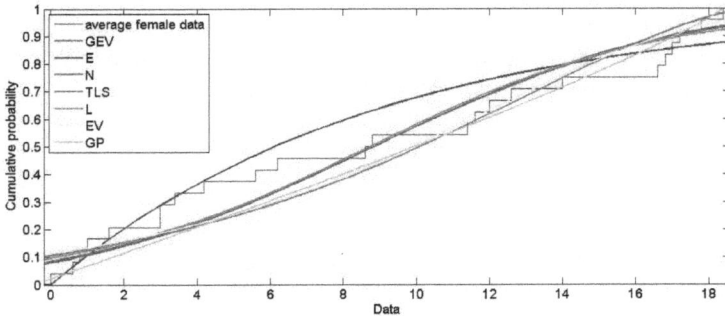

Figure 2: Distribution fitting for average female data with 6 distributions

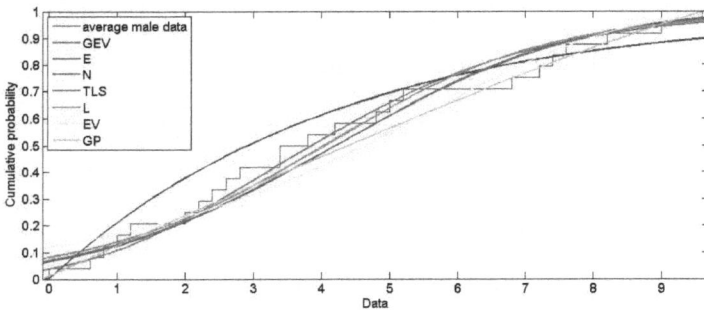

Figure 3: Distribution fitting for average male data with 6 distributions

4.2   Kolmogorov-Smirnov test

The Kolmogorov-Smirnov test (KS-test) is used to assess the level of proximity between two datasets (Marsaglia 2003). In our case, we used the one-sample KS-test (MathWorks Inc. 2005), which calculates a distance D between the empirical distribution function of the sample data and the standard distribution function. Moreover, we used the one-sample KS-test as a "goodness of fit", viz. a statistical model which describes how well a set of observations can fit a standard distribution (Massey 1951). The test calculates the distance D as:

$$D = \max(|F(x) - G(x)|) \tag{5}$$

where $F(x)$ is the hypothesized function and $G(x)$ is the standard distribution.

We applied the KS-test into the average of the test data for both genders' data sets (female and male) and with standard distributions. Parameters for standard distributions were extracted from "dfittool", "raylfit", "gamfit" and "wblfit" Matlab's functions. The alpha value that used for all tests was *0.01* instead of default *0.05*. This alpha value represents the probability that the test fails if Matlab returns that hypothesis is true (Papoulis and Pillai 2002). The other values that we have calculated beyond the logical *h* (*h=1* the hypothesis is rejected, *h=0* the hypothesis is true) is the p-value *(p)* and the test statistic *(k)*. Assuming that the hypothesis is true, *p* is the probability of getting a test statistic at least as high as the one that was actually calculated (Stuart, Ord *et al.* 1994; Bharath 2010). However, *p* is not the probability that the null hypothesis is true (Marsaglia 2003). A statistic value on which the result is based about to accept or reject a hypothesis is the test statistic *k* (Bharath 2010). More specifically, *k* is the maximum difference between the curves, viz. the hypothesized and the standard (Papoulis and Pillai 2002). Therefore, the criterion for comparison between distributions is the lowest *k* value. Results for female and male fitting tests are presented in tables 1 and 2.

Distr.	N	GEV	E	TLS	L	EV	GP	R	G	W
h	0	0	0	0	0	0	0	0	0	0
p	0.6918	0.5088	0.3546	0.6524	0.7186	0.5578	0.5426	0.1058	0.3384	0.3535
k	0.139	0.1613	0.1829	0.1437	0.1357	0.1552	0.1571	0.2401	0.1854	0.1831

Table 1: Average female fitting

Distr.	N	GEV	E	TLS	L	EV	GP	R	G	W
h	0	0	0	0	0	0	0	0	0	0
p	0.8877	0.7922	0.4479	0.8731	0.3314	0.6536	0.5205	0.5707	0.7691	0.4095
k	0.1127	0.1265	0.1694	0.1150	0.1866	0.1436	0.1598	0.1536	0.1295	0.1747

Table 2: Average Male fitting

5   Discussion on results

Based on the fitting that are presented in tables 1 and 2, we conclude that the hypothesis of average experimental data CDF fitting with standard CDFs is true for all distributions of both female and male profiles' average of test data. Indeed, for concluding on which distribution can fit more accurately to the captured data set, we used as a criterion the lowest *k* value (Papoulis and Pillai 2002).

From table 1 it can be extracted that female data set best fits on the Logistic distribution (CDF) with $\mu = 8.73565$ and $\sigma = 3.92103$.

$$F_{female}(t) = \frac{1}{1 + e^{-(t-8.73565)/3.92103}}$$

$$(6)$$

Similarly, male data set best fits (Table 2) on the Normal distribution (CDF) with $\mu = 4.21667$ and $\sigma = 2.85287$.

$$F_{male}(t) = \frac{1}{2.85287\sqrt{2\pi}} \int_{-\infty}^{t} e^{-(x-4.21667)^2/16.277} dx = \frac{1}{2}[1 + erf\left(\frac{t-4.21667}{2.85287\sqrt{2}}\right)]$$

$$(7)$$

Where *erf* is so-called *error function* (Spiegel, Srinivasan *et al.* 2000).

The above results were extracted from the average data set. In order to verify that the data set of each profile satisfactorily fits the above corresponding distributions, we used again the KS-test. At this point the hypothesis was that the corresponding data set did not differ significantly with (6) for the female profiles and with (7) for male profiles. Table 3 below denotes that hypothesis is true for 9 out of 10 data sets. The hypothesis is rejected only for the first female profile.

Profile	Female 1	Female 2	Female 3	Female 4	Female 5
KS-Test	1	0	0	0	0
Profile	Male 1	Male 2	Male 3	Male 4	Male 5
KS-Test	0	0	0	0	0

Table 3: Implementing KS tests in all profiles' data

In order to calculate the corresponding survival functions, formulas (6) and (7) yield from equation (1) as formulas (8) and (9).

$$S_{female}(t) = 1 - \frac{1}{1 + e^{-(t-8.73565)/3.92103}}$$
(8)

$$S_{male}(t) = \frac{1}{2}[1 - erf\left(\frac{t - 4.21667}{2.85287\sqrt{2}}\right)]$$
(9)

Similarly, to calculate hazard functions, formulas (8) and (9) yield from equation (3) as formulas (10) and (11) (MathWorks Inc. 1999):

$$\lambda_{female}(t) = \frac{0.255035e^{0.255035t}}{9.32778 + e^{0.255035t}}$$
(10)

$$\lambda_{male}(t) = \frac{0.279678e^{-0.0614336(-4.21667+t)^2}}{1 - erf[-1.04514 + 0.247858t]}$$
(11)

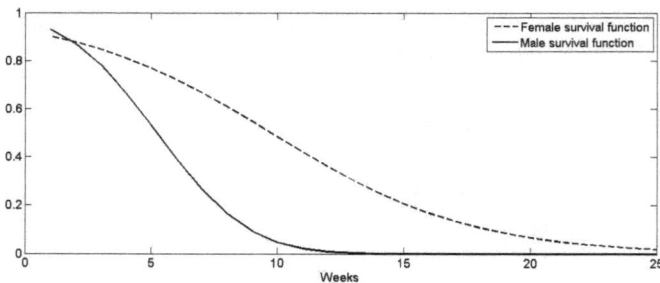

Figure 4: Survival Functions plot

Figures 4 and 5 depict the graphs of the calculated survival and hazard functions, respectively. It is indicative that even though incoming hazards for female profile are more in absolute numbers, the surge in the rate of occurrence in male hazards results in sharper curve in male survival function. This is more obvious in Figure 5.

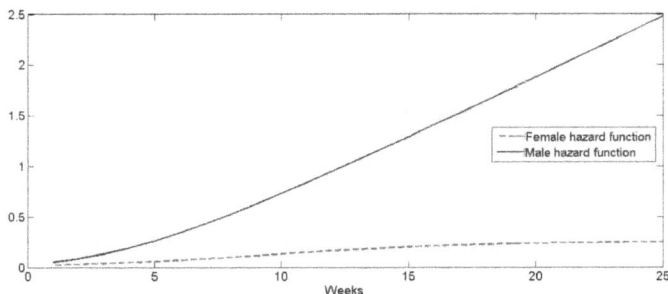

Figure 5: Hazard functions $\lambda(t)$ plot

6   Conclusions

In this work we studied the relation of minor users' hazards in social networks with the exposure time. Our results demonstrated that online hazards for minor users follow specific statistical distributions for each gender. In particular, results shown that female profiles follow the *Logistic* distribution whereas male profiles follow the *Normal* distribution. These results provide us the opportunity to predict the incoming hazards for each new child registered profile. Such a statistical prediction can be very useful on creating defenses against online hazards. Moreover, the presented research work reveals that incoming hazards for children are increasing as a function of the exposed time. Therefore, when developing detection mechanisms the sensitivity of the detection threshold should be adjusted on the curves depicted above for optimum performance purposes.

7   References

"Child Sexual Abuse." Retrieved 9 November 2011, from http://www.nlm.nih.gov/medlineplus/childsexualabuse.html.

Allison, P. D. and Books24x7 Inc. (2010). *Survival analysis using SAS a practical guide*, second edition. Cary, N.C., SAS Pub.

Armagh, D. S., N. L. Battaglia, et al. (2006). Use of computers in the sexual exploitation of children. *Portable guides to investigating child abuse*. Washington, DC, U.S. Dept. of Justice, Office of Justice Programs, Office of Juvenile Justice and Delinquency Prevention.

Balakrishnan, N. and C. R. Rao (2004). *Advances in survival analysis*. Amsterdam ; Boston, Elsevier.

Berson, I. (2003). "Grooming Cybervictims: The Psychosocial Effects of Online Exploitation for Youth." *Journal of School Violence* **2**(1).

Bharath, R. (2010). "Nonparametric statistics for non-statisticians: a step-by-step approach." *Choice: Current Reviews for Academic Libraries* **47**(7): 1324-1324.

Facebook. (2012). "Data use policy." Retrieved 23 December, 2011, from http://www.facebook.com/about/privacy/.

Facebook. (2012). "Statistics." Retrieved 6 January, 2012, from http://www.facebook.com/press/info.php?statistics.

Kontostathis, A., Lynne Edwards, Amanda Leatherman (2009). Text Mining and Cybercrime. *Text Mining: Application and Theory*. E. Michael W. Berry and Jacob Kogan, John Wiley & Sons.

Le, C. T. (1997). *Applied survival analysis*. New York, Wiley. ISBN 0-471-17085-2

Marsaglia, G., W. Tsang, and J. Wang (2003). "Evaluating Kolmogorov's Distribution." *Journal of Statistical Software* **8**(18).

Massey, F. J. (1951). "The Kolmogorov-Smirnov Test for Goodness of Fit." *Journal of the American Statistical Association* **46**(253): 68-78.

MathWorks Inc. (1999). *MATLAB : the language of technical computing*. Natick, MA, MathWorks.

MathWorks Inc. (2005). *Simulink® : simulation and model-based design : using Simulink*. Natick, MA, MathWorks.

Michalopoulos D., Mavridis I. and Vitsas V. (2010). Towards a Risk Management Based Approach for Protecting Internet Conversations. *9th European Conference on Information Warfare and Security, ECIW 2010*: 201-208.

Michalopoulos D. and Mavridis I. (2010). Surveying privacy leaks through online social networks *14th Panhellenic Conference on Informatics, PCI 2010*. **art. no. 5600443**: 184-187.

Miller, R. G., G. Gong, et al. (1981). *Survival analysis*. New York, Wiley.

O'Connell, R. (2003) "A typology of child cybersexploitation and online grooming practices " *Cyberspace Research Unit*, University of Central Lancashire.

Olson, L. N., Daggs, J. L., Ellevold, B. L. and Rogers, T. K. K. (2007). "Entrapping the Innocent: Toward a Theory of Child Sexual Predators Luring Communication." *Communication Theory* **17**: 231-251.

Papoulis, A. and S. U. Pillai (2002). *Probability, random variables, and stochastic processes*. Boston, McGraw-Hill.

Spiegel, M. R., R. A. Srinivasan, et al. (2000). Schaum's outline of theory and problems of probability and statistics. *Schaum's outline series*. New York, McGraw-Hill.

Stuart, A., J. K. Ord, et al. (1994). *Kendall's Advanced theory of statistics*. London, Edward Arnold.

Ethical Guidelines for Cyber-related Services Aimed at the Younger Generations

N. Kortjan, R. von Solms and J. van Niekerk

PO Box 77000, Nelson Mandela Metropolitan University, Port Elizabeth 6031, South Africa

e-mail: s208045801@live.nmmu.ac.za; Rossouw.VonSolms@nmmu.ac.za; Johan.VanNiekerk@nmmu.ac.za

Abstract

Ethics together with the law should be able to govern the tendencies of cyber users in order to create a virtual world with disciplined users. One of the major challenges in achieving such outcomes is the lack of a solid ethical base, specifically with the Younger Generation. The way in which the Internet is used by this generation not only affects them personally but also in their professional capacities. This paper argues towards and suggests a set of ethical guidelines that will assist in eradicating unethical behavior. It furthermore provides questions that a person should ask themselves, to evaluate whether or not they have applied the guidelines.

Keywords

Younger generation, Internet, Ethics, Law, Unethical Behaviors, Cyber usage

1   Introduction

Technology has always had the sole purpose of enhancing the means of living (Ermann *et al.* 1997). One of these enhancements is the invention of the Internet. The Internet has had an extraordinary influence on the way in which human beings do things (Hauptman, 1996). It is evident that the Internet has become part of how the world functions, specifically in communication (Kiesler and Sproull, 1992). Therefore, online activities are nowadays second nature to many people spanning different generations. These generations can be divided into various age groups, as listed in Table 1.

Generation name	Ages in 2010
Teens	Ages 12-17
Millenials (Gen-Y)	Ages 18-33
Gen-X	Ages 34-45
Younger Boomers	Ages 46-55
Older Boomers	Ages 56-64
Silent Generation	Ages 65-73
G.I Generation	Ages 74+

Table 1: Generation Distinctions (PEW Internet, 2010)

For the purposes of this paper the focus will be the Teens and/or Millenials generation groupings which will jointly be referred to as the Younger Generation. As reported in PEW Internet the Younger Generation uses the Internet the most (PEW Internet, 2010). The problem is in the behaviour exhibited of this generation, while using the Internet. The behaviour of this generation definitely poses some ethical concerns. Berdik (2007) suggests that this is due to the abstract nature of the Internet and the inability of users to align their behavior in the real world and the virtual world experienced on the Internet. The objective of this paper is not to address legal issues, but merely to attempt to put legality in context with ethics. The aim of this paper therefore, is to formulate guidelines that will assist in addressing these ethical implications of the Younger Generation whilst communicating online. These guidelines will be extended by a series of easy questions that a person should ask him/herself, to evaluate whether or not he/she has applied the proposed guidelines and therefore communicated in an ethical manner.

The upcoming sections will elaborate on the influence that the Internet has on the Younger Generation. A clear definition of ethics and the law, the relationship between these two concepts as well as their role in cyber usage will be provided. Behaviours that are considered ethically questionable and illegal will be cited. Furthermore, the proposed ethical guidelines will be revealed and followed by concluding clarifications.

2   The Internet in the Society

The Internet is widely used for many purposes by individuals today. These users of the Internet span various generations with each generation favoring certain services and functions. How these services and functions are used is determined by many factors including: what it is used for, who it is supposed to influence and how responsible the user is. Thus, this section will study the impact that the Internet has on individual and also in a wider sense on the society.

Each generation in society utilizes the Internet in a unique manner. The difference of the generations regarding Internet usage has been highlighted by PEW Internet (2010). These statistics point out that each generation does in fact utilize different Internet services. Moreover, the Millenials prove to be using the Internet the most and the G.I Generation use it the least.

The way in which the Internet is used can either construct or destruct, depending on who uses it, how it is used and the reasons thereof. One of the ways in which the Internet destructs is how it manifests criminals. The Internet has not only simplified the good things, it has also given criminals a platform to grow and proliferate. The lack of security and control over cyber usage is also an advantage to criminals as it permits criminals new ways to commit old crimes (Cyberethics - Ethics in the Age of the Internet, n.d.). As a result, the Internet is dubbed as the Wide Wild West of the information age. This is mainly because of its lack of control and restraints. Thus, the Internet serves as a potential threat to society (Cyberethics - Ethics in the Age of the Internet, n.d.).Except for the fact that potential criminals flourish on the Internet,

Gaungrong (1998), states that the Internet corrupts people's minds, influences and changes people's moral perspectives and ethical values and therefore can have a negative effect on the individual (Gaungrong, 1998). It has also affected different generation groupings in different ways. Sir Burton (2008), states that the Younger Generation mainly uses the Internet to "share" information, while the older generation prefers to use the Internet to "know" and therefore to find information (Burton, 2008). When using the Internet, individuals mostly remain anonymous making it easy for one to partake in atypical Internet behaviour (Freestone and Mitchell, 2004). Thus the Internet definitely has a 'dark side'.

On the other hand, while the Internet is used for many wrong and negative reasons, for responsible people it is indeed a very useful technology. *"Responsible people want to use the Web for research, communication, and instruction"* (Berdik, 2007). Taking into consideration what inadequate control exists on the Internet, it is up to the individual to oversee how to behave in cyber space. Moreover, to reflect the implications of such behavior against what is socially and professionally acceptable. Therefore, it is important that one continuously be alerted to proper behavioral norms while online.

From this section it is clear that different generation groupings use the Internet for different purposes. Further, the positive as well negative sides of the Internet has briefly been highlighted. With this in mind, the following section will introduce the law and ethics, together with how they can assist in attending to this questionable behaviour. It will also focus on defining the law and ethics, together with how they relate.

3 A transparency on the Law and Ethics

The importance of the law and ethics in relation to cyber usage is very important, as these should dictate the way in which an individual communicates in cyberspace. It is important to note that defining the law is solely attempted to put legality in context with ethics. This section will provide clarity on how ethics and the law are related and furthermore stipulate the role they play in cyber usage. The term "cyber usage" will be used to its optimum, referring to how the Internet is used.

3.1 Defining the Law

The law, as defined by Fuchs, Bichler and Raffl (2009) is *"social norms defined by the government. Norms that are sanctioned with the help of the state-monopoly of the means of compulsion organized in the form of the executive system. They consist of the police system, the military system, and the prison system and the judiciary system"*. Alternatively, the law has also been defined by Curzon (1986) as the *"written and unwritten body of rules. These rules are largely derived from custom and formal enactment. They are recognized as binding among people who constitute a community or state, so that they will be imposed upon and enforce among those parsons by appropriate sanctions"*. There are other classifications of the law but they all share the same notions, which are rules, monitoring, compliance and control. Following are some descriptions of ethics.

3.2   Defining Ethics

Elaboration on the law is achieved and following is an expansion on ethics. Brockett and Heimstra (2004) defines ethics as simply being the study of right and wrong, of good and evil, in human conduct. Adeola (n.d.) also explains ethics as a principal branch of philosophy in the study of value or quality. Ethics further incorporate the analysis of concepts such as right, wrong, good, evil, justice and responsibility. They help members of a society to know what to do and what is not to be done. With ethics forming part of the Internet era, the term "cyberethics" has developed. For Richard Spinello, cyberethics is about norms that guide *"acting well in this new realm of cyberspace"* (Spinello, 2003). It is rather easy to extract the commonality of these definitions, which are right and wrong in human conduct. While the law is not left to any individual to decide, ethics allow people the choice to decide what is acceptable or not to the society. With the law and ethics defined it is only rational to move on to explaining how they relate.

3.3   The Relationship between the Law and Ethics

Adeola (n.d.) elaborates on the relationship between ethics and the law, suggesting that indeed they do relate. In areas where law is silent or permits, ethics come in and raise the standard to a level where everyone is content. Each generation applies ethics according to its own context, background and area of influence. Not complying with those ethics though does not necessarily bring about punishment. Ethics, together with the law, should mold the behavior of an individual to what is legally and socially acceptable.

Hauptman (1996) believes that the traditional base of ethics is enough to withstand any technology inventions. He views the nature of the Internet as rebellious and suggests that its presence should call for ethics rather than netiquette. On the contrary, it has to be acknowledged that the Internet is not responsible for this rebellious nature, but rather makes it easier for users to act in such a manner. Despite the fact that the role of ethics in cyber usage of the Younger Generation is still uncertain, the law has been visibly implemented in directing cyber usage. One of the ways in which the law is implemented is through copyright laws (Harris and Dumas, 2009). These laws should ideally prohibit illegal behavior of the Younger Generation towards intellectual property. But, it seems to be ineffective as plagiarism and illegal downloading of music and/or software are becoming common practice amongst the generation of today (Harris and Dumas, 2009). The inadequacy of the law affirms the need for ethic intervention.

Sensitizing ethics and the law is now achieved, together with how these concepts relate to one another. Moreover the role they play in cyber usage is now realized. According to the above mentioned descriptions of ethics, it is safe to argue that for ethics to be effective people should be convinced that some behaviour is in fact not acceptable to other people. To accomplish this, perhaps some form of awareness and education is required. Once that is accomplished then individuals might treat online unethical behaviours as thoughtful as physical unethical behaviours. Subsequent is an exploration of some unethical behaviors and illegal behaviors on the Internet.

4   Unethical and Illegal behaviors on cyberspace

Individuals have different views of what is regarded right or wrong as well as what is ethical or unethical. With the law and ethics defined in the prior section, this section will cover a few examples of typical unethical behaviours. It will be done in comparison to some examples of illegal behaviours. It will explore the extant in which the Younger Generation is deemed to act in an ethical manner when active in cyberspace. It will furthermore provide facts from literature on how this generation is affected by its behaviour personally and professionally.

According to Du Plooy (2010) this generation shares inappropriate information and it also makes undesirable statements that are regarded as "hate speech". McMasters (1999) defines "hate speech" as that which offends, threatens, or insults groups based on race, colour, religion, national origin, gender, sexual orientation, disability or a number of other traits. Although "hate speech" is in most cases not unlawful it is unethical. It is present in any form of communication online, such as in emails, social networks, status updates, chat rooms and blogs. This generation portrays no shame in speaking their minds online without considering the implications (Du Plooy, 2010). That is promoted by the intangible nature of the Internet (Du Plooy, 2010; Baum, 2005). The lack of fear of punishment encourages people to act in an indecent manner and Freestone and Mitchell (2004) credits the Internet for paving the way for many new forms of aberrant behaviour. The Internet is the "new environment for unethical behaviour" and it allows the Younger Generations to misbehave (Freestone and Mitchell, 2004). It can be concluded that the Younger Generation is prone to unethical behaviour while active on the Internet.

The Younger Generation not only behaves unethically but is often victim to such behaviour (Brown *et al.* 2006). This transpires in a form of cyber bullying and cyber stalking. Meloy and Gothard (1995) define stalking as "*the wilful, malicious and repeated following and harassing of another person that threatens his or her safety*". Tokunaga (2010) reports on cyber bullying as "*the use of information and communication technologies to support deliberate, repeated, and hostile behaviour by an individual or group that is intended to harm others*". Dehue, Bolman and Vollink (2008) delimits three conditions that must be met for a situation to be considered cyber bullying. The first condition is that the behaviours must be repeated. The second is the bullying should involve psychological torment, and third is that it must be carried out with intent. These definitions purposely state the expression "repeated" suggesting that if the acts are repeated, they move away from unethical to being illegal. For example, if one is sent one malicious email they cannot claim that they are being cyber stalked. Likewise, if one is harmed in any form of way electronically only once, one cannot claim that one is cyber bullied. From a legal point of view, limited states and countries have cyber bullying acts that assist in combating this offense. One of which is Nevada in the USA (Hinduja, Patchin, 2011). However, such a law is not defined in South Africa (South African Law Reform Commission, 2006).

Unethical behaviour affects the Younger Generation personally, typically through cyber bullying and cyber stalking and it also affects this generation professionally. This behaviour not only negatively impacts the society but includes the corporate world (Freestone and Mitchell, 2004). Alverson (1999) claims that every generation in American history has separate personality traits and that applies even for today's generation. Filipczak (1994) also states that the older generation complains about the Younger Generation's work ethic, and considers it as the lack of a work ethic. At work place the Younger Generation has a different ethical stance from the older generation (Govitvatana, 2001). The negligence of this generation regarding information affects the way in which they should appreciate information at work.

In the UK, on January 9th 2008, the theft of a Ministry of Defence (MOD) laptop from a naval recruiter's car led to an intense investigation (Burton, 2008). This investigation was conducted by Sir Edmund Burton. He reported on the impact that personal behaviour has on the professional behaviour. One of the issues that were identified in the Burton Report (2008) is that the Younger Generation adds to a culture of information security ignorance. Sir Burton (2008) states that the Younger Generation of MOD staff is not inculcated with the same culture of protecting information as their counterparts from previous generations. This poses as a major consequence of the unethical behaviour of today's generation in general.

From what has been recited, the following can be concluded:

1. The Younger Generation struggles to align their virtual lives to their real lives.
2. The Younger Generation is prone to be unethical while active online.
3. On occasion the Younger Generation is unaware of the consequences of their unethical behaviour.
4. Often the actions that are labelled unethical have negative impact.
5. The Younger Generation might be dubbed as the weakest link when it comes to information security.

The above statements will be addressed by some ethical guidelines in the following section. The guidelines are applicable when one is to communicate online.

5   Ethical Guidelines

The Younger Generation has been dubbed as acting unethically to a large extent in the previous section. Its behavior online has affirmed the necessity of ethical intervention. This section will introduce ethical guidelines that will address the five statements that were made in the aforementioned section. These guidelines are listed and explained below in Table 2. This section will furthermore provide questions that a person should ask themselves before posting or communicating online, to evaluate whether or not they have applied the proposed guidelines.

Guideline	Justification
1. A person should be fully aware of what they are about to do online as well as the consequence of that action.	It is visible that in some instances people act without considering the implications of those actions (Du Plooy, 2010). It would help if people took time to evaluate their actions, and to know entirely what they are about to do before doing it.
2. The intention that one has while communicating online, should be positive.	If a person's intention is positive, then hate speech and cyber bullying can be mitigated. Since both of these offences require the intension to harm people (Dehue *et al.* 2008; McMasters, 1999).
3. If the content of the information that one is to post online might be deemed as defamatory other people, one should have the consent of every person that is involved.	Since society at large has different views of what is regarded ethical and unethical (Baum, 2005). It is important that before sharing information that seems appropriate to you, to consult everyone involved. This is to avoid conflict of values.
4. Before one posts information through the Internet, one should check whether or not they are giving too much information, specifically private information that might cause harm.	Information security is everybody's responsibility (von Solms and von Solms, 2009). Therefore it is up to every individual to ensure that they are not giving too much information that is potentially harmful to them.
5. An individual should be in their right state of mind while posting something online. This is to avoid being driven by anger and posting something one might regret.	Anger or any other emotion can cause one to act abnormally (Loewenstein and Lerner, 2003). One should be in a clear state of mind when active online, so as to enable conscious decision making.
6. A person must be certain that what they do online aligns with what they would do in physical life.	The abstract nature of the Internet promotes "two-faced" personalities (Berdik, 2007). If one would attempt to act as they would in real life, then some uncalled for behaviors would be eliminated.
7. While online, one should attempt to say things that they would also appreciate receiving.	It is reported that the Younger Generation fails to consider the implications and consequences of their actions online (du Plooy, 2010).Taking that into account, assessing how one would accept a behavior if it was directed to them can assist this generation in taking responsibility for its actions.

Table 2: Ethical Guidelines

Based on the proposed guidelines, it is important that Internet users are able to evaluate themselves. Below as Figure 1 is a flowchart with five easy questions to evaluate whether one has applied the above mentioned guidelines. The decisions made by users must lead to "Ethical – Go Ahead" in the flowchart below. If so, what the user is about to communicate should be free of any unethical content. If not, the user has to reconsider the content of the information they are about to communicate.

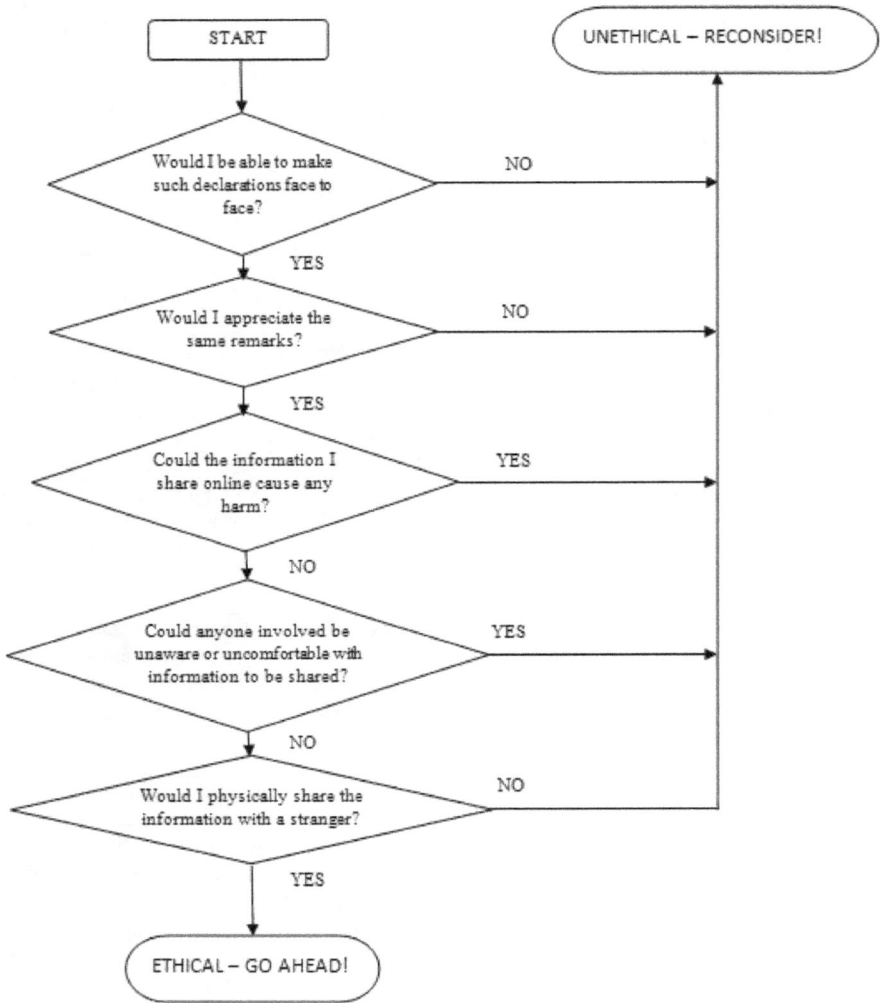

Figure 1: Five Point Self-Evaluation Flowchart

The notion is to apply the proposed guidelines, aiming at eliminating the chance of being unethical. Once that is done, one is to go through the self-evaluation flowchart to ensure that the guidelines are appropriately implemented. With the guidelines and flowchart established, the prospect for an ethical tomorrow is imaginable.

6   Conclusion

Having the Internet as a common resource has impacted on how the world operates. This resource has affected various generation groupings differently. It has affected the Younger Generation in a rather negative manner personally and professionally. The way in which the Internet is used today renders it destructive. It has contributed to the increase of cyber criminals. In addition, it continues to serve as a platform where people deviate from what they truly are in actual reality. The law has become inadequate in regulating the behaviors of users while active online. That lack of control calls for ethics. The proposed ethical guidelines aim to adjust the cases of unethical behavior of the Younger Generation in a positive sense. They aim to arouse the sense of responsibility amongst cyber users and also to contribute to a tomorrow with responsible users.

7   References

Adeola, O. (n.d.). *"Law and Ethics"* www.goodluck4ever.hubpages.com/hub/Law-and-Ethics-Relatioships, (Accessed 5 May 2011)

Alverson, M. (1999). "The New Generation Gap", *Woman in Business,* Vol. 51, No. 3, pp14-17.

Baum, J. J. (2005). "CyberEthics: The New Frontier", *Tech Trends,* Vol. 49, No. 6, pp56-58.

Berdik, C. (2007, 3 12). *"BU Today News and Events"*, www.bu.edu/today/node/2763 ,(Accessed 27 April 2011)

Brockett, R. G., & Hiemstra, R. (2004). *Towards Ethical Practice,* Krieger Publishing Company, Malabar, FL, ISBN: 978-0334043379.

Brown, K., Jackson, M., & Cassidy, W. (2006, December 18). Cyber-Bullying: Developing Policy to Direct Responses that are Equitable and Effective in Addressing this Special Form of Bullying. *Canadian Journal of Educational Administration and Policy*(57).

Burton, E. (2008). *Report into the loss of MOD Personal Data.* UK: Ministry of Defence.

Chen, J., Chen, C., & Yang, H.-H. (2008). "An empirical evaluation of key factors contributing to internet abuse in the workplace", *Industrial Management & Data Systems,* Vol. 108, No. 1, pp87-106.

Curzon, L. B. (1986). *A dictionary of law* Pitman Publishing, London. ISBN 13: 9780712104395

Cyberethics - Ethics in the Age of the Internet. (n.d.) www.123helpme.com/view.asp?id=22369 (Accessed 3 May 2011)

Dehue, F., Bolman, C., & Vollink, T. (2008). "Cyberbullying: Youngsters' experiences and parental perception", *CyberPsychology & Behavior,* Vol. 11, No. 2, pp217-223.

du Plooy, D. (2010, March 25). *"Net hate speech 'not unusual"*, www.news24.com/SouthAfrica/News/Net-hate-speech-not-unusual-20100325 (Accessed 15 August 2011)

Ermann, D. M., Williams, M. B., & Shauf, M. S. (1997). *Computers, Ethics, and Society.* Oxford University Press, Melbourne, Vic.

Filipczak, B. (1994). "It's just a job generation X at work", *Training,* Vol. 31, No. 4, pp21-27.

Freestone, O., & Mitchell, V. W. (2004). "Generation Y Attidudes towards e-ethics and Internet-related Misbehaviours", *Journal of Business,* Vol. 54, No. 2, pp121-8.

Fuchs, C., Bichler, R., & Raffl, C. (2009). "Cyberethics and Co-operation in the Information Society", *Science and Engineering Ethics,* Vol. 15, No. 4, pp447-466.

Gaungrong, R. (1998). The Negetive Impact of the Internet and Its Solutions. *The Chinese Defense Science and Technology Information Monthly*(121).

Govitvatana, W. V. (2001). *GENERATION GAP IN THE WORKPLACE BETWEEN BABY BOOMERS AND GENERATION X.* University of Wisconsin-Stout.

Harris, L. C., & Dumas, A. (2009, December). Online Customer misbehaviour: an application of neutralization theory. *Marketing Theory,* pp. 379-402.

Hauptman, R. (1996). "Cyberethics and Social Stability", *Ethics & Behavior,* Vol. 6, No. 2 pp161-163.

Hinduja, S., & Patchin, J. (2011). *State Cyberbullying Law: A Brief Review of State Cyberbullying Laws and Policies.* United States: Cyberbullying Research Center.

Kiesler, S., & Sproull, L. (1992, June). "Group decision making and communication technology", *Organizational Behavior and Human Decision Processes,* Vol. 52, No. 1, pp96-123.

Loewenstein, G., & Lerner, J. S. (2003). *The role of affect in decision making.* London: Oxford University Press.

McMasters, P. K. (1999). ""Must a Civil Society Be a Censored Society?" Human Rights". *Journal of Individual Rights & Responsibilities,* Vol. 26, No. 4, pp1-7.

Meloy, J. R., & Gothard, S. (1995). "Demographic and clinical comparison of obsessional followers and offenders with mental disorders", *American Journal of Psychiatry,* Vol. 152, No. 2, pp258-263.

PEW Internet. (2010). *Generations 2010.* Washington, Pew Research Center, D.C..

South African Law Reform Commission. (2006). *Stalking.* South Africa: South African Law Reform Commission.

Spinello, R. A. (2003). *Cyberethics, Morality and Law in Cyberspace.* Sudbury, Massachuetts: Jones and Bartlett.

Tokunaga, R. S. (2010). "Following you home from school: A critical review and synthesis of research on cyberbullying victimization", *Computers in Human Behavior,* Vol. 26, No. 3, pp277-287.

von Solms, R., & von Solms, B. (2009). *Information Security Governance,* Springer, New York, ISBN: 978-1-905824-07-6

Woon, I. M., & Pee, L. G. (2004). *Behavioral Factors Affecting Internet Abuse in the Workplace – An Empirical Investigation.* Washington D.C.

Author Index